Transfer of Learning in Professional and Vocational Education

The notion of transfer of learning underpins all education, yet it has rarely been explored in terms of professional or vocational education. In this book the authors unpack the concept of transfer of learning, examine it in relation to current debates in education, and show how it can be used most effectively to benefit students.

The first part of the book looks at:

- what transfer of learning means
- how it operates
- the implications for teaching
- issues such as assessment, competence, outcomes

The book is also concerned with practical issues of how to teach to encourage transfer. In the second part, contributors present case studies from social work which show how specific teaching methods can be used to make the mazimum use of the student's previous experience. These include:

- personal construct psychology
- enquiry and action learning
- intentional observation
- critical incident analysis
- reflective diaries
- process recording
- information technology

Good practice examples are presented in enough detail to enable teachers and practice supervisors to apply them directly in their work with students. Combining an accessible presentation of the underlying theory with case studies which explain how to put theory into practice, this a text which is relevant to 'teaching for transfer' in any professional or vocational context.

Viviene E. Cree is a Lecturer in Social Work, University of Edinburgh.
Cathlin Macaulay is a Research Consultant, University of Edinburgh.

Transfer of Learning in Professional and Vocational Education

Edited by Viviene E. Cree and Cathlin Macaulay

London and New York

First published 2000
by Routledge
11 New Fetter Lane, London EC4P 4EE

Simultaneously published in the USA and Canada
by Routledge
29 West 35th Street, New York, NY 10001

Routledge is an imprint of the Taylor & Francis Group

Typeset in Galliard and Gill Sans by
Prepress Projects Ltd, Perth, Scotland
Printed and bound in Great Britain by
Biddles Ltd, Guildford and King's Lynn

British Library Cataloguing in Publication Data
A catalogue record for this book is available
from the British Library

Library of Congress Cataloging in Publication Data
ISBN 0-415-20418-6 (hbk)
ISBN 0-415-20419-4 (pbk)

Contents

Illustrations

Figures

Boxes

Contributors

Yvonne Channer is a senior lecturer at Sheffield Hallam University. Her work as a social work educator has enabled her to develop a research interest in the strength of Black communities and teaching and learning issues. Her publications include articles on social work education and practice and the schooling of Black African Caribbean children.

Gary Clapton is a qualified social worker and practice teacher, who works as a practice teacher and training officer for City of Edinburgh Social Work Department and as a social worker and counsellor in a Scottish adoption agency. He has had articles on practice teaching, anti-discriminatory practice, child sexual abuse and birth fathers published.

Viviene E. Cree is a lecturer in social work at the University of Edinburgh and is a qualified social worker and practice teacher. Her published work includes writing on social work education, transfer of learning, the history of social work, sociology and social work, and she has co-edited a book on feminist work with men. She is currently researching Scottish children affected by HIV or AIDS.

Ralph Davidson was a senior lecturer in social work at the University of Edinburgh until 1999. He formerly worked in social services as a childcare officer, senior childcare officer, area officer and practice teacher. Recent publications include books on poverty and community care.

Hilary Davies has worked as a lecturer in social work at Glasgow University and as senior practice teacher and staff development and training officer with Barnardo's, Scotland. She is currently involved in disability equality and homelessness and in counselling people with visual impairment. Publications include articles on group supervision, group care teaching in social work education and practice teaching.

Nick Gould is reader in social work in the Department of Social and Policy Sciences at the University of Bath. Previously, he was a social worker in local authority and forensic psychiatric settings. He has written widely on social work education, information management and the development of qualitative methodologies. Publications include books and articles on social work education and a co-edited book on reflective learning.

Pam Green Lister is a qualified social worker and lecturer in the Department of Social Policy and Social Work at the University of Glasgow. Before this, she taught at Queen's College, Glasgow, and Glasgow Caledonian University. Pam is writing up her doctoral thesis on creative writing and women survivors of sexual abuse. She has published articles on community work, child protection and women and language.

Hazel Kemshall is Professor of Community and Criminal Justice at DeMontfort University. Before this, she was a senior lecturer at Birmingham University after ten years working as a probation officer and manager. Hazel's research interests are women offenders, quality assurance and offender risk assessment and management and she has published numerous articles and books in these areas.

Helen Kinloch has worked in social work education in Aberdeen and Stirling Universities, with Barnardo's, Scotland as training manager and as manager of the Tom Allan Centre Counselling Service in Glasgow. Currently she is engaged in pastoral care training, counselling and counselling supervision. Publications include writing on group care and social work education and practice teaching.

Pat Le Riche is a lecturer in social work at Goldsmith's College, London. She has had social work practice experience in a range of agencies in London and south-east England and has worked as a lecturer with the Open University and the Universities of Kent and London. Publications include articles on feminism and older women, social work education, and articles and a co-edited book on observation in social work.

Cathlin Macaulay has worked as a research fellow at the Edinburgh Centre for Social Welfare Research. She has worked on a number of research projects to do with student learning and social work education. Publications include articles and reports on education, the Gaelic language, mature students, social work education and transfer of learning.

Mike Tait is a qualified community worker and practice teacher based in the voluntary sector in Scotland. He has played a key role in the development of practice teacher training, equal opportunities' policies in selection for social work training, and self-advocacy for people with learning difficulties. He is an adviser to People First (Scotland) and is the company secretary.

Karen Tanner is a lecturer in social work at Goldsmith's College, London. Before this, she worked as a social worker in generic and specialist settings, as a child protection adviser and a hospital-based social worker, working with children who have leukaemia. Publications include articles and a co-edited book on observation in social work.

Liz Timms is a lecturer in social work at the University of Edinburgh. Previously she worked as a lecturer in Australia and New Zealand and at Moray House College, Edinburgh. She is seconded part time to a European project to develop transnational-collaborative learning using computer mediated communication. Publications include articles on new technology and social networks.

Acknowledgements

Thanks to Geraldine Doherty and Liz Wolff-Cochrane from the Central Council for Education and Training in Social Work and to Fiona Paterson from the Scottish Executive's Central Research Unit for their continuing interest in and support for the transfer of learning agenda in social work education.

Preface

Transfer of learning underpins education and, indeed, is a fundamental part of life. The aim of this book is to examine what is meant by 'transfer of learning', to look at its role within higher and professional education and to provide a range of methods by which transfer of learning might be encouraged within the specific context of social work education. Although the book is rooted in the experience of social work educators and practitioners, we hope that it will be of interest to all those involved in education and training.

Because transfer of learning is such a broad concept, choices have had to be made about what should be included and what should be left out of this volume. In the interests of presenting a coherent book, we have focused on qualifying training in social work, and specifically on educational as opposed to vocational aspects of transfer. This is not to suggest that other aspects, such as the transfer of learning from education to work, or pre- and post-qualifying training, are unimportant. On the contrary, we believe that by looking in depth at one aspect of the educational experience (that is qualifying training in social work), lessons can be learned that have applicability across all learning contexts.

Transfer of learning has particular relevance in providing a means of reconciling apparently incompatible aims and objectives in higher and professional education. In the present climate, education is being pulled between the demands of the social conscience, on the one hand, and the needs of the national economy on the other. This anti-synergy can be seen to be operating particularly in the caring professions – social work, health care and teaching. The need to provide a caring, personal service that emphasises democratisation and the empowerment of the individual service user takes place within a context that is increasingly aimed at standardisation and uniformity, which is bureaucratised, regulated and governed by rules and procedures. These conflicts can be placed within an overall framework of resource cutbacks and 'downsizing', paralleled by an increasing awareness of contingency and uncertainty among professional workers and educators about what constitutes knowledge, expertise and 'good enough' practice.

Social work education and practice in the UK exemplifies these shifts and uncertainties in its current reorganisation, and it is not clear what the shape of social work will be in the years to come. Finding ways of dealing with this change and impermanence is a fundamental feature of working life, and of professional education.

> Graduates are likely to change their jobs at least five times during their careers; even if they do not change jobs, their jobs will change. So in a sense one has to prepare them for the unknown, or at best, the dimly known.
>
> (Brown 1997: 2)

But how can this be achieved? How can we prepare students for 'the unknown', or 'the dimly known'? We will argue that transfer of learning offers a possible way forward – a way of building on what we know and how to make an imaginative leap into a new or different situation.

Transfer of learning is, we believe, a means of getting 'back to basics'. It is about recognising the human, recognising that all learning starts from the unique ways in which individuals experience the world. In terms of the curriculum, it is about trying to design an educational experience that recognises this uniqueness as well as the continual flux of the world in which we live. We cannot offer a blueprint for defining transfer of learning and how it may be taught, but we hope, by 'unpacking' the concept and giving examples of how it may be facilitated, to provide a stimulus for those providing any kind of education.

Our own interest in transfer of learning arises out of an earlier study funded by the Central Council for Education and Training in Social Work (CCETSW) and the Scottish Office. We conducted a literature review and interviews with social work practice teachers, lecturers and educationalists and wrote up the findings as a report, 'Transfer of Learning: A Study' (Cree *et al*. 1998). During the course of our investigation, we came across social work lecturers and practice teachers who demonstrated special interest in teaching for transfer; they have contributed to this edited volume.

The book falls into two parts. The first part provides an overview of transfer of learning and places it within contemporary educational debates. In Chapter 1, Cathlin Macaulay examines the concept of transfer of learning and looks at how it might operate as a process psychologically and in relation to education. She summarises some of the teaching methods through which individuals might be encouraged to integrate their life knowledge and formal knowledge (from their community of practice), using this as a basis for comprehending new, potentially confusing situations and taking appropriate professional actions. In Chapter 2, Viviene Cree examines assessment in higher education looking particularly at how transfer of learning may be evidenced and placed within such a framework. In Chapter 3, Hazel Kemshall examines the current climate of professional/vocational education, contrasting the emphasis on developing educational criteria based on behavioural outcomes with the increasing awareness of risk and contingency in decision-making processes and examining the role that transfer of learning may have in terms of reconciling these competing constituents.

The second part of the book describes various methods that might be used to facilitate transfer of learning within the teaching context. Although these methods are currently used by educators and practitioners in social work, they are relevant and accessible to anyone working in education. In Chapter 4, Nick Gould describes the use of repertory grids as a technique to heighten students' awareness of their actions in relation to service users and other workers. Viviene Cree and Ralph Davidson outline in Chapter 5, enquiry and action learning (EAL), a process of learning in small groups through the problematising and research of given case study scenarios. Karen Tanner and Pat Le Riche discuss the use of observation as a method of developing reflective and reflexive practice in Chapter 6. Mike Tait details in Chapter 7 the many ways in which the reflective diary may be used as a means of developing self-awareness among students in a practice agency. In Chapter 8, Gary Clapton points out the usefulness of the process recording in developing a sense of the complexity of an interaction and in enabling the intuitive process to emerge. Hilary Davies and Helen Kinloch focus on critical incident analysis (CIA) and how it may be used to explore and reflect on different aspects of practice in Chapter 9. The final three chapters move sideways slightly, examining facilitation of transfer of learning in relation to the experience of particular groups of students. In Chapter 10, Pam Green Lister shows how course organisation based around the needs of carers attracts mature women students whose individual experiences are used as an integral aspect of developing good working practice. Yvonne Channer points out in Chapter 11 that social work courses need to take on board and value the experiences those from 'minority' groups such as Black Christian students, whose views have, traditionally, been marginalised. Finally, Liz Timms discusses, in Chapter 12, a specific usage of the Internet to teach community work students in Finland, Sweden, Scotland and Germany.

Throughout, the authors are concerned with showing the importance of reflectivity, reflexivity and mindfulness in the educational process. These qualities are enhanced by educational courses that, most importantly, use the experience of the learner as a central focus and in using a variety of teaching methods, encourage cognitive flexibility and versatility and the ability to make connections.

Viviene E. Cree and Cathlin Macaulay
Edinburgh
August 2000

Bibliography

Brown, G. (1997) *Assessing Student Learning in Higher Education*, London: Routledge.

Cree, V.E., Macaulay, C. and Loney, H. (1998) *Transfer of Learning: A Study*, Edinburgh: Scottish Office Central Research Unit and CCETSW.

Chapter 1

Transfer of learning

Cathlin Macaulay

Transfer of learning has been described as 'the ultimate aim of teaching'. However, achieving this goal is regarded as 'one of teaching's most formidable problems' (McKeough *et al.* 1995: vii). Transfer of learning has been of interest to academics working in a number of different fields – psychology, philosophy, schooling, adult education and vocational/professional education. In terms of social work education in the UK, it is one of the central tenets of the professional qualification – the Diploma in Social Work – binding the elements of a disparate curriculum with a diverse range of objectives.

Yet what is transfer of learning? How can it be taught? The purpose of this introductory chapter is to unpack the concept of transfer of learning before examining some of the ways in which it may be facilitated, particularly in social work education. The material for this discussion is based on a small-scale study (funded by the Central Council for Education and Training in Social Work and the Scottish Office) that involved a review of research on transfer of learning in the fields of social work, education, nursing studies and cognitive psychology, and interviews with fourteen social work educators.

What is transfer of learning?

There is a considerable diversity of opinion regarding the definition of transfer of learning and particularly in evidencing it. There is little research on transfer of learning as such – most studies form the addendum to another debate and are grounded in the predispositions of the authors towards a particular theory or model of learning or education. (This lack of conceptual consistency may, in fact, be a feature of educational debate in general.) However, at a level at which most protagonists would not disagree, transfer of learning can be defined as 'prior learning affecting new learning or performance' (Marini and Genereux 1995: 2). Within an instructional setting, transfer can be seen to involve three elements – learner, task and context:

> The new learning or performance can differ from original learning in terms of the task involved (as when students apply what they have learned on practice problems to solving a new problem), and/ or the context involved (as when students apply their classroom learning to performing tasks at home or work). The basic elements involved in transfer are thus the learner, the instructional tasks (including learning materials and practice problems), the instructional context (the physical and social setting, including the instruction and support provided by the teacher, the behavior [sic] of other students, and the norms and expectations inherent in the setting), the transfer task, and the transfer context.
>
> (Marini and Genereux 1995: 2)

The notion of transfer is not new. Assumptions about transfer of learning have long informed the development of educational programmes. A case that is often quoted is the considered virtue of a classical education – a belief that learning Latin or mathematics was a necessary precondition for the study of any other discipline in that these subjects trained the mind and that the skills so developed were transferable. In fact, these subjects were no more likely to develop habits of mind than might any other perhaps more utilitarian subject (Thorndyke 1924). Nevertheless, the belief that they did led, until recent years, to qualifications in Latin and mathematics being necessary for entry into certain universities. Although this assumption is no longer tenable, similar (unfounded) arguments may be seen to be operating in the current debate about generic and core skills (Bridges 1994; Marginson 1994).

Transfer of learning, then, should not be taken for granted. Even the existence of transfer of learning as an identifiable phenomenon has been questioned. Reviewing the evidence from experimental psychology, Detterman (1993: 7) asserts that 'transfer is very difficult to obtain'. He concedes the possibility of verifying transfer between situations that are highly similar: 'Transfer occurs, when it occurs, because of common elements in the two situations' (Detterman 1993: 6); by which he means when the contents of two situations are obviously and superficially alike (as an example, learning Latin helps when learning French since many French words come directly from Latin). The existence of 'near' transfer or 'specific' transfer has been demonstrated by many empirical researchers.

Early behaviourist theory, focusing on observation and measurement, established that behaviour could be influenced or shaped. For example, a specific stimulus could induce a specific response in animals tested under laboratory controlled conditions:

> A study of transfer is by definition a two-stage experiment comprising a training phase and a test phase. The basic question is how training provided during the first stage influences performance during the second stage ... the presence of significant transfer effect, whether positive or negative, implies that at least some of the responses established during the training phase are carried over to the test task.
>
> (Postman 1972, in Dickson and Bamford 1995: 93)

In terms of behaviourist theory, 'positive' transfer occurs if what is learned during the first phase enhances learning during the second phase. 'Negative' transfer occurs if what is learned during the first phase is in some way detrimental to learning during the second phase. Through experimental evidence, it was shown that responses learned during training were carried over to a test task that was very similar to the original learning situation, thus Thorndyke and his colleagues (1901) established the existence of what is called 'near' transfer. When two situations are obviously and superficially similar, subjects could apply what they had learned from the first situation to the second. The results of such behaviourist experiments have been highly influential in the development of educational programmes. Appropriate conditioning leads to an appropriate change in behaviour that is reinforced by systems of reward and feedback. Accordingly, the external aspects of learning involving the roles of the teacher and of assessment have been highlighted, perhaps at the expense of understanding the role of the learner and the process of learning. The use of the experimental method in social sciences has also led to a positivistic research paradigm on which much practice in social work has been based. However, this paradigm has been critiqued as social work increasingly recognises the role of contingency in making assessments (Fook 2000).

In terms of its implications for teaching and practice, 'far' or 'general' transfer of learning is of more significance. In contrast to 'near' transfer, 'general' transfer may encompass tasks or contexts that appear very different from those originally experienced:

> [E]xtent of transfer can conceivably range from near, specific, one

dimensional transfer (involving one task or context only slightly different from original learning), to the opposite extreme of far, general, multidimensional transfer (encompassing a wide variety of tasks and contexts very different from original learning).

(Marini and Genereux 1995: 6)

'General' transfer involves the ability to see underlying principles of similarity in situations that are not obviously alike. Although near transfer is relatively easy to verify within tightly controlled laboratory conditions, there is no empirical evidence to prove that 'general' transfer exists (Detterman 1993). Neither, however, is there any evidence to prove that it does not exist. A belief in the existence of transfer of learning is, then, based on an act of faith rather than factual evidence. This, however, is also the case insofar as learning itself is concerned. Despite the attempts of behaviourists (and to some extent information-processing theorists) the learning process itself remains something of a 'black box', as Collins points out:

We do not know how we manage to learn. There are various ideas such as positive and negative reinforcement, ostensive definition, the building of new concepts from old by logical extension, hard wiring of the brain for certain aspects of knowledge (such as linguistic structures, the ability to recognise elementary orientations and movements, and so forth) but these are all inadequate and insecure. One might say that the science of learning was still in the pre- or multi-paradigmatic stage. The evidence for this is that brand-new speculative 'theories' of learning can still grow out of nothing and yet not be completely implausible.

(Collins 1989: 207)

Although research to date has not empirically proved or disproved that transfer of learning exists, 'the idea's claims on our attention are considerable' (Whittington 1986: 574) because it is *necessary*: students have to be able to deal with situations in their practice that they will not encounter during the course of their formal education. In order to do so they have to be able to transfer what they have learned in earlier situations to new situations. There is no evidence to suggest that this does not or cannot happen, and in terms of everyday experience there is every reason to suppose that it does (Guberman and Greenfield 1991). Indeed, Fleishman argues that transfer of learning is a fact of life:

Transfer of learning ... is pervasive in everyday life, in the developing child and adult. Transfer takes place whenever our existing knowledge, abilities and skills affect the learning or performance of new tasks ... transfer of learning is seen as fundamental to all learning.

(Fleishman 1987: xi)

Given that transfer of learning in its general sense exists and is a fundamental aspect of education, the question is, how do we facilitate it? In order to do this it is necessary to understand the process by which transfer may occur. Moving away from the relatively narrow confines of experimental psychology towards psycho-social and cognitive theories of learning provides some elucidation.

The active learner

In terms of transfer of learning, the interface between prior experience or learning and its effect on new or novel situations is a crucial area. Constructivism, with its focus on the relationship between the learner and the sociocultural context of learning, has proved a useful way into examining transfer, and indeed it has also provided a philosophical basis for recent learning programmes within nursing education (Creedy *et al.* 1992; Cust 1995). Here, learning is seen as an active process in which 'learners strive for understanding and competence on the basis of their personal experience' (Cust 1995: 280). Motivation is seen as intrinsic: the learner has an innate propensity to seek knowledge about the world (Piaget 1972; Rogers 1975). Learning is constructivist because 'old knowledge is always revised, reorganised and even reinterpreted in order to reconcile it with new input' (Cust 1995: 281). The concept of 'viability' is important too as learners seek to make sense of what they see and experience. Viability depends on:

[T]he fit between the existing knowledge of the individual and the way it reflects what the learner continuously observes and experiences. The structure of knowledge is based on what the individual experiences and how it is interpreted through their filters of interest, values and affect. These interpretations lead to the prioritisation and categorisation of what the learner experiences.

(Billet 1994: 38)

Learning becomes meaningful and therefore effective through making the links between past and present experience. The interaction between the individual and social experience can be described in terms of Vygotsky's principle of appropriation: 'the individualised process of constructing meaning from socially and contextually defined knowledge using the individual's idiosyncratic structuring of knowledge and understanding' (Billet 1994: 40). Within professional/vocational education, contextually defined knowledge is that which is relevant to the 'community of practice' to which the learner is aspiring to become a member.

The concept of the centrality of the learner (as opposed to the learning task) has, for some time, been a basic tenet of non-formal adult education (Knowles 1983; Mezirow 1983; Freire 1983). The experience the learner brings to the educational arena forms a basis for developing programmes that are relevant to their needs. The dispositions of the learner, the feelings s/he brings to the task, are important as learning involves the development of identity (Rogers 1975). Learning is effortful, so the learner needs to feel that the time and energy expended will be worthwhile (Billet 1994). Although a lack of confidence or anxiety is likely to impede the process of learning, more positive feelings, such as that of self-efficacy or a deep interest in the subject, are likely to facilitate it. Adult educators emphasise the importance of personalising education by integrating the experience of the learners with that which they are learning. This ensures that learning is both relevant and authentic and that it does not become spurious intellectualisation. In this sense the experience of the learner is not merely seen as something to take account of – it is crucial to the learning process (Boud and Miller 1996; Freire 1983; Mezirow 1983).

Within this learner-centred concept of learning, knowledge is not given but is actively acquired and interpreted by the individual. In this context, transfer of learning will be facilitated by creating a suitable climate for learning, acknowledging that the feelings and attitudes of the learner are as important as their cognitive strategies in dealing with the learning task, enhancing their capacity for self-direction, and allowing time for reflection and making connections between prior and present experience. Collaborative or andragogic models facilitate this kind of learning more effectively than the traditional top-down or didactic approaches to teaching (Knowles 1983).

Psycho-social theories of cognition emphasise the role of the active learner. Cognitive psychology has not specifically explored transfer of learning in any depth, although it has provided a repertoire of information on learning as such, focusing, by analogy and inference, on internal mental structures and processes. Schema theory gives us some insight into how knowledge is constructed and stored; information-processing theory gives an insight into how knowledge is accessed and retrieved.

Schema theory and information processing

According to schema theory, knowledge is stored in the memory in the form of mental models or representations known as schemata:

> Schemata are coherent knowledge structures that are stored in memory. They arise from and mentally represent frequently experienced situations such as those pertaining to recognising people, executing a tennis stroke, visiting the doctor, remembering the route to work, understanding the nature of a theory and reading a textbook. These contextually based mental entities profoundly influence all aspects of learning including perception, comprehension, memory, reasoning and problem solving.
>
> (Cust 1995: 283)

Schemata, the building bricks of cognition, may be stored and used in the form of concepts, procedures, images and episodes (Brooks and Dansereau 1987). The organisation of knowledge here is a highly integrative one as individual schemata are held to contain both propositional/conceptual knowledge and procedures for action (Gould 1996). The activity through which schema are formed, modified and retrieved may be described according to information-processing theory in terms of three main events or stages:

> [F]irst, a (preconscious) stage in which, through selective perception, certain aspects of the environment are given attention and filtered 'upwards' for conscious processing; second, active mental engagement with the new input so as to make personal sense of it, using selectively recalled prior learning in the process; and finally, a structuring of the resultant learning in such a way that it can be stored usefully in long term memory as a basis for future learning.
>
> (Atkins *et al*. 1993: 50)

From this perspective, we can see that transfer will probably depend on how a memory search is initiated, the kinds of memory nodes accessed and the extent of their connectedness to other nodes in memory (Salomon and Perkins 1989). On a day-to-day level, this activity is largely subconscious. However, within a formal education setting, students need to have an awareness of their own learning process. Variously described as 'knowing about one's knowing' or 'learning about learning', metacognitive awareness has been described as a key aspect of transfer (Marini and Genereux 1995; Brooks and Dansereau 1987).

Metacognition is the knowledge of and regulation of cognition, involving aspects such as the planning, organisation and evaluation of learning (Cust 1995). As Nisbet and Shucksmith (1986: 40) point out, 'Meaningful learning requires a *deliberate* effort on the part of learners to relate new knowledge to relevant concepts they already possess'.

The activities by which the learner enables transfer to occur involve a variety of cognitive processing techniques, for example connecting, relating, structuring, re-structuring, collecting, adapting, applying, refining, memorising, analysing, synthesising, comparing, evaluating, imaging, problem-solving, generalising, abstracting etc. (Atkins *et al.* 1993). A prime ability involved in transfer of learning is that which allows the student to identify similarities between the new or novel situation and previous situations. A common way of describing this process is 'generalisation'. Gardiner sees generalisation as the primary process of transfer of learning:

> By the transfer of learning I mean using these parts of the overall learning process (having the experience, recognising what is salient, building up patterns, making patterns of patterns which become generalisations, and then the recognition in new situations that the earlier generalisations may be appropriate or relevant) to make use of earlier experiences in new situations. Thus both the generalisation from particular experiences and the application of these generalisations are both essential components in the transfer of learning.
>
> (Gardiner 1984: 100)

This emphasis on generalisation is taken by a number of authors, particularly in social work, and it has sometimes become synonymous with transfer of learning. However, as well as the ability to see 'likeness' in situations, the ability to discriminate is essential (Harris 1985; Sternberg 1994). Thus, generalisation and discrimination may be regarded as being dialectical: one needs the ability to discriminate in order not to overgeneralise.

From a slightly different conceptual base the discussion of transfer has been based on the activity of abstraction: the abstraction of general principles from a particular learning experience that then aid the learner in dealing with another situation. The process of abstraction has been described as:

> [T]he extraction from or identification in a learned unit of material,

in a situation or in a behaviour, some generic or basic qualities, attributes or patterns of elements. These extracted qualities are represented in some symbolic manner accessible to consciousness and, being devoid of contextual specificity, afford application to other instances. Abstraction thus involves both decontextualisation and re-representation of the decontextualised information in a new, more general form.... Abstractions therefore have the form of a rule, principle, label, schematic pattern, prototype or category. This makes it clear how abstraction leads to transfer. It yields a re-representation that subsumes a greater range of cases.

(Salomon and Perkins 1989: 125)

Abstraction provides a bridge from one context to another. *Mindful* abstraction is 'the deliberate, usually metacognitively guided and effortful, decontextualisation of a principle, main idea, strategy or procedure, which then becomes a candidate for transfer' (Salomon and Perkins 1989: 126).

Research suggests that if links are explicitly made between 'unlike' tasks as part of an educational programme, the ability of students to see underlying principles in different situations will be enhanced (Gick and Holyoak 1987; Guberman and Greenfield 1991). Active learning whereby individuals extract the principles of a situation for themselves facilitates greater understanding and farther transfer than passive learning. Active learning enables the student to engage with a situation and to experience its complexity at first hand. Mindfulness is required because the principle must be understood in order for an appropriate schema to be developed. The notion of mindfulness relates to the idea of 'reflection-in-action' encapsulated by Schön (1983, 1987), and to the adult educator Mezirow's (1983) description of 'critical reflectivity'.

The nature of knowledge and its use in theory and practice

Having explored the way in which transfer of learning may operate in terms of cognitive processes, we now turn to the social construction of knowledge and how this may influence transfer. Recent epistemological debate suggests that traditional ways of conceptualising 'knowledge' and 'skills' as separate entities has been misleading, and this area has been reconceptualised under the general rubric of knowledge. Knowledge involved in action or while undertaking a task includes conceptual knowledge (knowing that), procedural knowledge (knowing how) and strategic knowledge (knowing what to do when) (Cust 1995).

Conceptual knowledge (sometimes referred to as propositional or declarative knowledge) consists of concepts, facts, propositions and theories. These may be acquired through experience or through comprehension of written and verbal materials. Conceptual knowledge has been described as 'a mental model representing the world involving the object of the procedure' (Hatano 1982 in Guberman and Greenfield 1991: 248). Procedural knowledge involved in cognitive and psychomotor skills specifies actions to be taken when the right conditions are present. Strategic knowledge (sometimes referred to as conditional knowledge) is an awareness of when to use conceptual and procedural knowledge and why (Gott 1989; Stevenson 1994).

Conceptual, procedural and strategic knowledge are underpinned by what could be described as 'personal' knowledge based on the individual's own idiosyncratic apprehension of experience (Eraut 1994). These aspects of knowledge are seen as highly interactive by contemporary learning theorists, and in order to facilitate transfer they need to be developed simultaneously so that rich linkages are made between them (Gagne 1970; Sternberg 1994; Billet 1994; Cust 1995; Eraut 1994; Stevenson 1994). Within this paradigm, 'learning' knowledge and 'using' knowledge are not seen as separate processes but rather as part of the same process: using knowledge transforms it so that it is no longer the same knowledge (Eraut 1994). This has been described in terms of 'vertical transfer' – 'the use of existing knowledge and skills to acquire new conceptual knowledge'– and 'lateral transfer' – 'the application of existing knowledge and skills in novel contexts' (Guberman and Greenfield 1991: 254).

This reconceptualisation of knowledge as incorporating both information and skills is important in terms of teaching in that it bridges two classic theories of instruction, the doctrine of formal discipline, in which learning strategies or 'skills' are emphasised, and the Gradgrindian notion of teaching 'facts, facts, facts', when teaching of information is emphasised.

Within a postmodernist climate, enabling individuals to enhance their capacities for the creation of, and application of, knowledge is regarded as a principle task in professional education, particularly social work (Gould 1996; Fook 2000). Various studies suggest that students' understanding and use of conceptual knowledge or theory occurs most effectively through learning that is based on experience and which allows time for reflection on experience (Kolb 1984; Boud and Miller 1996; Gould and Taylor 1996). Kolb elucidates:

[L]earning, and therefore knowing, requires both a grasp or figurative representation of experience and some transformation of that representation ... Learning, the creation of knowledge and meaning, occurs though the active extension and grounding of ideas *and* experiences in the external world and through internal reflection about the attributes of these experiences and ideas.

(Kolb 1984: 42, 52)

Professional knowledge may be derived through practice and the systematic analysis of that experience (Gould 1996).

Transfer of learning as a subconscious process occurs continuously; the individual is constantly reconstructing old knowledge on the basis of new experience and developing a new schema. As a conscious process within an educational or vocational framework, transfer of learning takes on another dimension. It is not enough merely to make connections. It is necessary to make appropriate and relevant connections. Positive transfer occurs when appropriate connections are made. Negative transfer refers to an inappropriate application of past models to new situations and may occur as a result of an incomplete or incorrect schema. For example, students often enter higher education with a conception of learning as a process of memorisation (a procedure that may have proved effective in attaining the qualification to gain entrance to a course) rather than as developing understanding and interpreting reality. This often leads to the use of 'surface' learning strategies involving rote learning rather than 'deep processing', which involves an intention to understand complex ideas and make connections between new concepts and previous knowledge (Entwistle 1987).

The concept of positive and negative transfer is particularly relevant in terms of the relationship between theory and practice in social work. In her study of social work students on practice placements, Secker (1993) proposed a typology of practice in which three approaches – the 'everyday social' approach, the 'fragmented' approach and the 'fluent' approach – were distinguished on the basis of the knowledge that underpinned each approach and the ways in which that knowledge was used. Students using the 'everyday social' approach did not draw at all on the kind of knowledge that is usually described as theoretical, but instead they operated solely on knowledge derived from their personal lives. The practice of students using the 'fragmented' approach was characterised by conflicts between their everyday and theoretical knowledge, which resulted in dilemmas about how to act in the course of interactions with service users and others. Those using the 'fluent approach' were able to creatively amalgamate different sources of knowledge, both personal and theoretical (Secker 1993: 24–5).

The 'everyday social' approach can be likened to negative transfer or inappropriate transfer. Here, the student treated service users as if they were friends, family or casual acquaintances, people for whom the student had no professional duty. Secker described this as working with an unconscious theoretical framework that did not provide the student with the knowledge/skills necessary to deal with situations they may have either not personally experienced or were afraid of (Secker 1993: 30–3; Ryan *et al*. 1995). The 'fragmented' approach involved conflict between the 'everyday social' approach and the stated intention of the student to apply more 'theory' to new situations, indicating that students had not developed an integrated knowledge base. Secker found that students using this approach were very self-conscious of their theoretical justifications, and their reports were consequently very ego-centred (Secker 1993: 46–7). Finally, the 'fluent approach' was demonstrated by a minority of students able to select and apply relevant knowledge, thus resolving the dilemmas that characterised the 'fragmented' approach:

> The main difference lay in the fact that in the context of this approach the students did not rely on ready made theoretical explanations in the form in which they were handed on by teachers and others to make sense of the situations they described. Instead they made use of this ready made knowledge in constructing their own theories.
>
> (Secker 1993: 78)

Within professional education and work settings, the process of transfer of learning involves the *appropriate* selection of knowledge to assess and deal with a new situation. This is an iterative process, requiring both forward and backward reaching: forward reaching in the sense of developing models or principles that may be used in the future; backward reaching in the sense of looking to see whether models developed in the past may help make sense of a new and difficult situation. The importance of using 'grounded' theory, that is assessing the situation in order to access appropriate theoretical perspectives rather than imposing theory in a 'top-down' way has been emphasised by Ellerman (1998: 42): 'It is when professionals no longer struggle to make practice conform to structures imposed by a priori notions that they can begin to bridge the gap between social work theory and everyday practice'. In this context, studies of expertise offer some insight into transfer of learning.

Expertise and transfer of learning

Schön (1987) outlined the importance of apprehension as a mode of knowing in his examination of artistry in social work practice. He indicates that such 'artistry' can be examined by studying the performance of unusually competent performers. Recent studies within vocational groups as diverse as nurses and workers in the coal industry suggest that transfer of learning is the hallmark of expertise (Atkins *et al.* 1993; Benbenishty 1992; Benner 1984; Billet 1994; Creedy *et al.* 1992; Guberman and Greenfield 1991). Stevenson explains:

> Expertise consists in the ability to coordinate the use of conceptual knowledge, specific skills and general procedures when confronting problematic situations ... individual conceptual and procedural knowledge are patterned by communities of practice, in various functional contexts; and ... the development of expertise is reliant on both the embedding of knowledge in such contexts and its dis-embedding (abstraction) so that its applicability in new contexts is perceived ... it is the ability to transfer which comprises expertise.
>
> (Stevenson 1994: 1, 20)

Experts differ from novices in terms of the speed with which they reach the appropriate solution to a particular problem. They reach the stage where they can come to an *intuitive* grasp of the situation without wasteful consideration of a large range of alternative diagnoses and solutions (Benner 1984; Atkins *et al.* 1993; Gould 1996). Experts engage fully with a situation, are open to change and uncertainty and are able to handle complexity (Fook 2000). Assessment rather than reasoning is crucial. Expertise is regarded as encompassing creativity, artistry and critical thinking; and these involve much more than the simple, linear application of routine skills. Only when a problem is particularly difficult or different from prior cases do experts fall back on analytical procedures (hypo-deductive reasoning) in order to find a solution, and even then this kind of reasoning is schema driven. Cust elucidates:

> The long held view was that problems are solved, bottom up, by applying general reasoning or logical thinking strategies in a step-by-step fashion so that several possible solutions are generated and then tested systematically... These strategies were considered to be independent of the problem solver's existing knowledge and the type of problem involved. Current research findings suggest an alternative, top-down knowledge-based explanation accounts for the marked differences in novice and expert problem solvers... When they encounter familiar problems, experts carefully assess the problem, taking more time to do so than novices. Then, rather than

trying out several possible solutions as novices do, a schema is selected which, once adapted to the problem is likely to effectively represent the problem as well as suggesting a solution procedure to execute. Employing these processes, experts typically solve problems more quickly and accurately than novices.

(Cust 1995: 286)

Expertise is facilitated by knowledge, context-related knowledge, through examples and experience of practice (Billet 1994; Stevenson 1994; Fook *et al*. 1997). The knowledge of experts is well organised into clusters that permit them to recognise meaningful patterns and principles, that is, into schemata. As well as recognising patterns, their knowledge enables them to perceive aspects of the situation that are not salient; in this way, experts are questioning and discriminative. By building up a repertoire or index of practice, the practitioner is able to 'home in on' a case, to see where it is similar to previous cases and to initiate a set of procedures for action. The development of expertise, then, requires integration of conceptual, procedural, strategic and personal knowledge and, as such, cannot be facilitated by a general heuristic skill learned out of its context of use (Atkins *et al*. 1993; Marginson 1994).

Another way in which the study of expertise elucidates transfer of learning concerns the role of the 'teacher' or facilitator. We have seen that transfer involves the abilities of interpretation, abstraction and transformation of experience and that learners need to be guided in the process of abstracting principles from the learning situation. Transfer of learning 'must be cued, primed and guided; it seldom occurs spontaneously' (Perkins and Salomon, 1989, in Marginson 1994: 20). The apprenticeship model, whereby the learner is facilitated by an expert in the role, has been advocated in this respect (Billet 1994; Gott 1989), as has that of the 'coach' (Schön 1983). Within social work, this role is normally taken by the practice teacher whose primary function may be seen as that of enabling the learner to transfer learning from one task to another or from one context to another:

Transfer of learning is not something which is automatic and linear in its manifestation, but is likely to require structured support and facilitation from practice teachers. If students are to move towards complex but coherent personal models of practice then a function of practice teaching is to help students articulate their assumptions or constructs and to make connections between them.

(Gould 1993: 86)

Implications for teaching and learning

It can be seen that transfer of learning is a complex process that cannot be explained or 'proved' easily. It cannot be regarded as a unitary theory or model of learning but, rather, underpins all learning. Using a basic definition of 'prior learning affecting new learning or performance', it is helpful to 'unpack' the concept by examining ways in which the previous knowledge and experience of learners affect their ability to deal with new situations, and by looking at the processes by which transfer may occur, that is examining the conceptualisation of knowledge and how it may be stored within the mind and accessed, retrieved, used, processed and transformed. I will conclude with a brief summary of how transfer of learning may be facilitated in social work education in relation to the elements involved in transfer as outlined earlier – learner, task and context.

The learner

The essential task of professional education and, in particular, of social work education has been described as the enhancement of the knowledge creating capacities of individuals (Gould 1996). Individuals vary in terms of their ability to transfer learning appropriately: for some the ability to see connections and to use their knowledge effectively is almost a natural ability, for others more guidance is required. Adults entering professional education courses arrive with an often unarticulated set of preconceptions, or anticipatory schemata, about what they will learn and how they will learn, based on their own personal histories. In order to facilitate the ability to transfer it is useful to enact the process within the curriculum by allowing these models, preconceptions or assumptions to be brought to the fore. This implies a pedagogy that values and uses the individual experiences which students bring to learning, recognises the importance of the feelings and attitudes of students in enabling or inhibiting their progress, allows time for reflection, encourages a 'deep' as opposed to a 'surface' approach to learning and promotes autonomy and active learning.

For mature students, the experience of education can lead to a significant change or disruption in their personal lives in both practical and emotional terms. At a practical level, institutions might respond by reorganising course timetables so that they fit in with home and childcare responsibilities (see Chapter 11). At an emotional level, creating a suitable 'climate of care' enables students to feel safe in sharing their feelings, stresses and anxieties; sharing such experience is, in itself, a valuable resource. Learning starts from within; knowing and appreciating the emotional world of self and others is a fundamental task of social work education.

Climate setting, the provision of a safe environment, is also important in terms of challenging inappropriate behaviour. The problem of 'values' is one that perennially haunts the social work profession. Research suggests that students can go through the motions of evidencing anti-discriminatory practice without internalising it if courses allow the 'pathologisation' of certain belief systems and, by implication, certain students, rather than enabling them to be accommodated appropriately within a framework of professional ethics (Marsh and Triseliotis 1996). Holding strong religious beliefs is not necessarily incompatible with being an effective social worker and may sometimes enable more empathy between worker and service user (see Chapter 12). Within a postmodernist paradigm, the task of budding practitioners is to get to 'know themselves' and to use this knowing as a way of gaining access to the differing perspectives of other people. Ellerman (1998) suggests that one way of doing this may be through discourse analysis in which students write about particular issues from a variety of different points of view (e.g. their own, lone parent, practice teacher, etc.). This is also a means of encouraging reflexivity.

Adults have different life experiences and different modes of making sense of these life experiences. Research has shown that students also have different ways of learning and handling knowledge. These have variously been described as learning styles (Pask 1976) or approaches (Entwistle 1992). Pask (1976) differentiates serialist and holist learning styles. 'Serialists' break down the learning task into small steps, which they master in turn. 'Holists' need an overall picture and proceed by relating different parts of the tasks to that picture. Learners are regarded as having a predisposition to use one style rather than another, but whether this is innate or influenced by previous educational experience is a matter of conjecture. There has been some debate whether teaching styles should 'match' the predominant learning styles of the students (and to some extent these have been linked to subject areas with 'serialists' congregating in science and 'holists' being more attracted to the arts); those who advocate that matching should take place indicate that students are less anxious and learn more effectively if this is the case. It has been argued, on the other hand, that deliberate mismatching introduces cognitive dissonance, which encourages students to challenge preconceptions.

Work on 'deep' and 'surface' learning approaches indicates that, although students have a predisposition to use one or other approach, the learning environment can shift students from a 'deep' to a 'surface' approach or vice versa. In terms of professional education, it is obviously more desirable to foster 'deep' approaches; yet, as Biggs points out, it is 'rather easier to induce a surface than a deep approach … It is very easy to make students anxious, cynical or simply overworked – all excellent soils for surface strategies to flourish – but much more difficult to make them curious' (Biggs 1990 in Atkins *et al.* 1993: 56).

In terms of encouraging transfer of learning, it is necessary to use a variety of teaching methods (Milligan 1998; Entwistle 1992). This enhances learning and cognitive flexibility by providing a mixture of learning tasks and processes – a repertoire of possibilities – from which learners are able to pick their learning procedure. It also enhances metacognitive awareness: the ability to select a suitable strategy for dealing with the task in hand. In the context of social work, creativity and artistry have been noted as important aspects of expertise and these may be encouraged by developing areas not normally encountered on the curriculum such as creative writing, literature, art and meditation (Gould and Taylor 1996).

The task

For curiosity to be sustained, students have to be active learners, making connections between their own unique experience and the knowledge acquired from their community of practice. In relation to the learning task, appropriate transfer of learning requires that the original learning must be in place and be understood, the learner must be able to see and understand the connections between the original learning and the new learning and there must be sufficient opportunity to try out this new learning in practice. Transfer of learning will thus be facilitated by a learning experience that is well taught and well integrated with previous knowledge, teaching methods which seek to enhance the ability of students to make connections and ample scope for putting learning into practice.

Learning involves change: the modification of existing schemata, the interpretation, categorisation of and application of knowledge. As indicated, knowledge is a broad concept implying both action and reflection. It is not enough to teach students knowledge for practice; students have to learn to use knowledge in practice and to revise this knowledge in the light of their practice. The role of the teacher or facilitator is crucial in terms of enabling students to map professional knowledge or know-how, to 'challenge students with alternative ways of interpreting experiences and present them with ideas and behaviours that cause them to examine critically their values and ways of acting and assumptions' (Brookfield 1986: 23, in Taylor 1996: 85). In contemporary social work, practitioners need to engage with contingency and the uncertain conditions under which they will practice; they need to be able to 'read' situations and 'problematise'; and they need to take appropriate action based on the different sources of knowledge that they have accessed.

Theory and practice, then, need to be closely interlinked. Facilitators need to structure examples of practice in a such a way as to bring the transferable elements – concepts and principles – into consciousness and point out their more general applicability (Nisbet and Shucksmith 1986: 21). Butler and Elliot (1995: 19) indicate that if students are taught factors associated with a general principle they can apply them to a range of situations; for example, if loss is taken as a general principle, such factors may be applied to a range of different kinds of loss such as bereavement, amputation, unemployment or divorce.

Educators reiterate the importance of building up an index of examples of good practice on which the student may call when faced with a new and problematic situation (Stevenson 1994). Enquiry and action learning (EAL) encourages students to work together to build up their knowledge of a domain by accessing a particular case study or 'problem' using a variety of methods and resources, books, tapes, expert consultants, role-playing, back-up lectures and workshops; the variety enables them to test and revise their ideas continually (see Chapter 5). Such methods, which encourage group-based discussion and discovery, facilitate 'deep' processing and transfer of learning (Brooks and Dansereau 1987; Resnick 1990). As Ehrenherg (1983: 82–3) points out: 'people learn better, faster and retain longer when they have frequent and appropriate opportunities to verbalise and share what they are learning with other learners or with instructors'.

Other methods used within the context of an educational institution may include problem-based learning (PBL), role-playing, critical incident analysis (CIA), video simulations and vignettes. These provide a basis for this index of experience, allowing students to explore the important facets of a case while being a step removed from 'messy' reality where time is of the essence. Such methods enable students to articulate their 'anticipatory' schema, whether based on personal experience or formal theory or a mixture of both and to critically analyse these models and revise them within a safe environment. Within practice placements, closer to the 'hard edge', the role of the supervisor is crucial in enabling the students to see links between the theories they have constructed and the reality they encounter. Where methods such as PBL or EAL are used, teaching needs to ensure that the students are clear about the nature of their learning – that there is no 'right answer' to be uncovered – but rather a puzzle which might have a number of resolutions, thus encouraging students to be inquiring and sceptical.

As well as providing a range of practice experiences, case studies or examples may be devised with the intent of helping students to overcome common misconceptions (Creedy *et al.* 1992). As an add-on to this kind of discursive method, computer-assisted learning may be used to reinforce learning; one study demonstrated that hypertext learning environments that explicitly related abstract and case-specific knowledge prepared students to use such knowledge in new situations (Jacobson *et al.* 1995).

Reflection has a fundamental place in transfer of learning. Experience is initially apprehended at the level of impressions: a period of reflective thinking is required before it is either assimilated into existing schemata of experience or induces those schemata to change in order to accommodate it. Including time for reflection, away from 'busywork', is crucially important in terms of the demands of coursework and future practice. Reflection may be an aspect of any kind of teaching, but methods that specifically encourage the process of reflection include the use of learning logs, journals, reflective diaries, process recordings, CIA, intentional observation and personal construct theory (see Chapters 4–9).

It must be emphasised that a student-centred curriculum such as outlined here does not imply less work for the teacher/facilitator. The range of knowledge required in promoting group discussions or use of reflective diaries, critical incidents, etc. probably exceeds that required by conventional teaching methods. In addition, for this kind of curriculum to be effective, there is more onus on the facilitator to be open and responsive to what the students bring: in other words, to practice reflexivity (Rossiter 1996).

The context

The learning context is influenced by the curriculum, the educational or professional framework within which it is located, the institution and society in general. In terms of the curriculum, the way in which knowledge is organised through the teaching process is of key importance in terms of developing the learner's own patterns of representing knowledge and for enabling recall and retrieval strategies. Aspects such as overloading encourage anxiety and stress on the part of the student and militate against teaching for transfer. In social work education, the integration of theory and practice, and learning and application is important both within the institutional context of learning and within the practice placement. A learning environment that is caring, safe and challenging will enable the student to progress. As a process that is largely internal to the individual, transfer of learning is difficult to evidence empirically and may not lend itself to traditional educational assessment or outcome measures; methods such as the one-off examination may, in fact, operate against it. Alternative methods of assessment and feedback include self-assessment exercises, observation and the use of vignettes, all of which involve the active learner (Cree *et al*. 1998).

Outside the institution there are many pressures that encourage less than ideal conditions for learning. The drive to 'marketisation' of education, the increase in student numbers without a corresponding increase in staff in many colleges and universities means that students may have less individual attention and staff have less preparation time for the production of learning materials. This is exacerbated by the 'knowledge explosion', which makes it harder to keep up to date with the field and to select appropriate curriculum materials without overloading students. At best, such pressures may promote the use of peer group learning, computer-aided learning and sharing of resources, and examples of best practice, between courses. Militating against this, however, are the traditional demarcation lines of particular departments and institutions and the current climate of teaching and research assessment exercises that promote competition for the limited resources available. We have argued that transfer of learning requires a process-based model of education rather than a product-based one; yet the development of 'packaged education' and the increasing emphases on modularisation, documentable transferable skills and outcome-led curricula may lead to an increasingly fragmented notion of what education is about and how it can be assessed (Cree *et al*. 1998).

In tandem with changes in educational ethos are debates within social work itself. These largely concern its role and meaning as a profession – of which there are many competing discourses, most of which stress its intangible and ambivalent nature – within a framework of practice that has become more rigidly bureaucratised and proceduralised. Workers within agencies are frequently overstretched and have little time to keep up to date with new legislation, never mind find the space for reflective practice. No wonder social workers sometimes find themselves in the role of 'double agent' as they seek to take account of the competing needs of the agency and the service user:

These developments bring social work uncomfortably close to a confrontation with its own contradictory reality. On the one hand it is inescapably concerned with the resolution of human conflicts and collective action dilemmas by negotiated means that aim at agreed solutions. On the other, its organised formal expression, especially since its incorporation into welfare states, has been increasingly concerned with statutory enforcement and the rationing of scarce resources. Practice balances precariously between these two elements, drawing on knowledge from each for its improvisations and strategies for survival.

(Jones and Jordan 1996: 266–7)

In the face of this, one of the central dilemmas of social work education, or indeed any professional education, is how the ideals of the profession can be maintained, or even harnessed, while enabling budding practitioners to deal with the messy, chaotic and contradictory reality that they will encounter. Jones and Jordan argue the importance, in this respect, of cognitive flexibility, and knowledge developed from practice:

Social work education can do little but react to these developments.... More hopefully it can provide opportunities for practitioners and students to reflect critically and flexibly on their experiences, and to develop intelligent strategies within the new frameworks. All this will require educators and trainers to reinterpret the relationship between knowledge and practice .... The real integration between theory and practice will not come from a ponderous, rigid body of knowledge, but from the humility to learn from practitioners' experiences.

(Jones and Jordan 1996: 266)

Putting transfer of learning at the centre of the curriculum, with its emphasis on developing and enhancing cognitive flexibility, as a way of coping with the knowledge revolution, as a way of coping with the contradictory demands of practice, as a way of coping with contingency and ambiguity, and as a way of coping with the increasing complexity of the social work task, might, just might, provide an answer.

Acknowledgement

Thanks to the editor of the journal *Social Work Education* for kindly allowing me to draw on some material originally published in an earlier draft as an article entitled 'Transfer of learning: concept and process', 18(2): 183–94.

Bibliography

Atkins, M.J., Beattie, J. and Dockrell, W.B. (1993) *Assessment Issues in Higher Education,* Newcastle upon Tyne: School of Education, University of Newcastle upon Tyne.

Barnett, R. (1994) *The Limits of Competence: Knowledge, Higher Education and Society,* Buckingham: The Society for Research into Higher Education.

Benbenishty, R. (1992) 'An overview of methods to elicit and model expert clinical judgment and decision making', *Social Service Review* December: 598–616.

Benner, P. (1984) *From Novice to Expert,* Menlo Park, CA: Addison-Wesley.

Bennett, N., Buckingham, D. and Dunne, E. (1994) *Personal Transferable Skills,* Exeter: University of Exeter.

Biggs, J. (1990) 'Teaching for desired learning outcomes', in N. Entwistle (ed.) *Handbook of Educational Ideas and Practices,* London: Routledge.

Billett, S. (1994) 'Authenticity in workplace learning settings', in J. Stevenson (ed.), *Cognition at Work. The Development of Vocational Expertise,* Leabrook, Australia: National Centre for Vocational Education Research Ltd.

Boud, D. and Miller, N. (eds) (1996) *Working with Experience: Animating Learning,* London: Routledge.

Bridges, D. (1994) 'Transferable skills: a philosophical perspective', in D. Bridges (ed.) *Transferable Skills in Higher Education,* Norwich: University of East Anglia.

Brookfield, S. (1986) *Understanding and Facilitating Adult Learning,* Milton Keynes: Open University Press.

Brooks, L.W. and Dansereau, D.F. (1987) 'Transfer of information: an instructional perspective', in S.M. Cormier and J.D. Hagman (eds) *Transfer of Learning. Contemporary Research and Applications,* San Diego: Academic Press.

Burgess, H. (1992) *Problem-led Learning for Social Work: the Enquiry and Action Approach,* London: Whiting and Birch.

Butler, B. and Elliott, D. (1985) *Teaching and Learning for Practice,* Aldershot: Gower.

Central Council for Education and Training in Social Work (1995) *Assuring Quality in the Diploma in Social Work – 1: Rules and Requirements for the DipSW,* London: CCETSW.

—— (1995) *Assuring Quality in the Diploma in Social Work – 2: Approval, Review and Inspection of DipSW Programmes,* London: CCETSW.

Channer, Y. (1996) 'Adult learning and practice teaching: issues for Black teachers and learners', *Social Work Education* 15: 57–68.

Collins, H.M. (1989) 'Learning through enculturation', in A. Gellatly, D. Rogers and J.A. Sloboda (eds) *Cognition and Social Worlds,* Oxford: Clarendon Press.

Cree, V.E., Macaulay, C. and Loney, H. (1998) *Transfer of Learning: A Study,* Edinburgh: Scottish Office Central Research Unit and CCETSW.

Creedy, D., Horsfall, I. and Hand, B. (1992) 'Problem-based learning in nurse education: an Australian view', *Journal of Advanced Nursing* 17: 727–33.

Cust, J. (1995) 'Recent cognitive perspectives on learning-implications for nurse education', *Nurse Education Today* 15: 280–90.

Detterman, D.K. (1993) 'The case for the prosecution: transfer as an epiphenomenon', in D.K. Detterman and R.J. Sternberg (eds) *Transfer on Trial: Intelligence, Cognition, and Instruction,* Norwood, NJ: Alex Publishing Corporation.

Dickson, D. and Bamford, D. (1995) 'Improving the interpersonal skills of social work students: the problem of transfer of training and what to do about it', *British Journal of Social Work* 25: 85–105.

Ehrenberg, L.M. (1983) 'How to ensure better transfer of learning', *Training and Development Journal* 37: 81–3.

Ellerman, A. (1998) 'Can discourse analysis enable reflective social work practice', *Social Work Education* 17(1): 35–44.

Entwistle, N. (1987) 'A model of the teaching-learning process', in J.T.E. Richardson, M.W. Eysenck and D.W. Piper (eds), *Student Learning,* Milton Keynes: The Society for Research into Higher Education, Open University Press.

—— (1990) 'Teaching and the quality of learning in higher education', in N. Entwistle (ed.) *Handbook of Educational Ideas and Practices,* London: Routledge.

—— (1992) *The Impact of Teaching on Learning Outcomes in Higher Education: A Literature Review,* Sheffield: USDU.

Entwistle, N. and Ramsden, P. (1983) *Understanding Student Learning,* Beckenham, Kent: Croom Helm Ltd.

Eraut, M. (1994) *Developing Professional Knowledge and Competence,* London: Falmer Press.

—— (1996) 'The new discourse of vocational education and training: a framework for clarifying assumptions, challenging rhetoric and planning useful theoretically informed research', ECER Conference Paper, 1–13, Seville.

Fleishman, E.A. (1987) Foreword, in S.M. Cormier and J.D. Hagman (eds) *Transfer of Learning. Contemporary Research and Applications,* San Diego: Academic Press.

Fook, J. (2000) 'Deconstructing and reconstructing professional expertise', in Fawcett, B., Featherstone, B. and Fook, J. and Rossiter, A. (eds) *Practice and Research in Postmodern Feminist Perspectives,* London: Routledge.

Fook, J., Ryan, M. and Hawkins, L. (1997) 'Towards a theory of social work expertise', *British Journal of Social Work* 27(2): 399–417.

Freire, P. (1983) 'Education and conscientizao', in M. Tight (ed.) *Education for Adults: Adult Learning and Education*, Beckenham, Kent: Open University/Croom Helm.

Gagne, R.M. (1970) *The Conditions of Learning*, London: Holt, Rinehart and Winston.

Gardiner, D.W.G. (1984) 'Learning for transfer', *Issues in Social Work Education* 4(2): 95–105.

—— (1988) 'Improving student's learning – setting an agenda for quality in the 1990s', *Issues in Social Work Education* 8: 3–10.

—— (1989) *The Anatomy of Supervision: developing learning and professional competence for social work students*, Milton Keynes: The Society for Research into Higher Education and The Open University.

Gibbs, G., Rust, C., Jenkins, A. and Jacques, D. (1994) *Developing Students' Transferable Skills*, Oxford: The Oxford Centre for Staff Development.

Gick, M.L. and Holyoak, K.J. (1987) 'The cognitive basis of knowledge transfer', in S.M. Cormier and J.D. Hagman (eds) *Transfer of Learning. Contemporary Research and Applications*, San Diego: Academic Press.

Gott, S. (1989) 'Apprenticeship instruction for real world tasks: the co-ordination of procedures, mental models and strategies', *Review of Research in Education* 1(15): 97–169.

Gould, N. (1993) 'Cognitive change and learning from practice: a longitudinal study of social work students', *Social Work Education* 12(1): 77–87.

—— (1996) 'Social work education and the crisis of the professions' in N. Gould and I. Taylor (eds) *Reflective Learning for Social Work*, Aldershot: Arena.

Gould N. and Taylor I. (eds) *Reflective Learning for Social Work*, Aldershot: Arena.

Guberman, S.R., and Greenfield, P.M. (1991) 'Learning and transfer in everyday cognition', *Cognitive Development* 6: 233–60.

Harris, R.J. (1985) 'The transfer of learning in social work education', in R.J. Harris (ed.) *Educating Social Workers*, Leicester: Association of Teachers in Social Work Education.

Jacobson M.J., Spriro R, Spiro J. (1995) Hypertext learning environments, cognitive flexibility and the transfer of complex knowledge: an empirical investigation. *Journal of Computing Research* 12(4): 301–33.

Jinks, G.H. (1991) 'Making the most of practical placements: what the nurse teacher can do to maximize the benefits for students', *Nurse Education Today* 11: 127–33.

Jones, M. and Jordan, B. (1996) 'Knowledge and practice in social work', in S. Jackson and M. Preston-Shoot (eds) *Educating Social Workers in a Changing Policy Context*, London: Whiting and Birch.

Knowles, M.S. (1972) 'Innovations in teaching styles and approaches based upon adult learning', *Journal of Education for Social Work* 8: 32–9.

Knowles, M.S. (1983) 'Andragogy: an emerging technology for adult learning', in M. Tight (ed.) *Education for Adults: Adult Learning and Education,* Beckenham, Kent: Open University/Croom Helm.

Kolb, D.A. (1976) *Learning Style Inventory: Technical Manual,* Newton, MA: Institute for Development Research.

Kolb, D.A. (1984) *Experiential Learning,* New York: Prentice Hall.

McKeough, A., Lupart J. and Marini A. (eds) (1995) *Teaching for Transfer. Fostering Generalization in Learning,* Mahwah, NJ: Lawrence Erlbaum Associates, Inc.

Marginson, S. (1994) *The Transfer of Skills and Knowledge from Education to Work,* Melbourne: Centre for the Study of Higher Education.

Marini, A. and Genereux, R. (1995) 'The challenge of teaching for transfer', in A. McKeough, J. Lupart and A. Marini (eds) *Teaching for Transfer. Fostering Generalization in Learning,* Mahwah, NJ: Lawrence Erlbaum Associates, Inc.

Marsh, P. and Triseliotis, J. (1996) *Ready to Practise? Social Workers and Probation Officers: their Training and First Year in Work,* Aldershot: Avebury.

Martin, E. and Ramsden, P. (1987) 'Learning skills, or skill in learning', in J.T.E. Richardson, M.W. Eysenck and D.W. Piper (eds) *Student Learning: Research in Education and Cognitive Psychology,* Milton Keynes: SRHE and Open University Press.

Marton, F. and Saljo, R. (1984) 'Approaches to learning', in F. Marton, D. Hounsell and N. Entwistle (eds) *The Experience of Learning,* Edinburgh: Scottish Academic Press.

Mezirow, J. (1983) 'A critical theory of adult learning and education' in M. Tight (ed.) *Education for Adults: Adult Learning and Education,* Beckenham, Kent: Open University/Croom Helm.

Milligan F. (1999) Beyond the rhetoric of problem based learning: emancipatory limits and links with andragogy. Paper presented at the Nurse Education Tomorrow conference, Durham, 1999.

Nisbet, J. and Shucksmith, J. (1986) *Learning to Learn,* London: Routledge and Kegan Paul.

Papell, C.P. and Skolnik, L. (1992) 'The reflective practitioner: a contemporary paradigm's relevance for social work education', *Journal of Social Work Education* 28: 18–26.

Pask, G. (1976) 'Styles and strategies of learning', *British Journal of Educational Psychology* 46: 4–11.

Piaget, J. (1972) *Psychology and Epistemology*, P. Wells (translator), Harmondsworth: Penguin Books.

Pietroni, M. (1995) 'Nature and aims of professional education. A postmodern perspective', in M. Yelloly (ed.) *Learning and Teaching in Social Work. Towards Reflective Practice,* London: Jessica Kingsley Publishers.

Postman, L. (1972) 'Transfer, interference and forgetting', in J.W. Kling and L.A. Riggs (eds) *Woodworth and Schlosberg's Experimental Psychology*, London: Methuen and Co., Ltd.

Ramsden, P., Beswick, D. and Bowden, J. (1987) 'Learning processes and learning skills', in J.T.E. Richardson, M.W. Eysenck and D.W. Piper (eds) *Student Learning: Research in Education and Cognitive Psychology*, Milton Keynes: SRHE and Open University.

Resnick, L. (1990) 'Instruction and the cultivation of thinking', in N. Entwistle (ed.) *Handbook of Educational Ideas and Practices*, London: Routledge.

Rogers, C. (1975) 'Freedom to learn', in N. Entwistle and D. Hounsell (eds) *How Students Learn*, Lancaster: University of Lancaster.

Rogers, C. (1983) *Freedom to Learn for the 80s*, Columbus, OH: Charles E. Merrill.

Rossiter, A. (1996) 'Finding meaning for social work in transitional times: reflections of change', in N. Gould and I. Taylor (eds) *Reflective Learning for Social Work*, Aldershot: Arena.

Ryan, M., Fook, J. and Hawkins, L. (1995) 'From beginner to graduate social worker: preliminary findings of an Australian longitudinal study', *British Journal of Social Work* 25: 17–35.

Salomon, G. and Perkins, D.N. (1989) 'Rocky roads to transfer: rethinking mechanisms of a neglected phenomenon', *Educational Psychologist* 24(2): 113–42.

Schön, D.A. (1983) *The Reflective Practitioner: How Professionals Think in Action*, London: Temple Smith.

—— (1987) *Educating the Reflective Practitioner*, San Francisco: Jossey-Bass.

Secker, J. (1993) *From Theory to Practice in Social Work*, Aldershot: Avebury.

Sternberg, R.J. (1994) *Thinking and Problem Solving*, London: Academic Press.

Stevenson, J. (1994) 'Vocational expertise', in J. Stevenson (ed.) *Cognition at Work. The Development of Vocational Expertise*, Leabrook, Australia: National Centre for Vocational Research Ltd.

Taylor, I. (1996) 'Facilitating reflective learning' in N. Gould and I. Taylor (eds) *Reflective Learning for Social Work*, Aldershot: Arena.

Thorndyke E. L. and Woodworth R. S. (1901) The influence of improvement in one mental function upon the efficiency of other functions. *Psychological Review* 8: 247–61.

Thorndyke E. L. (1924) Mental discipline in high school studies. *Journal of Educational Psychology* 15: 1–22.

Tight, M. (1983) *Education for Adults*. Vol. 1: *Adult Learning and Education*, London: Croom Helm and Open University.

Whittington, C. (1986) 'Literature review: transfer of learning in social work education', *British Journal of Social Work*, 16: 571–7.

Chapter 2

The challenge of assessment

Viviene E. Cree

Introduction

Assessment in education is a challenge for students and teaching staff alike. Students frequently find themselves forced to leap-frog across what can seem like countless assessment hurdles in the course of their training. At the same time, teachers (lecturers, tutors and practice teachers) need to ensure that assessment tasks are as effective and fair as possible. It has been argued that the assessment process may either facilitate or inhibit transfer of learning, depending on its nature, systems and procedures (Cree *et al.* 1998). In this chapter I will develop this idea more fully, identifying the problems and pitfalls in assessment, as well as the potential for good practice and the encouragement of transfer of learning. Before doing so, however, it is necessary to clarify what is meant by assessment in the context of higher education and social work education.

Definitions: what is assessment?

Assessment is of central importance to students' learning (Brown *et al.* 1997). It sets parameters on what students think of as important, how they spend their time and how they see themselves as learners and even as human beings. Brown *et al.* (1997: 7) argue that 'If you want to change student learning then change the methods of assessment'.

But what is assessment? The term is derived from the Latin *ad sedere* – to sit beside – the implication being that it is primarily concerned with collaboration rather than inspection (Brockbank and McGill 1998). In the real world of assessment in higher and professional education, the experience of being assessed may be very different from this. Brown offers an explanation of assessment:

Assessment consists, essentially, of taking a sample of what students do, making inferences and estimating the worth of their actions … The behaviours sampled may be specific to a course or they may be more general. They may be related to explicit or implicit criteria. The sampling may be undertaken by the students themselves, their peers, their tutors or employers with whom they are working. On the basis of the sample that is taken, inferences are made about a person's achievements, potential, intelligence, aptitudes, attitudes, motivations and, perhaps, personality and an estimate of worth in the form of grades, marks or recommendations is made.

(Brown *et al*. 1997: 8)

Assessment is, then, the process of sampling students' work and drawing inferences from that sample. Beyond this broad description, a number of specific questions emerge. How is the sample to be chosen? By whom? When should the sample be taken? What about students' work that is not included in the sample? How are the inferences to be made? Again, by whom?

A useful framework for carrying out assessments is provided by the educationalist Loacker. He identifies six steps in the procedure:

Determine what is to be assessed: in order to achieve this, we must first ask the question – what constitutes distinction or competence in our field?

Design the means and criteria of assessment: this may mean setting aside or at least re-examining existing tests and looking more broadly at what might be part of the assessment process.

Assess: take care to apply the criteria, and identify any significant signs of ability that the criteria might not include.

Interpret results: ask the question – what do the results tell us about the student's learning, progress and needs for future direction?

Give feedback: feedback contributes to the dynamic picture that students are building of their own abilities.

Use feedback: feedback must connect to the broader picture of each student's development, so that improvements can be made to teaching itself.

(Loacker 1988: 20–3)

This framework clearly indicates the importance of identifying the component parts of the assessment process. Yet there is a sense in which it poses more questions than it answers. How do we determine competence? What criteria should we apply and by whose standards? Who interprets the results and against what standards? In practice, assessment may be criterion-referenced (where students' work is measured against certain fixed criteria), norm-referenced (where students' work is ranked against that of their peers) or self-referenced (where students set their own targets and measure themselves against those). It may be either summative (carried out for grading purposes, often at the end of a course of training) or formative (carried out to assist students' learning, usually during the course of their training). All these factors will have an influence on the nature of assessment and the kinds of assessment methods adopted.

Assessment in higher education has three very different, sometimes overlapping, purposes (Rowntree 1987):

- Diagnosis/appraisal (examining what an individual student has learnt and suggesting where to go from there);
- Marking/grading (grading students' performance against one another or against a standard);
- Evaluation (assessing how far students have learned what they have been taught; thus, how successful teaching has been).

The vast majority of research and literature on assessment has been concerned with the use of assessment for marking and grading, rather than for either diagnosis or evaluation (Rowntree 1987). This chapter will attempt to keep all three purposes of assessment in mind, examining the ways in which transfer of learning may be influenced by the many procedures that are used to assess student learning.

Trends in assessment

Assessment in higher education

During the 1970s, a shift took place in ways of thinking about assessment in higher education, characterised by Brown *et al.* (1997: 13) as 'down with exams; up with coursework'. Other aspects of this shift may be outlined as follows:

From	*Towards*
Written examinations	Coursework
Tutor-led assessment	Student-led assessment
Implicit criteria	Explicit criteria
Competition	Collaboration (self and peer assessment)
Product assessment	Process assessment
Objectives	Outcomes
Content	Competencies
Course assessment	Modular assessment
Advanced levels	Assessed prior learning (APL)

(Brown *et al.* 1997: 13)

This list encapsulates some of the trends in assessment over the last twenty-five years. It may also, however, be seen as something of a 'wish-list'. Higher education has been slow to adopt new ideas. It is often the so-called 'new' universities, the former polytechnics and technical colleges, (renamed universities in 1992) that have taken on and developed notions such as modularisation and accreditation of prior learning (APL). Despite the rhetoric, higher education institutions have been reluctant to move away completely from examinations, and frequently the notion of continuous assessment has been treated as an addition, rather than an alternative to the end-of-course examination. Similarly, although there may have been a shift in the direction of peer assessment and self-assessment, this has usually been a 'value-added' extra to more conventional assessment methods. This may, in part, be because peer and self-assessment methods can lead to difficulties in achieving consistency and fair comparisons across student groups (Brown *et al.* 1997: 10).[1] It may also, however, reflect the reality that the increase in students entering higher education in the 1980s and 1990s has tended to make assessment processes more proceduralised and rule-driven. Pressure from central bodies such as the Higher Education Funding Council has also tended to increase the formality of documentation and, again, the replacement of discretion with fixed rules (Higher Education Quality Council 1997: 8).

There is tension within the changing assessment practices detailed above. An emphasis on outcomes, for example, may be at odds with the idea of incremental learning and process-based assessment. The familiar questions re-emerge: what is assessment, and what is it for? If the learning objectives are to open students' minds and broaden their experience, then the chosen assessment methods will be very different from those that set out to assess a specific piece of knowledge or skill.

The shift to competency and modular approaches in higher education must be seen as part of a wider project to make education more relevant and useful to employers and in the workplace. Competence-based training (CBT) appeared in teacher training courses in the USA in the late 1960s, but it was not taken up in the UK until 1989 with the development of National Vocational Qualifications (NVQs) (Atkins *et al.* 1993; Ford and Hayes 1996). Competence has been defined as 'the ability to perform to recognised standards' (Jessup 1991: 40). Competency approaches thus carry with them the tantalising promise that it is possible to identify not only what students or employees can do, but also how this performance measures up to an agreed standard. The central concern of education and training becomes the outcome of the learning/training process; there is little interest in the process itself, since it is understood that individuals will reach the point of outcome in different ways.

Employers , however, do not constitute the only group that has been pushing for changes in the organisation and delivery of higher education. As a more diverse group of students has entered higher education (Silver and Silver 1997), so there have been calls to recognise and accredit the previous learning experiences of non-traditional entrants. APL and APEL (accreditation of experiential prior learning) schemes have made it possible for mature students with experience of work or family commitments to undertake degree courses and to achieve some recognition of their existing learning. APL and more specifically APEL schemes have brought new challenges for assessment, because ways have had to be found for the measurement and accreditation of experience that until now has not been formally assessed (Brown *et al.* 1997; Reeve and Smith 1996).

Assessment in social work education

Changes in assessment in social work education in the UK must be placed in the context of two, very different pressures. On the one hand, changes may be seen as mirroring the wider changes taking place in assessment in higher education in general. On the other hand, they reflect the very particular situation of social work and its struggle for professional status.

Social work assessment and assessment in higher education

Two key features of contemporary social work education in the UK reflect the shift already described in relation to higher education as a whole. These are the adoption of a competency approach and the development of modularisation.

The origins of a competency approach in UK social work can be found with the introduction by the Central Council of Education and Training in Social Work of a new qualification in social work, the Diploma in Social Work (DipSW) in April 1989 (CCETSW 1989). The new qualification replaced two former qualifying awards and for the first time specified the knowledge, skills and values needed for competent social work practice (CCETSW 1995). It also made it a requirement that academic institutions would work with employers in partnership to provide programmes of social work education. Three years later the DipSW was under review,[2] and by 1995 a revised DipSW redefined the purpose, knowledge skills and values of the profession and presented a set of competences and practice requirements that had to be met by all qualifying students. The new DipSW also set out to promote wider and more flexible routes to education and training in social work: non-graduate, undergraduate, post-graduate; college, university and employer-based; modular, distance learning and part-time courses (Vass 1996: 3–4).

The competency model outlined in the DipSW takes as its starting point the desired outcome of training; in this case, the competent social worker. Six behavioural objectives ('competences') are designated, which all students must be able to demonstrate by the point of qualification. These are:

- communicate and engage
- promote and enable
- assess and plan
- intervene and provide services
- work in organisations
- develop professional competence.

The core competences are said to be based on and can only be achieved through the *transfer* of knowledge, skills and values (CCETSW 1995: 3). Thus transfer of learning underpins all social work programmes, although it is not defined as a specific competence.

The introduction of a competency approach to social work education has been welcomed by some commentators. O'Hagan (1996), for example, sees the spelling-out of 'evidence indicators' and 'practice requirements' as largely positive for students; it encourages them to think about what they are doing, and reminds them of the relevance of knowledge, skills and values to their practice. Others disagree profoundly, arguing that the competency model has led to a fragmented approach to learning, in which knowledge and skills are split up (Barnett 1994; Ford and Hayes 1996), and there may be a loss of focus on the development of values and beliefs (Bilson 1993). It is also claimed that focusing on the outcome of learning may lead to a devaluing of the process of achieving that learning (Shardlow and Doel 1996). Some social work writers raise even more basic questions about competence and competency, suggesting that these terms are at best illusory and at worst, misguided. Clark writes:

> The pursuit of 'competence' is a false trail for social work, as in all higher occupations. In such roles job content can never be reduced to predefinable observable behaviours. No set of 'competences' can ever in principle cover adequately the range and complexity of tasks and issues to be addressed; further it is not practically possible to create properly validated objective tests of competence. For these reasons, purporting to train students to achieve competence is perverting professional education.
>
> (Clark 1997: 55)

Competency approaches have been accompanied, in some social work programmes, by the introduction of modular courses. The modularisation of learning, as already stated, is part of the drive to make education more systematic and identifiable, as well as more flexible to meet the needs of an expanding and changing student population. The development of modular, credit-based courses in social work may be seen as enabling students to acquire credits from a variety of sources and to enter and exit training at different points (Reeve and Smith 1996). Modularisation, on the other hand, with its discrete units of learning, has been seen as carrying with it dangers of splitting and compartmentalisation, discouraging students from making connections between different areas of the curriculum (Cree *et al*. 1998).

Social work and the struggle for professional status

There is another key issue that must be considered as part of the underlying picture of assessment in social work education, that is social work's claim to professional status. The introduction of ever-tighter regulations for curriculum and assessment in social work education must be understood as part of an ongoing struggle to define and control the social work task (Cree 1995). Since its beginnings in nineteenth-century philanthropy and the Poor Law, social work has fought to achieve the professional standing and position of other, 'older' professional groupings such as lawyers, doctors and the clergy. In this struggle, social work education has played a central role. As Jones (1979: 72) points out, 'social work courses have exercised important regulatory and unifying functions within the profession, and are regarded by social work leaders themselves as one of the crucial places where the social work perspective is established and sustained'. Jones suggests that social work education should be understood as having two principal functions, external and internal. At the external level, social work education aims to 'forge a professional and expert identity for social work' and 'claim a slice of social welfare activity for itself' (Jones 1979: 73). At the internal level, it sets out to socialise social workers into the norms and values of the profession. This theme is picked up by Hugman (1991), who argues that professionalisation is a prime example of what he calls 'exclusionary closure based on credentials'. Credentials (qualifications) enable an occupation to keep out those who do not meet the standard expectations; the more successful an occupation is in gaining control over the establishment and award of qualifications, the greater the degree of closure it will have achieved. Hugman (1991) argues that exclusionary closure affects not only those who enter a profession but also those who are allowed to practise a profession. It defines boundaries between one profession and another, and it provides foundations for power exercised by professionals in relation to service users.

If we accept this conceptualisation of professionalisation, the assessment of social work students becomes more than simply a neutral, technical activity carried out on individual students. Instead, it is a highly political process, reflecting the interests and objectives of specific interest-groups within social work and within society. The shift towards a competency approach in social work education and the introduction of greater controls over what is taught and what is assessed in social work training may be seen to reflect the relative success of employers and governments in winning control of the social work profession.[3] Dominelli (1997) puts this cogently:

> DipSW has been the vehicle through which CCETSW has technocratised social work education and shifted the balance of power away from professional academics and practitioners on to employers. Bureaucratic controls have superseded professional ones as relationship building in social work becomes supplanted by practical competences endorsed by government and employers. These changes reflect a move away from training as an educational process concerned with socialising professionals into the best traditions of the profession towards the technical transmission of approved skills.
>
> (Dominelli 1997: 194)

The critical professional

Dominelli (1997) presents what is rather a depressing view of changes that have affected social work education; Clark (1997) likewise raises fundamental questions about the adoption of a competency approach as a framework for professional education. Given that social work education is located in a context of increasing bureaucratic control and regulation, how can we ensure that social work retains its value-base? More specifically, what place is there for anti-oppressive practice here? Batsleer and Humphries (2000) suggest that the notion of the 'critical professional' goes some way towards bridging this gap. The critical professional appreciates the realities of structured inequalities in society and understands the inevitable contradictions in her/his role. From this perspective, educators and practitioners can, to an extent, work in the interests of the students and service users with whom they are working to 'challenge the hegemony of the market' (Batsleer and Humphries 2000: 12). Drawing on the insights of Donald Schön (1983, 1987) and David Kolb (1984), Issett offers a model for the critical professional:

1   Recognises that professional knowledge is imperfect and can always be improved;
2   Realises that technical expertise is necessary but that there are not formulaic answers to complex questions – what Schön has called 'indeterminate zones of practice';
3   Operates within an integrated personal/professional/political value-base which uses an analysis of power relations and commitment to anti-oppressive practice, that seeks to understand and change the social and political context affecting practice;
4   Builds a cycle of critical reflection to maximise the capacity for critical thought, and produces a sense of professional freedom and a connection with rather than a distance from clients (Pietroni 1995: 43);
5   Needs a safe supportive environment in which to honestly reflect and practice;
6   Listens and learns from ways of reflecting in different cultures and groups.

(Issett 2000: 129–30)

The concept of the critical professional provides a useful backdrop for an examination of the issues concerned with assessment in general and assessment of transfer of learning in particular.

Issues in assessment

Three key issues must be addressed whenever and wherever assessment takes place: its impact on how and what students learn; the problem of subjectivity; and the role of assessment in the evaluation of teaching.

The impact of assessment on students' learning

It has already been stated that assessment methods play a major role in determining how and what students learn. As Wergin writes:

> If we have learned anything from educational research over the last fifty years, it is that students learn according to how they are tested. If we test students for factual recall, then they will memorize a set of facts. If we test them for their ability to analyze relationships, then they will begin to learn to think critically. If we assess how well they can apply classroom material to concrete problems, then they will learn to do that.
>
> (Wergin 1988: 5)

Assessment methods may influence students' learning, irrespective of the teaching methods that are embraced. In her discussion of enquiry and action learning (EAL) in social work education, Taylor (1993) points out that students who are faced with traditional evaluation and assessment methods reproduce conventional approaches to learning, even when the method of teaching is itself innovative. Entwistle (1990, 1995) suggests that open and collaborative assessment systems encourage 'deep' learning and the confidence to try out new approaches; overladen, restrictive assessment procedures, in contrast, create anxiety in students and lead them to adopt either a 'surface' or a 'strategic' approach to learning. The pressure that examinations bring has been specifically identified as leading students to skip courses and to neglect their wider learning objectives (Bennett et al. 1994).

The influence of assessment is not always, of course, detrimental to students' learning. Assessment may help to motivate students, encouraging them to learn and, more specifically, to prioritise certain aspects of the learning experience. It may enable students to structure their time and effort by legitimising certain kinds of activity and outlawing others, and by indicating what is to count as knowledge worth having and what is not (Rowntree 1987). Well-planned assessment mechanisms enable students to find out how they are progressing and give them feedback on their levels of understanding and pointers for the way ahead. Rowntree (1987) describes feedback, or 'knowledge of results', as 'the life-blood of learning': whenever students have said or done something of significance, they want to know how it is received (Rowntree 1987: 24). Brown (1997) notes that feedback is probably the best-tested principle in psychology. It has been found to be most effective when it is timely, perceived as relevant, encouraging and offers suggestions for improvement that are within a student's grasp (Brown 1997: 51). Self-evaluation, peer assessment and assessment by members of staff can all be useful ways of giving students a clear idea of how far they have reached, and how far they still have to go.

Subjectivity in assessment

Issues of subjectivity remain troublesome for assessment, whatever assessment tools are adopted. In reviewing written assessments (examinations, essays and short exercises), Heywood (1989) notes a lack of standardisation between institutions, departments and markers. A degree classification of 2.1 may be seen by individuals and employers to mean a different thing depending on the institution awarding the degree. There is also variation between faculties and departments within institutions in terms of the proportion and type of degrees awarded. Those studying an arts subject are more likely ultimately to be awarded a degree. Proportionately fewer science students are awarded a first class honours degree than in other disciplines (Heywood 1989).

A lack of standardisation exists both between and within individual markers. Not only are candidates' papers marked differently by different people, the same person will give different marks when they re-mark a paper. Studies of assessment suggest that there are many reasons why markers grade performance differently. Examination or essay questions are often open to a number of interpretations, thus the marker may be evaluating a different question from the one the student (or another marker) is responding to. Markers are subject to human error and fatigue; sometimes they may simply misread answers or overlook points. In addition, people bring with them certain predispositions to marking: some will tend to give high grades and others to give low grades.

Attempts, of course, are made to standardise the grades being awarded. Systems for the double-marking of written assignments may reduce the likelihood of individual error or bias. Arrangements to make the process of assessment fairer may include the introduction of anonymous marking of scripts, and the devising of marking frames for grading of essay scripts and examination papers (although given the subjectivity of an essay-type answer, this is not always appropriate). The external examiner/ assessor also plays an important role within universities and colleges in checking standards across and within courses. But none of these safeguards removes the reality that assessing a student's work is a complex, value-laden activity that inevitably involves a degree of subjective judgement on the part of the marker/evaluator. As Milton (1982: 22) writes somewhat provocatively: 'All classroom tests are subjective in one way or another. To seek objective evaluations about students is a waste of time – there are no such things….'

If subjectivity and standardisation are problematic in relation to the assessment of written work, then the scope for difficulties in assessment of professional practice is even greater. Studies have consistently demonstrated that the intense, one-to-one relationship of the social work student and practice teacher/assessor in social work education adds to the difficulty of maintaining objectivity in assessment (Collins and Ottley 1986; Ford and Jones 1987; Thompson *et al.* 1990). Practice teachers are more likely to value the performance of students whom they like, or whose learning style is similar to their own. Particular concerns have been raised in terms of ethnocentric bias in relation to the high proportion of Black students who fail social work programmes (Channer 1996; Graham 1999).[4] Institutions and social work programmes have set in place mechanisms to reduce the possibility of favouritism, personality clash or cultural disagreement. All programmes accredited by the social work education regulating body in the UK (up to 2001, the Central Council for Education and Training in Social Work, thereafter the Training Organisation in Personal Social Services) must have in place procedures for students' grievances and complaints. Some programmes, moreover, have designed specific schedules for observed practice that are used by practice teachers (Tanner and Le Riche 1996). Nevertheless, it remains a truism that what assessors look for and the interpretations that they make of what they find are intimately connected with personal world views and commonsense beliefs about social work, about learning and about human beings and the nature of experience.

The role of assessment in evaluation of teaching

Assessment, as we have seen, gives feedback to students about their knowledge and development. Assessment also gives feedback to teaching staff about the quality and utility of the teaching programme, its content, structure and style of delivery (Rowntree 1987). Although this may be considered to be a by-product of assessment, it is nevertheless the case that the performance of students provides useful information about the success or otherwise of teaching programmes. Where assessment exercises demonstrate that students have not understood a concept, or that their thinking is confused and unclear, instead of blaming the students for failing to grasp what has been taught, an alternative approach would suggest that teaching methods are examined to establish what is not working in a programme. This then enables teaching staff to make improvements that may benefit current and future generations of students (Rowntree 1987).

Assessment and transfer of learning

Transfer of learning is a difficult concept to pin down (Cree *et al*. 1998). It is a complex process in which the individual consciously and subconsciously makes sense of the world by relating previous experiences to a new situation. It is influenced by a range of factors, including specific characteristics in the individual learner, the learning and transfer tasks and the learning and transfer environments (see Chapter 1). Given its complexity, it is not surprising that different writers view the concept of transfer of learning quite differently. Importantly for this chapter, writers also disagree about possible criteria for assessing or evidencing transfer of learning (Biggs 1990; Gibbs *et al*. 1994). Two key theoretical assumptions stand out in this controversy, summed up in the notions of 'transferable' and 'transferring' skills.

A competency approach to education (pp. 31–3) brings with it the belief that it is possible to identify specific skills and competences that must be demonstrated by students at the point of qualification (Holmes 1994). Implicit in this is the notion that 'transferable' and 'generic' skills exist (Assiter 1995). Long lists of so-called transferable skills have been produced, frequently including skills such as verbal communication, written work, organisational and management skills, etc. Assessment of transfer of learning, according to this perspective, is quite straightforward. Tests are designed to assess whether or not, and to what degree, these skills have been evidenced.

However, the idea of 'transferable skills' has proved difficult to sustain in the real world of educational practice. Studies have demonstrated that skills which are commonly perceived to be transferable (for example interpersonal skills, communication skills, problem-solving skills, etc.) are not context-free behaviours fixed for all time and place. Rather, they are specific to knowledge, context and usage, and, as a result, may not necessarily be transferable in all times and places (Marginson 1994). An illustration of this is the fact that knowing how to write lengthy, theoretically oriented essays does not in itself prepare someone to write memos or short letters in an employment context.

A different conceptualisation to the notion of transferable skills is offered by Bridges (1994). He introduces the idea of 'transferring skills' – 'the competences that work on other competences' (Bridges 1994: 14) – or in the words of Marginson (1994), 'transferability skills'. These are not simple, task-oriented skills, but are rather 'higher-order' skills, such as 'learning to learn', 'knowing one's own knowing', making generalisations, discriminating, being flexible and creative. Transferring or transferability skills enable a person to be able to reflect on previous experience in a meaningful way and come up with imaginative solutions for the future. Marginson (1994) adds a note of caution. He asserts that above all else, an awareness of 'contingency' in the formation and use of skills and knowledge must remain at the heart of transfer. Learners must be aware of what they do not know, as well as what they know; real-life situations are inevitably complicated, and individuals inextricably play a part in the process within which they are involved.

The impact of assessment on students' transfer of learning

The general issues considered in relation to assessment have particular relevance for an examination of assessment and transfer of learning. It has already been stated that the ability to transfer learning is indicative of a deep approach to learning. Mechanisms set up to assess transfer of learning may in themselves either facilitate or inhibit the transfer of learning. Systems of assessment may encourage transfer of learning by enabling learners to value their own thought processes and prior experience and identify the conceptual links that they are making. On the other hand, assessment methods that are overly restrictive and burdensome may lead to students feeling 'de-skilled' and unable to make use of their existing knowledge and experience.

Aside from issues of the nature and quantity of assessment, there is also the question of who is doing the assessing. There has been extensive discussion within social work about issues of power in the supervisory and assessment relationship (for example, Channer and Stokes 1996; Clapton 1993; Collins et al. 1992; Elliott 1990; Ford and Jones 1987; Shardlow and Doel 1996; Thompson et al. 1990). This literature suggests that the activity of assessing students carries with it inevitable issues of power imbalance and the potential for oppression, based on status, gender, class, age, 'race'/ethnicity and disability. Whatever other structurally based privileges and advantages practice teachers and assessors in the academic setting may have, they have the additional power to pass or fail a student's work, and with this comes the possibility of coercion, control and oppression.

The supervisor–student relationship in social work education is an extraordinarily complex one. Early studies of practice teaching tended to stress the quasi-counselling relationship between the student and the practice teacher (e.g. Kadushin 1976). More recent literature has criticised the notion that supervision should be a kind of therapy being offered to students and has highlighted instead the need for an adult education model in supervision (Gardiner 1989; Doel 1990). The study by Collins *et al.* (1992) of practice teaching demonstrates the importance for students of practice teachers exercising four different, and at times contradictory, roles: assessor, manager, teacher and enabler. Research into student teachers on school-based placements similarly illustrates the value that students place on challenge as well as support in supervision (Cameron-Jones and O'Hara 1997). (See Chapter 6 for a further discussion of power in the practice teacher–student relationship.)

Subjectivity in assessment of transfer of learning

Issues of subjectivity also vex the assessment of transfer of learning. Finding unambiguous, incontrovertible evidence that transfer of learning has taken place is difficult. Students have different starting points, in terms of previous and current experience, cognitive skills and personality, feelings, experience of discrimination, etc. This means that any programme of assessment must take into account the reality that some students will begin training at a less (or more) advanced stage than others.

In addition, students learn from the *whole* experience of education; as Guberman and Greenfield (1991) have identified, there is no such thing as context-free learning. Research suggests that, faced with the same learning situation, individuals all learn different things (Green 1994). Consequently, students learn things that are not expected of them (and may not, therefore, be examined) as well as things which are tested for, and for which evidence can be found. They also learn in different ways and at different rates: for some, the transfer of learning experience may not be fully internalised until well after the assessment event is completed (Sawdon 1986). What works for one student (in terms of their learning experience and the tools used to assess it) may therefore not work for another (Cree *et al.* 1998).

Assessing transfer of learning as a gauge of the quality of education

Just as student grades offer an indication about the successfulness of teaching, so assessment of transfer of learning gives pointers to the quality of the learning environment as a whole. If students are able to transfer learning readily, we can be fairly certain that the learning context is open and generally supportive. In contrast, when students are unable to transfer learning, we need to look to factors in the educational environment, such as organisational pressure, institutional discrimination and poor teaching as well as factors in the individual student's personality and cognitive ability.

Factors in the transfer and learning task, as well as the learning and transfer context may have a detrimental impact on a student's ability to transfer learning. When original learning is not well understood and is separated from practice, transfer of learning may be inhibited. In addition, factors in the context of both the academic and the practice world may have an adverse influence on transfer of learning, including student poverty, large class sizes, cutbacks in service provision and low morale among colleagues and other professionals. The ability to transfer learning then becomes a kind of 'litmus test' for the whole process of education. If it is not happening, then we need to find new ways of organising and delivering the educational product.

Assessing transfer of learning: practical aspects

The focus of the chapter so far has been to examine the concept of assessment and to consider the relationship between assessment and transfer of learning. I will now offer some practical suggestions for assessing transfer of learning in social work education. In doing so, all the issues raised already must remain at the forefront; there can be no easy solutions to questions about subjectivity, power and control, indeterminacy and contingency (Cree 2000). Nevertheless, assessment methods must be found that are, at the very least, less discriminatory and more inclusive and, at the best, may even facilitate the process of transfer of learning.

The process of assessing transfer of learning: what to assess?

One of the first choices to be made in assessing transfer of learning is to decide what to assess: what, precisely, do we think of as evidence of transfer of learning? Transfer of learning is a complex, highly individual process that varies from student to student. There are, however, key characteristics that are involved in transfer of learning, and these can be sought as indicators or clues that transfer is taking place, or has taken place:

1   Being an active leaner – seeking out knowledge and learning.
2   Being able to reflect on previous experience and knowledge.
3   Being able to see patterns and to make relevant connections between different experiences and sources of knowledge.
4   Being open and flexible, able to compare and discriminate critically.
5   Being able to use abstract principles appropriately.
6   Being able to integrate personal knowledge and experience with professional knowledge and experience.

Where to assess transfer of learning?

Closely connected with the question 'what to assess?' is the issue of where to seek evidence of transfer of learning. Transfer of learning is likely to be found (and so assessed) in the continuous relationship between the student and the practice teacher/tutor, between the student and the practice agency, and between the student and the educational institution (Cree *et al.* 1998). It will therefore be evidenced in supervision and tutorial discussions, in student groups and classrooms and in the preparation of learning tasks for supervision and tutorials.

Transfer of learning may also be demonstrated in a whole range of assessed and non-assessed written work: in practice studies and reports, dissertations, process recordings, learning logs and perhaps even in examination papers, when a student makes useful connections between theory and practice or past and present experience or learning. The issue here is not the assessment tool *per se*, but the way the assessment method is used, and the kind of question that is asked.

Transfer of learning will also be found in practice with service users, when a student purposefully and creatively draws on his/her experiences of life or work. The assessment of practice raises particular ethical issues for students and service users. Direct observation of practice and making recordings of meetings with service users may be experienced negatively by service users, if they feel that confidentiality and comfort is undermined. Service users must be able to make an informed choice about whether or not their exchanges are observed by a third party (Evans 1990: 43).

When to assess transfer of learning?

Rowntree (1987) counsels against prescribing too early what is to be valued in a student's work. He points out that to do so risks 'closing our eyes against evidence of valuable student learning that happens to lie outside our prior specifications' (Rowntree 1987: 82). Research into assessment demonstrates that students learn best through an assessment design which is 'step-up' in character, building on basic knowledge and skills into more and more complex learning (Bryce and McCall 1990).

Because of the nature of transfer of learning, it is difficult to envisage a simple 'step-up' approach to its assessment. Students have very different starting-points in terms of their ability to transfer learning, and this makes any generalised model difficult to sustain. Nevertheless, it seems likely that the assessment of transfer of learning will be enhanced by an exploration at the beginning of training of a student's existing knowledge, skills and experience and the ways the student learns most readily. This can then be the starting-point for a shared discussion that takes place at regular intervals throughout the course of training.

How to assess transfer of learning?

The assessment of transfer of learning should be located in the context of an overall programme of assessment that takes account of both the incremental nature of learning and the importance of individual creativity. It will be essential to use different methods of assessment and hence different kinds of evidence: first, to build up an overall picture of a student's work [Shardlow and Doel (1993) call this the 'correspondence principle'] and, second, to allow for individual variations between students.

Assessment of direct practice with service users

Before direct observation of practice takes place, there must be clear expectations about assessment and the role of practice teacher and student in the assessment process, and an explicit contract between the practice teacher and student for the management of observed practice. The evidence that transfer of learning has taken place will either be visible during the encounter with the service user (when the student, for example, makes links between the current situation and a previous one) or will emerge in the debriefing discussion that takes place afterwards. Alternative methods that may lead to similar outcomes include the use of video or audio equipment to tape a meeting with a service user, role-playing or simulation exercises, or working alongside a student as a co-worker.

Assessment of oral and written evidence

Transfer of learning may be evidenced in a broad range of assessed and non-assessed oral and written work. However, it is the sessions and assignments that encourage reflection and conceptual thought that are more likely to demonstrate transfer of learning.

Learning logs/reflective diaries and process recordings may be especially useful. Some programmes invite students to keep diaries or logs throughout their training, whereas on other courses they are kept on placement only. Tutors or practice teachers may give written or verbal feedback, thus giving another perspective on the learning experience. Although reflective diaries/learning logs are not formally assessed, they are important places for demonstrating that transfer of learning is taking or has taken place. Students often make use of material from reflective diaries as evidence of learning transfer in their contributions to practice reports. Moreover, writing helps students to revisit and reflect on an experience in which they may have been too involved with at the time to have paid much conscious attention to. They can also go back to the same experience many times and see their own professional growth taking place. (See Chapter 7 on the use of reflective diaries.)

Process recordings are a conventional tool of supervision, long-used by practice teachers to encourage students to get close to issues of feelings and the use of self in their contact with service users (Cree *et al*. 1998: 72). Process recordings tend to divide the writing up of the piece of interaction into three parts: a description of the action; what the student thought about this; and how the student felt about it. Some process recordings also ask students to reflect on what the service user may have been thinking and feeling. Process recordings provide a useful discussion tool in which evidence of transfer of learning, such as the relation between previous and new experiences, may emerge (see Chapter 9).

Taylor *et al*. (1999) recommend that students should be encouraged to create portfolios as an ongoing record, allowing them to see progress over time. This seems helpful in terms of facilitating the process of transfer of learning. Nevertheless, questions must be clarified from the outset about ownership of the portfolio and what happens if there is a difference in perception between the practice teacher and the student about the evidence that a portfolio contains (Kemshall 1993).

Assessment may incorporate 'single moments' as well as an ongoing process. Single moment assessments might include case vignettes or critical incidents. In a case vignette, students are allocated a piece of work and are invited to hypothesise on what the problem might be and how it might best be resolved in that particular setting. They might then be asked to address how this problem might be resolved in a different kind of setting. This is very similar to the use of the case scenario developed in EAL (see Chapter 5). Critical incident analysis is a detailed exploration by students of a specific piece of interaction that they have been involved in. It captures both what is unique and what is common about an event (Davis and Reid 1988: 306). It may be chosen by the student or the practice teacher/tutor according to specific criteria (e.g. an incident that went unusually well, one that was particularly demanding, or one that captured the essence of social work etc.) (see Cree *et al.* 1998: 75, and Chapter 8).

Self-assessment

Self-assessment plays a pivotal role in promoting transfer of learning. The Self-Assessment in Professional and Higher Education Project (SAPHE) supported by the Higher Education Funding Council in the UK, and backed by both CCETSW and the Law Society, demonstrates a range of different responses to self-assessment in practice. The four institutions and six departments involved in SAPHE piloted different kinds of self-assessment, from students marking their own and peers' essays, to students writing up self-evaluation sheets and learning logs and keeping portfolios of their work. Self-assessment was also introduced to the teaching of communication and interviewing skills.

In reviewing the SAPHE project, Burgess *et al.* (1999) argue that self-assessment can be a powerful tool to enhance learning, by encouraging students to become active not passive learners. Self-assessment helps learners to 'name their experience and therefore provides a means for exploring, appropriating and moving beyond it' (Boud *et al.* 1993: 32). Burgess *et al.* (1999) warn that self-assessment has significant resource implications. It must be properly planned: induction, guidance and support must be made available to teaching staff and students, through group discussion and in written form, at the start of self-assessment work and then later on as students engage more fully with the process (Burgess *et al.* 1999: 143). But self-assessment is worth the effort, Hinett and Thomas (1999: 9) assert, because assessing what is required is 'a key skill in the development of professional practice', and reflective practice is 'a skill for life, not just for professional practice'.

Feedback from service users

Social work as a professional body is increasingly concerned with seeking out and, where possible, making use of service users' views to improve policy and practice. Evans (1990) suggests that three main methods are possible for getting service user feedback, depending on the setting and the kind of information being sought: oral comments, written comments and questionnaires. He insists that 'client feedback' should be voluntary, but it is likely to be experienced positively by service users. It may not be easy to elicit clear evidence about transfer of learning from service users. Nevertheless, a direct question along the following lines might provide some illumination: 'How did X help you to make sense of what has happened to you?'

How to interpret evidence of transfer of learning?

A key issue in the assessment of transfer of learning is the question of interpretation. Do we judge students' work against some predetermined standard ('criterion-referenced' assessment), or do we compare them against the norm set by their colleagues ('norm-referenced' assessment)? Or do we ask students to assess their own work, through self-referenced assessment? Interpretation of evidence of transfer of learning is likely to use all three systems at different times. Although self-referenced assessment clearly has the advantage of allowing students to make connections and 'name' their own learning, other systems of interpretation will also be needed to bring a measure of standardisation and equity across student groups.

Conclusion

This chapter has turned out to be a wide-ranging discussion of assessment, transfer of learning and social work education. I have argued that we must be clear what assessment is for, as well as understanding what it is and how it operates. In the context of social work education, assessment of transfer of learning has the capacity to facilitate learning transfer: it makes visible the connections between past and present knowledge and experience; it highlights comparisons between different theoretical models; it encourages reflection on learning and experience. As such, assessment of transfer of learning may be regarded as a positive element in social work education. It can, however, as with all assessment systems, impede learning and act as a block to learning transfer. The onus is on social work educators to adopt assessment procedures that seek to facilitate transfer of learning – to build on the creative and reflective imperative that is central to the 'critical professional' (Batsleer and Humphries 2000). This is the real challenge of assessment.

Notes

1   For an outline of changing assessment practices in Scottish higher education, see Hounsell *et al.* (1996).
2   A critical element in the decision to review the new qualification was political and organisational pressure to soften Paper 30's anti-oppressive and anti-racist stance. (See Dominelli 1997; Vass 1996.)
3   This has been evidenced again in calls for a National Curriculum for social work training, on similar lines to the National Curriculum that has been introduced to school-based education in England and Wales (Association of Teachers in Social Work Education Conference, June 1999).
4   Similar concern has been raised about Black school students' experiences of assessment. Rowntree (1987: 41) indicates that several studies have shown that the performance of Black children can be lower when tested by a White person than when tested by someone of their own 'race'.

Bibliography

Assiter, A. (1995) 'Transferable skills: a response to the sceptics', in A. Assiter (ed.) *Transferable Skills in Higher Education*, London: Kogan Page.

Atkins, M.J., Beattie, J. and Dockrell, W.B. (1993) *Assessment Issues in Higher Education*, Newcastle upon Tyne: School of Education, University of Newcastle upon Tyne.

Barnett, R. (1994) *The Limits of Competence: Knowledge, Higher Education and Society*, Buckingham: The Society for Research into Higher Education.

Batsleer, J. and Humphries, B. (2000) *Welfare, Exclusion and Political Agency*, London: Routledge.

Bennett, N., Buckingham, D. and Dunne, E. (1994) *Personal Transferable Skills*, Exeter: University of Exeter.

Biggs, J. (1990) 'Teaching for desired learning outcomes' in N. Entwistle (ed.) *Handbook of Educational Ideas and Practices*, London: Routledge.

Bilson, A. (1993) 'Applying Bateson's theory of learning to social work education', *Social Work Education* 12(1): 46–61.

Boud, D., Cohen, R. and Walker, D. (1993) 'Understanding learning from experience', in D. Boud, R. Cohen and D. Walker (eds) *Using Experience for Learning*, Buckingham: SRHE and Open University Press.

Bridges, D. (1994) *Transferable Skills in Higher Education*, Norwich: University of East Anglia/ERTEC.

Brockbank, A. and McGill, I. (1998) *Facilitating Learning and Reflective Practice*, Buckingham: Open University Press.

Brown, G., Bull, J. and Pendlebury, M. (1997) *Assessing Student Learning in Higher Education*, London: Routledge.

Bryce, T. and McCall, J. (1990) 'Assessment of practical skills', in N. Entwistle (ed.) *Handbook of Educational Ideas and Practices*, London: Routledge.

Burgess, H., Baldwin, M., Dalrymple, J. and Thomas, J. (1999) 'Developing self-assessment in social work education', *Social Work Education* 18(2): 133–46.

Cameron-Jones, M. and O'Hara, P. (1997) 'Support and challenge in teacher education', *British Educational Research Journal* 23(1): 15–23.

Central Council for Education and Training in Social Work (1989) *Rules and Requirements for the Diploma in Social Work*, London: CCETSW Paper 30.

—— (1995) *Assuring Quality in the Diploma in Social Work – 1: Rules and Requirements for the DipSW*, London: CCETSW.

Channer, Y. (1996) 'Adult learning and practice teaching: issues for Black teachers and learners', *Social Work Education* 15(2): 57–68.

Channer, Y. and Stokes, I. (1996) 'Supervision issues for Black practice teachers', *Social Work Education* 15(2): 69–76.

Clapton, G. (1993) 'Anti-discriminatory practice teaching: power and powerlessness', *Journal of Training and Development* 3(2): 39–45.

Clark, C. (1997) 'Competence, knowledge and professional discipline', *Issues in Social Work Education* 16(2): 45–56.

Collins, S. and Ottley, G. (1986) 'Practice teacher: reflections, steps before reflection and some steps for the future', *Social Work Education* 6(1): 11–15.

Collins, S., Ottley, G. and McMurran, M. (1992) 'Student and practice teacher perceptions of the enabling role in practice teaching', *Social Work Education* 11(2): 20–40.

Cree, V.E. (1995) *From Public Streets to Private Lives. The Changing Task of Social Work*, Aldershot: Avebury.

—— (2000) *Sociology for Social Workers and Probation Officers*, London: Routledge.

Cree, V.E., Macaulay, C. and Loney, H. (1998) *Transfer of Learning. A Study*, Edinburgh: Scottish Office Central Research Unit and CCETSW.

Davis, I. and Reid, W. (1988) 'Event analysis in clinical practice and process research', *Social Casework* 69(5): 298–306.

Doel, M. (1990) 'Putting heart into the curriculum', *Community Care* 18(January): 20–2.

Dominelli, L. (1997) *Sociology for Social Work*, Basingstoke: Macmillan.

Elliott, N. (1990) *Practice Teaching and the Art of Social Work*, Norwich: University of East Anglia.

Entwistle, N. (1990) 'Teaching and the quality of learning in higher education', in N. Entwistle (ed.) *Handbook of Educational Ideas and Practices*, London: Routledge.

—— (1995) 'Defining quality in teaching: the research perspective', *SHEFC/British Council Conference on Quality Assessment in Higher Education, Edinburgh* September: pp. 1–15.

Evans, D. (1990) *Assessing Students' Competence to Practise in College and Practice Agency*, London: CCETSW.

Ford, K. and Jones, A. (1987) *Student Supervision*, Basingstoke: Macmillan.

Ford, P. and Hayes, P. (1996) *Educating for Social Work: Arguments for Optimism*, Aldershot: Avebury.

Gardiner, D. (1989) *The Anatomy of Supervision*, Milton Keynes: Open University Press.

Gibbs, G., Rust, C., Jenkins, A. and Jacques, D. (1994) *Developing Students' Transferable Skills*, Oxford: The Oxford Centre for Staff Development.

Graham, M.J. (1999) 'The African-centred world view: developing a paradigm for social work', *British Journal of Social Work* 29(2): 251–67.

Green, A. (1994) 'A psychological approach to identifying transferable skills and transfer skills', in D. Bridges (ed.) *Transferable Skills in Higher Education*, Norwich: University of East Anglia.

Guberman, S.R. and Greenfield, P.M. (1991) 'Learning and transfer in everyday cognition', *Cognitive Development* 6: 233–60.

Heywood, J. (1989) *Assessment in Higher Education*, Chichester: John Wiley & Sons Ltd.

Higher Education Quality Council (1997) *Assessment in Higher Education and the Role of 'Graduateness'*, London: HEQC.

Hinett, K. and Thomas, J. (1999) *Introduction to 'Self Assessment in Professional and Higher Education' (SAPHE),* Bristol: the University of Bristol in collaboration with the University of Bath, the University of the West of England and Southampton Institute.

Holmes, L. (1994) 'Competence, qualifications and transferability: beyond the limits of functional analysis', in D. Bridges (ed.) *Transferable Skills in Higher Education*, Norwich: University of East Anglia.

Hounsell, D., McCulloch, M. and Scott, M. (1996) *The ASSHE Inventory*, Edinburgh: University of Edinburgh.

Hugman, R. (1991) *Power in Caring Professions*, Basingstoke: Macmillan.

Issett, M. (2000) 'Critical professionals and reflective practice', in J. Batsleer and B. Humphries (eds) *Welfare, Exclusion and Political Agency*, London: Routledge.

Jessup, G. (1991) *Outcomes: NVQs and the Emerging Model of Education and Training*, London: Falmer Press.

Jones, C. (1979) 'Social work education, 1900–1977', in N. Parry, M. Rustin and C. Sataymurti (eds) *Social Work, Welfare and the State*, London: Edward Arnold.

Kadushin, A. (1976) *Supervision in Social Work*, New York: Columbia University Press.

Kemshall, H. (1993) 'Assessing competence: scientific process or subjective inference? Do we really see it?', *Social Work Education* 12(1): 36–45.

Kolb, D.A. (1984) *Experiential Learning*, New York: Prentice Hall.

Loacker, G. (1988) 'Faculty as a force to improve instruction through assessment', in J.H. McMillan (ed.) *Assessing Students' Learning*, San Francisco: Jossey-Bass.

Marginson, S. (1994) *The Transfer of Skills and Knowledge from Education to Work*, Melbourne: Centre for the Study of Higher Education.

Milton, O. (1982) *Will that Be on the Final?* Springfield, IL: Thomas.

O'Hagan, K. (1996) *Competence in Social Work Practice*, London: Jessica Kingsley Publishers.

Pietroni, M. (1995) 'Nature and aims of professional education. A postmodern perspective', in M. Yelloly and M. Henkel (eds) *Learning and Teaching in Social Work. Towards Reflective Practice*, London: Jessica Kingsley Publishers.

Ramsden, P. (1992) *Learning to Teach in Higher Education*, London: Routledge.

Reeve, F. and Smith, I. (1996) *Accrediting Prior Experiential Learning. A Manual for Good Practice in Higher Education*, Glasgow: Glasgow Caledonian University, Centre for Continuing Education.

Rowntree, D. (1987) *Assessing Students: How Shall We Know Them?*, London: Kogan Page.

Sawdon, D.T. (1986) Transferability and all that', in D.T. Sawdon (ed.) *Making Connections in Practice Teaching*, London: NISW.

Schön, D.A. (1983) *The Reflective Practitioner: How Professionals Think in Action*, London: Temple Smith.

—— (1987) *Educating the Reflective Practitioner*, San Francisco: Jossey-Bass.

Shardlow, S. and Doel, M. (1996) *Practice Learning and Teaching*, Basingstoke: Macmillan.

Silver, H. and Silver, P. (1997) *Students. Changing Roles, Changing Lives*, Buckingham: SRHE and Open University press.

Tanner, K. and Le Riche, P. (1996) '"You see but you do not observe." The art of observation and its application to practice teaching', *Issues in Social Work Education* 15: 2.

Taylor, I. (1993) 'A case for social work evaluation of social work education', *British Journal of Social Work* 23: 123–38.

Taylor, I., Thomas, J. and Sage, H. (1999) 'Portfolios for learning and assessment: laying the foundations for continuing professional development', *Social Work Education* 18(2): 147–60.

Thompson, N., Osada, M. and Anderson, B. (1990) *Practice Teaching in Social Work*, Birmingham: Pepar.

Thorndike, R.L. and Hagen, E.R. (1977) *Measurement and Evaluation in Psychology and Education*, New York: Wiley.

Vass, A.A. (1996) *Social Work Competences. Core Knowledge, Values and Skills*, London: Sage.

Wergin, J.F. (1988) 'Basic issues and principles in classroom assessment', in McMillan, J.H. (ed.) *Assessing Students' Learning*, San Francisco: Jossey-Bass.

Chapter 3

Competence, risk assessment and transfer of learning

Hazel Kemshall

Introduction

The contention that higher education should positively contribute to the world of industry and the 'needs of society' is not entirely new (Barnett 1990; Holmes 1995; Silver and Brennan 1988). What is new is the prominence given to this connection in the curriculum, and, in particular, the new-found attention to 'transferable skills' (Holmes 1995). Although simplistic explanations include 'major structural changes in graduate employment patterns' (Holmes 1995: 21) and employer disappointment with the level of graduate skills (Otter 1992), a number of commentators have argued that such a development has to be placed within a broader political and economic context (Assiter 1995; Barnett 1994; Hyland 1991). Hyland (1991), in particular, notes the rise of an 'enterprise ethos in education', which has resulted in the need to justify higher educational activities in terms of industrial and economic rationalities. This in turn has led to an increased commercialisation of education at all levels and the use of managerialism as a mechanism to provide 'social legitimation and moral justification' for this new 'educational ethos' (Hyland 1991: 78). The contrast with pre-1970s educational liberalism could not be more stark.

This recent economic discourse on education is the context within which concerns about the transferability of learning in higher education and competence-based education in vocational training can be located. The primacy accorded to the 'requirements of industry and commerce' has led to the rise in vocational education characterised by curricula dominated by employer-led performance concerns (DES 1977, 1985). In higher education, this trend was expressed in the joint statement of the National Advisory Board and the University Grants Committee, which stated that 'The abilities most valued in industrial and commercial life as well as in public and social administration are the transferable intellectual and personal skills'. (NAB/UGC 1984: 1).

More recently the Dearing Report (1997) and the Garrick Report (1997) have argued for the notions of 'learning for life' and the 'learning society'. The emphasis here is upon the development of a flexible, highly skilled workforce in which people will be equipped for employment and life as citizens. Key themes are 'learning to learn', that is the development of critical reflection, analysis and reasoning, evaluation and problem-solving, and the development of basic skills in numeracy, literacy and information technology. The rise in competence-based education has been seen as part of this 'instrumental vocationalising' (Hyland 1993a: 57), and within an economic framing of education transfer of learning has become a key component.

This chapter will briefly review key issues in transferability, its link to competence-based education and the broader question of competence-based education's suitability in facilitating transfer of learning. In particular, it will explore the increasing ambiguity of many professional goals and tasks in areas such as social work, health and teaching, and the increased contingency of professional knowledge as professional roles and tasks are reconstituted. In this climate, transfer of learning is likely to be of increasing relevance, not least to hard-pressed professionals who are confronted with high degrees of uncertainty and who are frequently expected to adapt to new professional tasks. A key question is how transfer of learning is best facilitated and promoted by higher education.

Transfer of learning and competence-based education

Although transferability of knowledge and skills has gained prominence in current approaches to education, definitions of transferable skills and knowledge are elusive and varied (Cree *et al.* 1998). Within a predominantly economic discourse of education, a typical response has been a normative and positivistic one in which employer-related performance specifications uncritically predominate: '"skills" are treated as having some independent reality capable (in principle) of being identified and of being causally related to performance in a variety of settings' (Holmes 1995: 24). The issue of transferability is thereby reduced to one of accurate measurement techniques and evidence collection. This leaves unresolved a number of underlying difficulties such as what actually constitutes these skills, how they interrelate and how they are related to actual performance (Bridges 1992). The positivist framing of transferability and competence embodies a naive realism in which measurement techniques replace conceptual difficulties, and the socially constructed nature of transferability and competence concerns are obscured.

Similar critiques have been levelled at competence-based education. Implicit, normative statements of what constitutes appropriate education and what constitutes a desirable employee are also presented as largely uncontentious, as Eraut (1994: 159) indicates: 'The use of the word "competence" is not value-neutral'. In this context, competence often refers to the production of 'enterprising graduates' for the 'enterprise culture' (Assiter 1995; Corrigan *et al*. 1995; Training Agency 1989). The actual needs and desires of these graduates are largely ignored.

In considering transferable skills, two key issues have emerged. The first is the identification of those skills that can transfer across different cognitive domains or subject areas, and the second is the identification of those that transfer across various contexts and social settings. The former are most often referred to as 'core skills' such as numeracy, communication, study, problem-solving, personal and social skills, and information technology skills (National Curriculum Council 1990). The latter are seen as 'transferable skills' such as 'interpersonal communication, management skills and collaborative group working' that apply across a range of situations and locales (Bridges 1992: 9).

Various difficulties arise in the definition and pursuit of transferability. These occur most notably in terms of drawing clear boundaries between subject domains and hence identifying with reliability when transfer has occurred, and in working out the extent to which contexts and social settings are genuinely different and hence testing of transferability (Barrow 1987; Bridges 1992). One response to these difficulties has been the notion of 'meta-competence', that is the identification of the skills involved in the adaptation of skill or knowledge itself to new domains or situations, in essence the identification of the skill of transferability itself (Bridges 1992; Fleming 1991; Cree *et al*. 1998).

The pursuit of the meta-competence of transferability has, however, raised critical doubts about the appropriateness of competence-based education (Hyland 1992; 1993a). Collins (1991), for example, has dismissed it as a 'narrow technicist approach to education' designed to 'meet corporate needs' with both competences and the key ingredients of transferability constructed by employer rather than educational concerns (Collins 1991: 45). Critics have also argued against the positivistic behavioural reductionism of competence-based education with its roots in the functional analysis of work roles and the reduction of complex tasks to statements of performance outcomes against prespecified criteria (Hyland 1993a; Marshall 1991; Norris 1991).

Critiques of competence-based education essentially fall within two broad perspectives: the shortcomings of behavioural reductionism in terms of psychology and learning theory, and the epistemological shortcomings underpinning this approach. The behavioural critique, which draws attention to the reduction in creativity and laments the learning-to-order approach, has been well vented with Marshall (1991: 61), in particular, describing competence as being 'one-dimensional and prescriptive'. In addition, the uncertainty about the nature of competency and what actually underpins competences has led to epistemological concerns (Hyland 1992). The narrowness of employer-defined competences is seen as a particular problem. It is claimed that limited and mechanistic training may actually hinder professional development and transferability (Callender 1992). Marshall (1991: 63) suggests that although the NVQ framework may be effective in 'training basic skills', it is 'less effective as the level of skill and cognitive requirement increases', and, therefore, it would be 'ludicrous to apply the same model to all levels of training'. This has led to considerable debate about the appropriateness of competence-based education and training for professions such as teaching and the probation service (Hyland 1993b, Williams 1996).

The restrictive difficulties developing from the definition of narrow competences have in part been addressed by the notion of 'generic' competence 'which identifies the role-played by knowledge and understanding in the generation and development of competence' (Hyland 1993a: 59). In NVQ language this has resulted in a distinction between 'first order measures', which relate only to performance, and 'second order measures', which attempt to capture the underpinning knowledge, skills and understanding (Wolf 1990: 30). Generic competences have been designed to both ensure and measure 'the transferability of occupational skills so as to answer criticisms of narrowness of focus' (Hyland 1993a: 59, Raggatt 1991).

However, this has not entirely solved the epistemological difficulties. Writing from a constructivist position, Hyland (1992) argues that knowledge has to be inferred from observable performance. This is a process open to error, bias and a high degree of subjectivism (Kemshall 1993). It is also highly dependent upon the precise and adequate specification of 'outcome evidence' – only that knowledge which can be directly related to the performance, and only that which can be measured has any legitimacy. Competence-based education then remains 'epistemologically equivocal and theoretically suspect' (Hyland 1993a: 60). This is particularly exemplified by the disjuncture between theory and practice. The functionalist approach to knowledge and skill acquisition is viewed as particularly problematic in this regard. Eraut (1989) has been highly critical of the NVQ atheoretical approach to performance, stating that 'people use theory all the time ... it is their personal theories which determine how they interpret the world and their encounters with people and situations within it' (Eraut 1989: 65).

Assiter (1992: 18) has also rejected the functionalism of the competency approach and the pursuit of verification through the reduction of knowledge statements to observable, measurable forms. She argues for a broader conception of competence taken from Boyatzis (1982), in which competence is defined in terms of 'underlying characteristics' that enable 'effective action' and 'superior performance', a conceptualisation of competence which is not entirely amenable to positivistic techniques of measurement. Interestingly, the Training Agency began its conceptualisation of competence in these terms by stating that competence is 'the ability to perform the activities within an occupation ... competence is a wide concept which embodies the ability to transfer skills and knowledge to new situations within the occupational role' (Training Agency 1988: 1). In this conceptualisation, transfer of skills from one context to another is central, and 'is strikingly different from the recent NVQ focus on behaviours and outcomes of behaviour' (Assiter 1992: 23). The links with Bridges' (1992) notion of competence in the art of transfer itself are clear. Although it may be tempting to dismiss this as the illusory 'meta-competence' (Hyland 1992), the emphasis upon adaptability and applicability of knowledge and skills to new situations is useful.

This adaptability, with its emphasis upon problem solving in novel situations, and the applicability of existing knowledge to new contexts has been seen as the key to competent professional performance (Cree *et al.* 1998). Responsiveness and adaptability to new situations is seen as a key requirement of numerous professions and, therefore, a key ingredient of vocational education (Schön 1983).

Within social work, transfer of learning has a vital place because 'students cannot rehearse in training all the types of work which they will be required to undertake in their professional career' (Gardiner 1989: 134). The essential ambiguity and uncertainty of social work practice has been pointed out by Parton (1994). With its historical roots in discourses as diverse as law and psychiatry, social work has become a 'contested area and one subject to diverse and sometimes competing rationales and definitions' (Parton 1994: 95). This has been exacerbated by challenges to welfarism and the raison d'être of social work, coupled with disputes over the knowledge base of the profession and the level of its expertise (Carew 1979). The contingent nature of the social work task is increasingly apparent, correct resolutions are unknown and experts disagree:

> Problems cannot be overcome by quick technical fixes and there are no final resolutions to the dilemmas and difficulties encountered in social life ... Notions of ambivalence, contingency, risk and reflexivity are seen as integral to the (post) modern condition and its consequences.
>
> (Parton 1994: 104)

The question is whether competence-based vocational education can best equip professionals to respond to this ambiguity and contingency. This will be reviewed in the next section by considering professional responses to a highly ambiguous and contingent social work task: risk assessment and management.

Contingency, risk and transfer of learning

Contemporary society has been characterised as the 'risk society', a society in which the relentless pursuit of modernity has produced its own range of scientific, technological and environmental risks (Beck 1992: 30–1). However, the 'risk society' results not merely from a collection of new environmental hazards but also from a realisation of the contingent and uncertain nature of social life (Giddens 1990; Parton 1994). Social life no longer follows a 'predestined course' (Parton 1994: 104). The key underlying concern of the 'risk society' is the unpredictable nature of the future. Exposure to risk increases uncertainty and the possibility that one's future may contain unforeseen dangers, hence the desire to predict future risks and their potential negative outcomes. Strategies for risk assessment and risk management offer enticing mechanisms for accessing this uncertain future and enabling risk avoidance, essential for managing contingency (Kemshall et al. 1997; Parton 1996).

Uncertainty brings with it a number of consequences, not least increased anxiety, scepticism of expert opinion and diminished trust in both professionals and established institutions (Beck 1992). This was most recently expressed in both media coverage and public responses to the bovine spongiform encephalopathy (BSE) food scare (Miller and

Reilly 1996). There have been similar parallels in social work and criminal justice. For example, disputes over expert opinion on child abuse in Cleveland (Butler-Schloss 1988), the seminal Beckford report (London Borough of Brent 1985), and increased media and public anxiety over the ability of professionals to assess and regulate dangerous individuals in the community (Blom-Cooper *et al.* 1995). The disputed and contingent nature of expert professional knowledge raises the question of how we hold such experts to account for their activities when no-one can guarantee a certain outcome and the criteria for evaluating one set of activities against another are often unclear.

The growth of occupational standards and vocational competences can be viewed within this context. Their place in enhancing managerial accountability of professional performance is well documented (Hyland 1991). However, a key issue is whether this approach to vocational education facilitates professional performance in a world of contingency, or merely attempts to reduce professional and managerial anxieties over uncertainty. It has been suggested that competences are a response to conditions of postmodernity in that they represent a 'quest for certainty' (Taylor 1996: 159). As Howe (1994: 527) points out, 'The reduction of uncertainty underlines most occupational practices. To render safe and predictable, workable and reliable....'

In this context, transfer of learning may be seen as a key strategy in the management of contingency and uncertainty in professional practice. The limits of competence-based education in this regard can be discerned, primarily the restrictive nature of prespecified outcomes that militate against contingency, and the epistemological underpinnings which distance conceptual and strategic knowledge from procedural knowledge (Cust 1995; Eraut 1996). The latter is particularly significant, not only because of the importance of conceptual and strategic knowledge to transfer of learning but also to decision-making under conditions of uncertainty (Brearley 1982).

Howe has argued that attempts to establish a 'new certainty' have been based on procedures rather than expertise in 'diagnoses and therapeutic relationships', concentrating upon the 'what' rather than the 'why'. The prioritisation of performance over underlying theory and process has resulted in a transformation of social work practices to 'be task-orientated and performance related, quantifiable and measurable, product-minded and subject to quality controls. Procedure manuals and lists of competences define more and more what social workers should do and how they must do it' (Howe 1994: 528–9).

The essential character of social work has been transformed. The threat of contingency is reduced through increasing emphasis upon input–output ratios and performance criteria (McBeath and Webb 1991). The language and mechanisms of economic rationality are deployed to reduce the ambiguity of the social work enterprise. Competences provide not only access to performance but also assist in the reformulation of the social work discourse into an economic one.

In contrast, transfer of learning is process rather than product orientated. Described as the use of past experience or learning to make sense of novel situations, it is viewed as a way of coping with the highly changeable nature of the social work task (Cree *et al.* 1998). Risk in social work and probation practice provides a challenge to the transfer of learning. Intrinsically bound up with predicting a range of possible future outcomes, risk work involves the worker in constantly assessing the potentiality of novel situations and exploring the varied strategies through which such situations can be resolved (Kemshall *et al.* 1997). As an 'exercise in uncertainty', risk work provides an arena in which the possibility and utility of transferable learning can be tested Brearley (1982).

Risk and uncertainty: the possibilities and limits of transfer

Risk can be defined as 'the probability that a particular adverse event occurs during a stated period of time, or results from a particular challenge' (Royal Society 1992: 2). In the context of social work and probation, risk has become a key organising principle of service delivery. Risk here is defined as the 'uncertain prediction about future behaviour, with a chance that the future outcome of the behaviour will be harmful or negative' (Kemshall 1996: v). There is an important distinction to be made between risk and uncertainty; in essence the distinction between the predictable and the unpredictable, 'or more correctly the calculable and non-calculable forms of indeterminacy.' Parton (1998) indicates that the former is risk but the latter is uncertainty: 'It is my contention that the vast majority of social work ... is much better characterised in terms of uncertainty than risk, and that the notion of ambiguity is central to its operation' (Parton 1998: 23). Nursing and teaching practice have been seen in similar terms as 'ambiguous or ill-structured' (Cust 1995: 86); and professional practice generally as characterised by 'complexity, uncertainty, instability, uniqueness, and value conflict' (Schön 1983: 18). For these reasons, assessment 'cannot be resolved by recourse to neat, simple theoretical propositions that are the outcome of positivist research' (Cust 1995:285).

However, Kelly (1996) has offered just such a framework for the assessment of risk. He notes that the lack of a 'generally accepted theoretical framework' is a barrier to understanding 'the facts and knowledge (its) assessment procedures generate'; and, therefore, 'workers can be thrown back on their own accumulated knowledge or 'common sense' (Kelly 1996: 114). In these situations, the corrective approach of employer-led competences for risk are attractive. Kelly offers Brearley's (1982) situational and highly interactive model of risk assessment as a vehicle for evidence collection and assessment of risk performance standards. In so doing, Brearley's model is reduced to a snapshot, a static view of risk at odds with the dynamic methodology originally proposed. The highly contextualised nature of risk is diminished in favour of an objective construct amenable to competency-based measurement. This can result in difficulties, not least in attempting to transfer the competence across social care settings where the nature of risk may change (Kemshall and Pritchard 1997). As Wolf indicates:

> [K]nowledge and understanding are likely to be highly contextualised – and so, correspondingly, is competence. This means that it is difficult to infer from a single measure, or even quite a few measures, just how far competence extends ... This is, of course, the whole 'transfer' issue.
>
> (Wolf 1989: 44)

This 'contextualisation' was illustrated in a recent empirical study of probation officers that investigated the knowledge base used by staff in offender risk assessments (Kemshall 1998a). The study explored the extent to which technical knowledge on risk was deployed through the use of formal risk tools derived from research, such as the Offender Gravity Reconviction Score (Copas *et al.* 1994) or the Level of Service Inventory (Andrews 1995).

Although there was general acceptability that such 'tools can be useful', their impact upon decision-making varied. Respondents drew upon technical knowledge of actuarial risk indicators, but in terms of factors to be considered rather than as statistical factors in a probability calculation. Decision-making was characterised by high uncertainty and a number of 'it depends' that were situational and individual in nature. Risk was viewed by practitioners as a dynamic phenomenon, fraught by uncertain knowledge of current facts and uncertain future outcomes rather than as a static phenomenon amenable to probabilistic calculation. A typical response to a case scenario from a probation officer was:

> I think it very much depends. I would want to know a lot more about where the police are getting their information from; is it concrete proof; suspicions that she is continuing to offend are very vague. I would want to know a lot more information before I parted with mine, because the relationship I have with Joan is confidential; and yes I have information that she ... some months previously did have a [invalidity] book in her house, but I don't think that is enough to accuse her of something without a lot more information.

In these fluid situations of risk, professional knowledge is necessarily incomplete, tacit and practical (Jones and Joss 1995). In the absence of important knowledge and essential information, respondents literally 'wait and see' and engage in a process of reflective reasoning to decide on courses of action. For example, in deciding whether to inform the organisers of a luncheon club about an offender's previous conviction history, a probation officer indicated:

> I couldn't not do anything about it, I couldn't not take any action because I think it has got to be raised but I don't know whether I would tell them; I don't think I would do either of those things; I think the most likely would be to try and do it together.

This account illustrates the process of reflective reasoning used in situations of dilemma, particularly when dealing with incomplete information. Probation officers were also constrained in their decision-making by perceptions of roles and responsibilities, such as what it was 'appropriate to do', by legal considerations and whether they had the authority to act by ethical considerations about what it was 'proper to do' (for example breaching client confidentiality) and by what might be deemed managerially desirable. This is the delicate balance of risks, rights and responsibilities that all social workers are required to take account of (Kemshall and Pritchard 1997). Such decision-making usually contains a moral component (Parton et al. 1997). This consideration and other 'intangibles' are not usually encompassed by the competence approach:

> [C]ertain aspects of social work, such as the ability to think critically and creatively, the emotional quality of the interaction, and the thought processes and the values of the worker, tend to be excluded, because they are hard to observe and inaccessible to measurement.
> (Ford 1996: 30)

However, it is just such discretion which is seen as the key to 'artistry' (England 1986), a prerequisite of competent professional performance particularly in situations of 'indeterminacy' (Schön 1983). Values have a key role in the framing of assessment problems and in how actions are chosen for the resolutions of such problems (Brearley 1982; Schön 1983; Strachan and Tallant 1997). Values come into sharp focus in the exercise of roles and responsibilities. Brearley (1982) distinguishes between three types of responsibility: moral obligation, legal liability and organisational accountability (Brearley 1982: 15). These types of responsibility can conflict; for example, probation officers may feel a moral obligation towards the offender with whom they have a relationship, even though their organisational obligations may be to implement agency procedures and protect victims in order to avoid legal liability for their employers, procedures that may be detrimental to the well-being of their client. Different responsibilities may lead to the differing prioritisation of actions, not all of which will be conducive to the value-base of practitioners. This gap between values and actions is likely to be heightened when organisations introduce new tasks and responsibilities and alter the main role of the professional workforce. An emphasis on competences may lead to the concealment of such tensions beneath a subordination to the 'discipline of the market' (Nellis 1995: 13). In these situations, transfer of learning may be constrained by the expectations of the employer. One outcome is the possibility of a narrow transfer of learning in line with prespecified employer concerns. Market-led transfer can be potentially limiting. The tension for trainees between highly contextualised and employer-specific competences and the necessity for 'transportable skills' is very real.

The arena of practice uncertainty and the subsequent value-framing used to resolve it has been described by Schön (1983) as practice in the 'indeterminate zone'. Such uncertainty or 'indeterminacy' can be hidden by routinising practice and reducing dilemmas of problem framing and resolution to bureaucratic procedures (for example check-lists or competences). This is highly dependent upon an agreed view of the nature and likelihood of the risk in question and agreed goals and objectives for its regulation (for example the risk of radioactive discharge in the nuclear industry and the measures introduced for its prevention). Transferability to contexts where the nature and likelihood of risk is uncertain and goals and objectives contested can be problematic (Kemshall *et al.* 1997; Parton 1996). Risk decisions within these contexts are not merely matters of technical expertise, rather risk is viewed as situationally specific, highly variable and subject to a number of 'it depends' (Adams 1995). Risk is therefore viewed as a contested and conditional phenomenon, rooted in a complex interplay of individual subjective views, cultural belief and the specific context within which it is operationalised (Adams 1995; Beck 1992; Douglas 1986, 1992; Douglas and Wildavsky 1983).

This is most often expressed as a question of making decisions about which risks are acceptable, which can be tolerated, which risks are worth running and which are not. Such decisions have been characterised as decisions of value and belief as well as decisions of probabilistic calculation (Douglas 1986; Douglas and Wildavsky 1983). Parton captures this difference in social work risk decisions thus:

> As a consequence, systems, procedures and organisational frameworks which operate as if issues are resolvable in any kind of realist, scientific or calculative/probabilistic sense are in great danger of missing the point. We are in a situation where notions of artistic, situated judgements should be valued, and where organisations should concentrate on developing notions of mutual trust and be respectful of different points of view.
>
> (Parton 1998: 23)

The tension of opposing views (for example of rights, risks and responsibilities) is seen as an essential ingredient to maintaining alertness, flexibility and responsiveness in risk assessment and management (Dunsire 1978, 1990, 1992). Within this practice reality, workers in a study of probation practice engaged in strategic decision-making in order to manage the uncertainty of risk and the competing goals it gives rise to. In this sense, knowledge about risk is rarely 'just applied' but is mediated by concerns of value, strategic intent and avoidance of blame or self-risk. Risk decision-making is rooted in practical reasoning in which many factors play a part, and it is embedded in the sense-making practices that risk assessors use to navigate the indeterminate nature of their assessments (Kemshall 1998a). Respondents eschewed the static approach of technical risk instruments in favour of a more dynamic and contingent approach, recognising that 'Notions of ambiguity, complexity and uncertainty are the core of social work and should be built upon and not defined out. A commitment to uncertainty opens up creativity and novel ways of thinking' (Parton 1998: 23).

In summary, some significant implications can be drawn. Professional practice in social work is increasingly becoming characterised by uncertainty and competing risks. Workers encounter novel and indeed professionally challenging situations daily. These situations are managed through the use of strategic decision-making and the use of values to both frame and resolve problems. Assessment is increasingly about the identification and effective resolution of a number of 'it depends'. The reductionist and outcome-orientated approach of competences is unlikely to equip professionals to carry out the level of transfer of learning required by constant management of such innumerable imponderables. The question is: can professionals be facilitated to learn for such conditions of uncertainty, and, if so, how should it be done?

Transfer of learning for uncertainty

The key to professional performance is the ability to respond to ill-defined problems. Schon (1983) described this characteristic as 'practice wisdom', the essential artistry of the professional expert. The notion of 'expertise' has gained increased currency in approaches to the professional task. Cust (1995) describes the expert as having schema-driven knowledge, the almost unconscious or intuitive grasp of situations and their resolution as opposed to the hypo-deductive methodology of the novice. Transfer of learning is usually seen as the 'hallmark of expertise' as experts draw upon previous knowledge and experience to both frame and resolve problems (Cree *et al*. 1998). The distinction between novice and expert has often been expressed in terms of the speed and accuracy with which experts problem-solve. This is rooted in their ability to both generalise (that is to recognise patterns and relevance) and discriminate (that is to recognise difference) (Cree *et al*. 1998).

Such a view relocates attention away from the outcomes of knowledge to the process of its construction and use. Sheppard (1995) indicates that if process issues are considered then the divide between theoretical knowledge and 'practice wisdom' is less pronounced. The 'linking factor' between the theoretical knowledge products of social science and the practice wisdom of the field is 'the common methodology for understanding and reflecting upon situations' (Sheppard 1995: 269). He poses the 'heuristic device' of analytic induction derived from qualitative research into social interaction as this common methodology. The privileged position of positivism's expert researcher is rejected because 'as human beings social researchers are necessarily part of the human world they study ... and are captured by their common human status' (Sheppard 1995: 270). As such, social researchers must rely upon their 'common sense' knowledge of the world, the methodologies employed are 'merely refinements of those used in everyday life' (Sheppard 1995: 271). The interpretative methodology of the social researcher utilising analytic induction and the worker assessing case materials has numerous similarities, not least the search for meaning in data: 'Practice wisdom … is optimally developed through a retroductive process of hypothesis testing and reflection, involving an approach to evidence which is sceptical, and a principle of adopting hypotheses which are least likely to be wrong' (Sheppard 1995: 282).

The issue here is not the credibility of practice wisdom *per se*, but the extent to which practice routinely adopts these principles. Practitioners can be guilty of 'jumping to conclusions', failing to test, ignoring evidence and miscalculating the probability of a hypothesis being correct. This is compounded by practice wisdom that is highly personalised and not disseminated to the practice community, and practice knowledge that is developed and applied unsystematically. This can undermine precision and the 'accurate identification of relevant variables which may be subsequently built upon' (Sheppard 1995: 283).

This suggests that practice knowledge does not necessarily have to lack rigour, testability or validity, and it has the potential to negotiate complex and varying assessment situations. However, it must demonstrate key components such as critical awareness, routine scepticism, ability to check and validate hypotheses and avoidance of idiosyncratic practice. As Sheppard (1995: 285) indicates, 'critical awareness distinguishes mere experience from its intelligent use'.

However, expertise is not merely acquired, it requires prompting (Cree *et al.* 1998); nor is the concept of expertise itself entirely uncontentious:

> Too many theories of professional expertise tend to treat experts as infallible, in spite of much evidence to the contrary. Not only do professionals succumb to many of the common weaknesses which psychologists have shown to be regular features of human judgement; … some allow aspects of their expertise to decay and become … out of date.
>
> (Eraut 1994: 155)

The awareness of 'contingency' in the construction and application of knowledge and skill is essential to the notion of transfer (Marginson 1994). The uncertainty of risk practice in social work is one area in which this contingency is daily encountered (Kemshall 1998a, Kemshall *et al.* 1997). In effect, experts can quickly become novices when roles, responsibilities and tasks are radically changed. The use of existing schemata may result in inadequate decision-making based upon cognitive heuristics and stereotypes (Kemshall 1998a, Reason 1990). This may lead to costly assessment errors, which workers are often reluctant to revise in the light of new information (Munro 1996). In addition, contingency can be interpreted as threat, and uncertain problems may be routinised into certainties by accommodating them into existing practices or value-frames (Kemshall 1998a). Satyamurti (1981) described this as one strategy for achieving 'occupational survival'.

There are situations in which a degree of transfer may be occurring but from a largely redundant knowledge base. For example, the study of probation practice revealed that some officers carrying out risk assessments utilised a value-base rooted in rehabilitation and client need, and a knowledge base rooted in post-war case assessment (Kemshall 1998a). In this situation, training material on risk assessment methods, and an emphasis upon public protection values can have a low priority (Kemshall 1998b). Although officers were well able to recognise the contingent nature of risk (as illustrated above), the contingency of problem-solving and outcome solutions that naturally followed was seen as provoking much anxiety. In trying to make sense of their experience, probation practitioners drew inferences from the evidence presented in case situations. However, high error rates in such deductive reasoning have been found due to the process of 'similarity-matching' rather than the application of logic: information is more often used to confirm rather than to deny generalisations (Wason and Johnson-Laird 1972). In effect, 'short-cuts' to reasoning are taken to avoid what Bruner et al. (1956) called 'cognitive strain'; that is, reasoning against the normal habits and experiences of the thinker. The 'criterion of verisimilitude' compounds existing modes of thinking and prevents the exploration of more productive pathways (Reason 1990). This is likely to be exacerbated in those situations where existing knowledge is superseded or contested, or in situations of high uncertainty. This uncertainty is exactly the situation in current social work practice.

Given the nature of the social work task, how best can practitioners be facilitated to accept and effectively manage the contingency of their skills and knowledge, and the requirement to problem solve in novel and often disputed situations? Commentators concerned with the practice of social work 'under conditions of postmodernity' have argued for a 'more accepting attitude towards contingency' (Howe 1994; Parton 1994). This would involve 'taking responsibility for decisions and choices in a consciously reflexive way' (Parton 1994: 10). Two key questions are at the root of contemporary social work practice: 'How can we develop the art of judgement formation in the absence of fixed rules? And how can we continually attempt to remoralise individual and social life without falling prey to prejudice? (Parton 1994: 111).

The first question may be answered by considering the role of discourse analysis in facilitating reflective and reflexive social work practice. Ellerman (1998: 35) explores the issue of 'whether professionals who are self-conscious about the discourses within which they operate are more likely to be reflective practitioners'. Social work, she argues, is embedded in competing discourses, and as such competing understandings of the world. In this context, practitioners will be confronted with differing constructions of reality and differing claims to truth (for example between clients and workers, workers and managers). In this situation, it is essential for workers to be open to new ways of knowing, and more importantly to recognise how dominant 'regimes of truth' are established. Knowledge confers power, and in this sense 'those who control knowledge may do harm to others' (Ellerman 1998: 41). This connection between knowledge and power offers some possibility of tackling Parton's 're-moralisation' enterprise as the value and power base of differing discourses can be more clearly identified. This would produce practitioners capable of thinking 'about the complexities of practice instead of uncritically implementing employers' policies' (Ford 1996: 31).

Discourse analysis may aid practitioners in accepting uncertainty and in the management of contingency, as Ellerman points out:

> It is when professionals accept that problems cannot be definitely and conclusively solved, that fixed meanings do not exist and that 'truths' are not absolute, that they are open to exploring their own positions and to recognising the complexity and ambiguity of people's lives.
>
> (Ellermann 1998: 42)

This is very close to Eraut's (1994: 155–6) formulation of 'deliberate reflection', that is, critical reflection of even the routine tasks and self-evaluation of practice involving 'deep and serious consideration'. Ellermann is clear about the implications for social work education that 'must challenge the very notion of objective expertise'. Students and professionals need to adopt 'positions of uncertainty ... in order to develop understandings of the world that are historically, temporally and culturally specific as well as comparative' (Ellerman 1998: 42). Her broad suggestions for curriculum implementation involve:

- the deliberate deconstruction of key social work discourses;
- the deliberate adoption of differing discourses;

- comparative exercises which could involve the framing and resolution of problems from a range of discourses;
- the adoption of discourses contrary to a student's usual mode of operating;
- the deliberate introduction of uncertainties in 'safe' learning environments;
- the completion of reflective journals over time;
- the identification and critique of dominant discourses;
- exercises in which competing discourses have to be explored and mediated.

(Ellermann 1998: 42)

Ellerman concludes by suggesting that in this type of curriculum assessment would be concerned with 'deconstruction and self-questioning', and the 'emphasis of assessment' would 'shift from 'competence' to 'reflexivity' (Ellerman 1998: 43).

Conclusion

Although the era of postmodernity may be disputed (Smith and White 1997), the increasing uncertainty and contingency of the present age is recognised (Beck 1992; Giddens 1990; Lash *et al.* 1996). Social care professions find themselves exposed to uncertainty and risk, with consequences for both the workforce and social work educators. Professionals are likely to be confronted with continuously changing roles, responsibilities and tasks within which their expertise is challenged and sometimes de-legitimised. Although social care and probation practice have long been prey to legislative and ideological change, the difference now is the pace of change and the 'conditions of uncertainty' surrounding decision-making (Brearley 1982). As risk concerns become increasingly pervasive in organisational life and to service delivery, this uncertainty is likely to increase (Kemshall *et al.* 1997). This will require constant adaptation and an increased tolerance of both uncertainty in practice and the contingency of knowledge. Reflection on situations that do not have immediate answers is likely to result in anxiety and confusion (Taylor 1996). Transfer of learning will therefore be crucial; it will also be severely tested. Neither competence-based education nor reliance upon professional expertise is likely to meet the challenge of preparation for transfer of learning in this climate. Professionals must be equipped to function in practice situations in which their existing knowledge may be regularly superseded or contested, and in which competing knowledge claims and outcomes coexist. Parton (1994: 109) has suggested that we need not feel fearful of such relativism as the 'systematic cultivation of self-doubt ... opens up decision making and alternative possibilities'. Ellermann (1998) has offered practical and concrete examples of how such an approach could be embedded into the vocational curriculum. Her 'programme' may be seen as the beginning of a higher education agenda for the preparation of students for the uncertainty of professional life. In this context, preoccupations with transfer of learning are transformed beyond the pursuit of a meta-competence into the fostering of purposively reflective and reflexive professionals. As Taylor (1996) states, 'Reflective learning may be conceptualised as a response to postmodernism, as a positive and creative approach to the prospect of living with contingency (Taylor 1996: 159). Such an approach need not be 'at odds' with a market model of higher education, as reflective learning can foster transfer of learning, adaptability, flexibility, self-appraisal and 'lifelong' learning – all the hallmarks of the new education enterprise ethos.

The role for higher education in such a vocational curriculum would be to foster tolerance of uncertainty and a greater understanding of contingency. This will not be achieved through the use of reductive competences or indeed the top-down schema-based deductions of the expert. Rather the hypothetical deductive reasoning of the novice may be of the most help. Professionals are likely to lose their expertise quickly and to revisit the experience of the novice more frequently. This technique can be developed into a 'practice wisdom' based upon 'retroductive analysis' or the routine adoption of scepticism (Sheppard 1995). The key principles of this practice wisdom are an interactive process between data collection and theorising, constant hypothesis testing and reformulation, and the development of 'hypotheses least likely to be wrong' (Sheppard 1995: 281). This would include a more responsive stance to new information and situations, and a more provisional stance to knowledge claims. Such purposively reflective learning and provisionality requires a differing epistemological framework and alternative aims for vocational education. Pietroni (1995), following the work of Schön, argues that higher educational aims should be recast as:

- education for creativity and uncertainty;
- education for problem-solving and the exploration of discontinuity;
- continuous learning;
- partnership in learning.

(adapted from Pietroni 1995: 47–8)

Central to such aims is the testing of one's own and others' validity claims. Retroductive analysis and purposeful reflection will take place in a climate of 'constant flux' in 'a world where skills-mixes of a radically new kind are required and ethical dilemmas are often profound' (Pietroni 1995: 49). In this climate, transfer of learning and transferring skills may themselves need to be reconceptualised. The former may be better conceptualised as the ability to engage in retroductive analysis across a number of domains; and the second as the ability to deploy routine scepticism and to negotiate the contingency of professional life.

Bibliography

Adams, J. (1995) *Risk*, London: University College.

Adamson, C. (1997) 'Existential and clinical uncertainty in the medical encounter: an idiographic account of an illness trajectory defined by Inflammatory Bowel Disease and Avascular Necrosis', *Sociology of Health and Illness* 19(2): 133–59.

Andrews, D.A. (1995) 'The psychology of criminal conduct and effective treatment', in J, McGuire (ed.) *What Works: Reducing Offending. Guidelines from Research and Practice*, Chichester: John Wiley & Sons Ltd.

Assiter, A. (1992) 'Skills and knowledges: epistemological models underpinning different approaches to teaching and training', in D. Bridges (ed.) *Transferable Skills in Higher Education*, Norwich: University of East Anglia.

—— (1995) 'Transferable skills: a response to the sceptics', in A. Assiter (ed.) *Transferable Skills in Higher Education*, London: Kogan Page.

Atkins, M.J., Beattie, J. and Dockerell, W. B. (1993) *Assessment Issues in Higher Education*, Newcastle upon Tyne: School of Education, University of Newcastle.

Barnett, R. (1990) *The Idea of Higher Education*, Buckingham: Open University Press.

—— (1994) *The Limits of Competence*, Buckingham: SRHE and Open University Press.

Barrow, R. (1987) 'Skill talk', *Journal of Philosophy of Education* 21(2): 187–95.

Beck, U. (1992) *Risk Society: Towards a New Modernity*. London: Sage.

Benner, P. (1984) *From Novice to Expert*, Menlo Park, CA: Addison-Wesley.

Blom-Cooper, L., Hally, H. and Murphy, E. (1995) *The Falling Shadow: One Patient's Mental Health Care 1978–1993*, London: Duckworth.

Boyatzis, R.E. (1982) *The Competent Manager: A Model for Effective Performance*, New York: Wiley.

Brearley, C.P. (1982): *Risk and Social Work: Hazards and Helping*, London: Routledge and Kegan Paul.

Bridges, D. (1992) 'Transferable skills: a philosophical perspective', in D. Bridges (ed.) *Transferable Skills in Higher Education,* Norwich: University of East Anglia.

Bruner, J.S., Goodnow, J.J., and Austin, G.A. (1956) *A Study of Thinking,* New York: Science Editions.

Butler-Schloss (Lord) (1988) *Report of the Committee of Inquiry into Child Sexual Abuse in Cleveland 1987,* Presented to the Secretary of State for Social Services by the Right Honourable Lord Butler-Schloss DBE, Cm 412, London: HMSO.

Callender, C. (1992) *Will NVQs Work? Evidence from the Construction Industry,* University of Sussex, Institute of Manpower Studies.

Carew, R. (1979) 'The place of knowledge in social work activity', *British Journal of Social Work* 9(3): 349–64.

Collins, M. (1991) *Adult Education as Vocation,* London: Routledge.

Copas, J., Ditchfield, J. and Marshall, P. (1994) *Development of a New Reconviction Score,* Research Bulletin 36, London: HMSO.

Corrigan, P., Hayes, M. and Joyce, P. (1995) 'A modernist perspective on changes in the higher education curriculum', in A. Assiter (ed.) *Transferable Skills in Higher Education,* London: Kogan Page.

Cree, V., Macaulay, C. and Loney, H. (1998) *Transfer of Learning: A Study,* Edinburgh: The Scottish Office Central Research Unit.

Cust, J. (1995) 'Recent cognitive perspectives on learning – implications for nurse education', *Nurse Education Today* 15: 280–90.

Dearing Report (1997) *National Committee of Inquiry into Higher Education,* Chaired by Ron Dearing, London: Crown Copyright.

DeMontfort University (1998) *Scoping Study for Accredited Qualification Programmes for Prison Service Governors,* Submitted to the Prison Services Training Service, Leicester: DeMontfort University.

DES (1977) *Education in Schools: A Consultative Document,* London: HMSO.

—— (1985) *Better Schools: A Summary,* London: HMSO.

Douglas, M. (1986) *Risk Acceptability According to the Social Sciences,* London: Routledge and Kegan Paul.

—— (1992) *Risk and Blame,* London: Routledge.

Douglas, M. and Wildavsky, A. (1983) *Risk and Culture,* London: University of California Press.

Dreyfus, H.L. and Dreyfus, S.E. (1986a) *Mind over Machine: The Power of Human Intuition and Expertise in the Era of the Computer,* Oxford: Basil Blackwell.

—— (1986b) *A Five Stage Model of the Mental Activities Involved in Skill Acquisition*. Berkley: University of California.

Dunsire, A. (1978) *Control In A Bureaucracy: The Execution Process,* Vol. 2, Oxford: Martin Robertson.

—— (1990) 'Holistic governance', *Public Policy and Administration* 5(1): 4–19.

—— (1992) 'Modes of governance', in J. Kooiman (ed.) *Modern Governance,* London: Sage.

Ellermann, A. (1998) 'Can discourse analysis enable reflective social work practice?', *Social Work Education* 17(1): 35–44.

England, H. (1986) *Social Work as Art,* London: Allen and Unwin.

Eraut, M. (1985) 'knowledge creation and knowledge use in professional contexts', *Studies in Higher Education* 10(2): 117–33.

—— (1989) 'Initial teacher training and the NVQ model', in J. Burke (ed.) *Competency Based Education and Training,* London: Falmer Press.

—— (1994) *Developing Professional Knowledge and Competence,* London: Falmer Press.

Fleming, D. (1991) 'The concept of meta-competence', in *Competence and Assessment* 16: 9–12.

Flynn, N. (1993) *Public Sector Management,* London: Harvester Wheatsheaf.

Fook, J.K., Ryan, M. and Hawkins, L. (1997) 'Towards a theory of social work expertise', *British Journal of Social Work* 27: 399–417.

Ford, P. (1996) 'Competences: their use and misuse', in P. Ford and P. Hayes (eds) *Educating for Social Work: Arguments for Optimism,* Aldershot: Avebury.

Foucault, M. (1977) *Archaeology of Knowledge,* London: Tavistock Publications.

Gardiner, D.W.G. (1989) *The Anatomy of Supervision: Developing Learning and Professional Competence for Social Work Students,* Milton Keynes: The Society for Research into Higher Education and the Open University.

Garfinkel, E. (1967) *Studies in Ethnomethodology,* Englewood Cliffs, NJ: Prentice-Hall.

Garrick, R. (1997) *Higher Education in the Learning Society: Report of the Scottish Committee,* National Committee of Inquiry into Higher Education.

Giddens, A. (1990) *The Consequences of Modernity,* Cambridge: Polity Press.

Gross, R. D. (1987) *Psychology,* London: Edward Arnold.

Hartnett, A. and Naish, M. (eds) (1986) *Theory and Practice of Education,* London: Heinemann Educational.

Holmes, L. (1995) 'Skills: a social perspective', in A. Assiter (ed.) *Transferable Skills in Higher Education,* London: Kogan Page.

Howe, D. (1994) 'Modernity, postmodernity and social work', *British Journal of Social Work* 24: 513–32.

Hyland, T. (1991) 'Taking care of business: vocationalism, competence and the enterprise culture', *Educational Studies* 17(1): 77–87.

—— (1992) 'Meta-competence, metaphysics and vocational expertise', *Competence and Assessment* 20: 22–4.

—— (1993a) 'Competence, knowledge and education', *Journal of Philosophy of Education* 27(1): 57–68.

—— (1993b) 'Professional development and competence-based education', *Educational Studies* 19(1): 123–32.

—— (1994) 'Experiential learning, competence and critical practice in higher education', *Studies in Higher Education* 19(3): 327–39.

Jones, S. and Joss, R. (1995) 'Models of professionalism', in: M. Yelloly and M. Henkel (eds) *Learning and Teaching in Social Work*, London: Jessica Kingsley Publishers.

Kelly, G. (1996) 'Competence in risk analysis', in K. O'Hagan (ed.) *Competence in Social Work Practice: A Practical Guide for Professionals*, London: Jessica Kingsley Publishers.

Kemshall, H. (1993) 'Assessing competence: scientific process or subjective inference?' *Social Work Education* 12: 36–45.

—— (1996) *Reviewing Risk: A review of research on the assessment and management of risk and dangerousness: implications for policy and practice in the Probation Service*, A report for the Home Office Research and Statistics Directorate. London: Home Office.

—— (1998a) *Risk in Probation Practice*, Aldershot: Ashgate.

—— (1998b) *Risk Training for Senior Probation Officers: An Evaluation Report for Inner London Probation Service*, London: Inner London Probation Service.

Kemshall, H. and J. Pritchard (1997) (eds) *Good Practice in Risk Assessment and Risk Management: Protection, Rights and Responsibilities*, Vol. 2, London: Jessica Kingsley Publishers.

Kemshall, H., Parton, N., Walsh, M. and Waterson, J. (1997) 'Concepts of risk in relation to organisational structure and functioning within the personal social services and probation', *Social Policy and Administration* 31(3): 213–32.

Lash, S., Szerszynski, B. and Wynne, B. (eds) (1996) *Risk, Environment and Modernity: Towards a New Ecology*, London: Sage.

London Borough of Brent (1985) '*A Child in Trust: the Report of the Panel of Inquiry into the Circumstances Surrounding the death of Jasmine Beckford*', Presented to the Brent Borough Council and to Brent Health Authority by members of the Panel of Inquiry, London Borough of Brent.

McBeath, G. and Webb, S. (1991) 'Social work, modernity and postmodernity', *Sociological Review* 39(4): 745–62.

Marginson, S. (1994) *The Transfer of Skills and Knowledge from Education to Work*, Melbourne,: Centre for the Study of Higher Education.

Marshall, K. (1991) 'NVQs: An assessment of the "outcomes" approach to education and training', *Journal of Further and Higher Education* 15(3): 56–64.

Miller, D. and Reilly, J. (1996) 'Mad cows and Englishmen', *Planet* 117 (June): 118–19.

Munro, E. (1996) 'Avoidable and unavoidable mistakes in child protection work', *British Journal of Social Work* 26: 793–808.

NAB/UCG (1984) *Higher Education and the Needs of Society*, National Advisory Board for Public Sector Higher Education/University Grants Council, London.

National Curriculum Council (1990) *The Whole Curriculum, Curriculum Guidance 3*, York: National Curriculum Council.

Nellis, M. (1995) 'Probation training – the links with social work', in A. Vass and T. May (eds) *Working with Offenders*, London: Sage.

Norris, N. (1991) 'The trouble with competence', *Cambridge Journal of Education* 21(3): 331–41.

Otter, S. (1992) *Learning Outcomes in Higher Education*, Leicester: Unit for the Development of Adult Continuing Education.

Parton, N. (1994) 'Social work under conditions of (post) modernity', *Social Work and Social Sciences Review* 5(2): 93–112.

—— (1996) 'Social work, risk and the blaming system', in N. Parton (ed.) *Social Theory, Social Change and Social Work*, London: Routledge.

—— (1998) 'Risk, advanced liberalism and child welfare: the need to rediscover uncertainty and ambiguity', *British Journal of Social Work* 28: 5–27.

Parton, N., Thorpe, D. and Wattam, C. (1997) *Child Protection and the Moral Order*, Basingstoke: Macmillan.

Peters, R.S. (1996) *Ethics and Education*, London: Allen and Unwin.

Pietroni, M. (1995) 'The nature and aims of professional education for social workers: a postmodern perspective', in M. Yelloly and M. Henkel (eds) *Learning and Teaching in Social Work*, London: Jessica Kingsley Publishers.

Raggatt, P. (1991) 'Quality assurance and NVQs', in P. Raggatt and L. Unwin (eds) *Change and Intervention: Vocational Education and Training*, London: Falmer Press.

Reason, J. (1990) *Human Error*, Cambridge: Cambridge University Press.

Royal Society Study Group (1992) *Risk: Analysis, Perception and Management*, Royal Society report, London: Royal Society.

Salomon, G. and Perkins, D.N. (1989) 'Rocky roads to transfer: rethinking mechanisms of a neglected phenomenon', *Educational Psychologist* 24(2): 113–42.

Sataymurti, C. (1981) *Occupational Survival*, Oxford: Blackwell Publishers.

Schön, D. (1983) *The Reflective Practitioner: How Professionals Think in Action*, New York: Basic Books.

Sheppard, M. (1995) 'Social work, social science and practice wisdom', *British Journal of Social Work* 25: 265–93.

Silver, H. and Brennan, J. (1988) *A Liberal Vocationalism*, London: Methuen.

Smith, C. and White, S. (1997) 'Parton, Howe and postmodernity: a critical comment on mistaken identity', *British Journal of Social Work* 27: 275–95.

Strachan, R. and Tallant, C. (1997) 'Improving judgement and appreciating biases within the risk assessment process', in H. Kemshall and J. Pritchard (eds) *Good Practice in Risk Assessment and Risk Management: Protection, Rights and Responsibilities*, Vol. 2, London: Jessica Kingsley Publishers.

Taylor, I. (1996) 'Reflective learning, social work education and practice in the 21st century', in N. Gould and I. Taylor (eds) *Reflective Learning for Social Work*, Aldershot: Arena.

Training Agency (1988) *'Developing of Assessable Standards for National Certification: Guidance Note 2 – Deriving Standards by Reference to Functions'*, Sheffield: Training Agency.

—— Employment Department Group (1989) *Skills Bulletin*, No. 8, Spring. Sheffield: Training Agency.

Wason, P.C. and Johnson-Laird, R. (1972) *'Psychology of Reasoning: Structure and Content'*, London: Batsford.

Whittington, C. (1986) 'Literature review: transfer of learning in social work education', *British Journal of Social Work* 16: 571–7.

Whitty, G. (1985) 'The new right and the national curriculum: state control or market forces?', in B. Moon (ed.) *New Curriculum – National Curriculum*, London: Hodder and Stoughton.

Williams, B. (1996) 'Probation training: the defence of professionalism, *Social Work Education* 15(3): 5–19.

—— (1997) 'University-based social work education', *Canadian Social Work Review* 14(1): 69–81.

Wolf, A. (1989) 'Can competence and knowledge mix?', in J. W. Burke (ed.) *Competency Based Education and Training*, Lewes: Falmer Press.

—— (1990) 'Unwrapping knowledge and understanding from standards of competence', in H. Black and A. Wolf (eds) *Knowledge and Competence: Current Issues In Training And Education*, Sheffield: Careers and Occupational Information Centre.

Chapter 4

Personal construct theory and the transfer of learning

The history of a moment

Nick Gould

Sikander (Alexander the Great) went to a mystic, a fakir and asked him, 'Tell me, is the whole world just an idea, just imagination?'. The mystic took him to a bathing ghat here on the banks of the river and both of them stripped off and entered the water for a dip. 'Now dive under the water for a moment' said the fakir to Alexander. Sikander did. And what did he see in that moment? He forgot his kingly consciousness; he saw himself now a poor man with many little children starving and a wife as poor and miserable as he, all the cares of the world on them. And one day a terrible disaster happened to him.... But he gave a start and look! There he was back again as a king at the bathing ghat, dripping wet along with the fakir. He was struck with wonder. Of this tale Sachal said this: 'Sikander thought many years had passed, but it was merely the history of a moment'. So he said: 'You see, you are merely an idea'.

(eighteenth-century Sufi story, recounted in Wood 1997: 203)

Recent years have seen the emergence of the concept of lifelong learning. This is strongly embedded in changing forms of social structure and in particular the shift from conditions of modernity to postmodernity. This is associated with the effects of the globalisation of the world economy and its effects on flexibility of employment. However tenuous current understanding of the linkages between the macro economy and conditions of employment in social welfare may be, there is evidence that social workers will have to accept as a permanent condition of working life that the environment will change, and that over the course of a career individuals will change their place of employment several times. This transformation means that transfer of learning will be not just something to be demonstrated as a rite of passage by student social workers, but also a defining characteristic of social work expertise.

For many years the qualifying regulations for professional social work have referred to the need for social work students to demonstrate that they can transfer learning. This is something that, with a few exceptions, has been unproblematised before the writing of this book. This has always been at variance with my personal experience. When I have changed jobs, I have experienced a set of psychological reactions which when younger greatly troubled me, but which with greater experience I have come to recognise as 'normal' and, in the longer term, productive. These include the feelings on arriving at a new place of employment that I have no expertise to contribute to an organisation, the high levels of anxiety about my competence and relationships with new colleagues and the feeling that seemingly routine tasks are to me highly complex and time-consuming. I now feel sufficiently confident in my own abilities to recognise that these feelings are widely experienced and not dysfunctional. Despite this personal knowledge, we still expect student social workers to be able to adapt to new working environments and show learning within very short time-scales. At the time of writing, most British social workers have to do this within successive placements of fifty and eighty days, for instance, compared with periods of induction for university academics of between one and three years.

This chapter will suggest that one framework for helping students, practitioners and educators to make sense of these demands is personal construct psychology. There are striking synergies between personal construct psychology and theories of experiential learning, which can be drawn upon in order to provide a vocabulary for individuals to conceptualise and describe their experience of transferring learning. This may be valuable in helping to confront the uncomfortable aspects of transferring learning such as anxiety and feeling 'de-skilled' but also by using structured methods, such as repertory grids, creative understandings may be helped to emerge. Finally, opportunities and impediments for using this approach are considered in relation to other 'technologies' in social work education.

Personal construct psychology and theories of experiential learning

Personal construct psychology is premised upon a philosophical proposition that George Kelly (1955: 3) called constructive alternativism. In contrast to more fundamentalist constructive positions which contend that all realities are subjective, personal construct psychology accepts that there is an external reality but that apprehension of that reality is mediated by personal sense-making and is never interpretation free. The range of interpretations that might be made of an event reflect the biography of the individual, and to that extent are personal, but experience is also shaped by our social identities such as class, gender and ethnicity, so to that extent they are also patterned by collective experience. The concept of constructive alternativism is elaborated by the metaphor of 'the person as scientist', suggesting that the making of personal meaning is a dynamic process that proceeds by a process of experimentation. In taking an action, we are putting to the test hypotheses about the effects of our intervention. If the action has the expected outcome, then the hypothesis is confirmed until the next occasion. If the outcome is negative or unexpected, then our theory of the world is modified and on the next occasion we may put an adjusted hypothesis to the test.

This states the person as scientist metaphor at its simplest. We know that there is not always a perfect feedback loop between the consequences of behaviour and the modification of our beliefs about the world; indeed, there is a rich body of sociological evidence that scientists themselves often rationalise away experimental evidence which does not confirm a favoured hypothesis (Gilbert and Mulkay 1984; Collins 1992). There are other mediating influences such as the degree of centrality of a belief in our self-image, whether our social reference group overrides the lessons of personal experience, and so on. Nevertheless, this is a metaphor of learning that is persuasive and which agrees with other models of experiential learning. For example, Dewey (1963), a key figure in the American realist movement, considered that experience is the organising focus for learning, that experience is the crucible which fuses together observation and action with conceptual ideas. Lewin (1951) considered that experience initiated a feedback loop in which experience is transformed through observation and reflection into abstract concepts and generalisations, the implications from which are tested in new situations. Again, Piaget (1955) explains our capacity to adaptation towards abstract thought as accommodation of experience into existing mental representations or schemata, leading to reconstructed and adapted models of the world. In a well-known synthesis of these theories, Kolb (1984) sought to integrate these and other theories of experiential learning into a learning cycle that proceeds from experience to reflective observation to abstract conceptualisation to active experimentation and so on back to concrete experience.

As I have argued elsewhere (Gould 1989), at the risk of being over-reductionist, there is nevertheless a strong convergence between these contributions to a theory of experiential learning, reflection and personal construct psychology through the metaphor of 'experimentation'. Schön used the example of carpentry:

If the carpenter asks himself, what makes this structure stable? And begins to experiment to find out – trying one device now another – he is basically in the same business as the research scientist. He puts forward hypotheses and, within the constraints set by the practice context, tries to discriminate among them – taking as a disconfirmation of a hypothesis the failure to get the consequences predicted from it. The logic of his experimental inference is the same as that of the researcher's.

(Schön 1987: 71–2)

Thus, there are strong parallels between reflective theories of experiential learning and the epistemological assumptions and mental model of personal construct psychology. They all suggest a cyclical process of action, reflection, abstraction and experimentation. This provides us with a useful paradigm for thinking about processes relating to the transfer of learning and work needing to be done by students or practitioners moving to new contexts of practice. In short, if learning from experience is a cyclical process involving continuous loops, then endings and new beginnings invariably produce interrupted cycles of learning. Restarting within a new agency or with a client group means making a series of judgements between learning cycles that can be restarted in a new situation and those which no longer fit. Personal construct psychology may provide a series of concepts to bring to the teaching of practice that help learners to move forward productively.

Personal construct psychology and the transfer of learning

Repertory grid completion is a tool derived from personal construct psychology. Practitioners and researchers have used repertory grids to elicit various aspects of psychological functioning in a wide range of contexts. These have included the study of clinical areas such as thought disorder among people diagnosed as being schizophrenic (Bannister 1962), the treatment of stuttering (Dalton 1983), the dynamics of therapeutic groups (Dalton and Dunnett 1992) and the extensive use of grids as both a research and a learning methodology in educational settings (e.g. Thomas and Harri-Augstein 1985). The statistical analysis of repertory grid data can involve highly abstracted and complicated forms of statistical analysis. This notwithstanding, some of the concepts that emerged from Kelly's early theoretical and empirical research within personal construct psychology provide a useful vocabulary for reframing commonly used terms, such as anxiety, threat and hostility, for thinking about the transfer of learning.

Anxiety

Anxiety is 'the recognition that the events with which one is confronted lie outside the range of convenience of his [sic] construct system' (Kelly 1955: 495). Students, faced with a set of circumstances for which their existing understanding of practice has not prepared them, will feel anxious.

Threat

Threat is 'the awareness of an imminent comprehensive change in one's core structures' (Kelly 1955: 489). Social work is a form of practice that can challenge the most fundamental precepts we hold about the world. Sometimes these can operate at a personal level; there are high levels of anecdotal evidence accumulated by social work educators that re-evaluations of social roles and the exposure to empowerment theories places great strain upon existing family and personal relationships. Other attitudinal change can be more generalised, for example as individuals become aware of and unable to sustain prejudicial attitudes. All these processes of disconfirmation of previously held constructs become threats to the person.

Hostility

Hostility is 'the continued effort to extort validational evidence in favour of a type of social prediction which has already been recognised as a failure' (Kelly 1955: 510). When a student tries out a tested and favoured intervention learned in an earlier placement, it may not be effective in a new setting. Difficulty in accepting the need to modify the approach, but persisting in repetition of failing strategies or insufficiently modified strategies, can be communicated as hostility. Depending on the context, this can take the form of hostility towards service users, the practice teacher or other colleagues.

The following concepts are more specific to the technical analysis of repertory grids and are derived from the structural aspects of thinking revealed by grids.

Intensity

When a construct is used in a 'tight' way it is unvarying in the predictions that follow from it. Discriminatory and prejudicial construing often involve tight forms of construing, for example the notion that gay men will invariably be unsuitable foster parents. Conversely, 'loose' construing involves the application of constructs in ways which are so arbitrary that they are inconsistent. A community care assessment may be so imprecise and inconsistent in its use of language that no coherent formulation of a service user's needs emerges from it. Extreme and unvarying tightness or looseness of construing may, as indicated, be unproductive. However, Kelly (1955) also argued that the process of learning involves cyclical processes of moving between positions of relative tight and loose construing. When we first work in a new environment, anxiety can produce tightness of construing as we react to uncertainty by trying to get at least some fixed points in terms of what we think. As we become more comfortable with the situation we can afford to relax our construing and allow ourselves to test out new categories to analyse and understand the environment. The measurement of movement between tight and loose construing can be measured from repertory grid data and is referred to as the intensity score. The statistical method for calculating intensity need not detain us here, but the underlying concepts give us a vocabulary and reference point for exploring how rigidity of thinking can impair student functioning in a new practice setting.

Cognitive complexity

A criticism of reflective theories of learning can be that they lack operational markers to denote what may be involved in learning. One indicator of learning that has some theoretical support is the idea that reflective learning should lead to more complexity of thought about practice. Personal construct psychology does not own the concept of cognitive complexity, but there have been serious attempts to define and measure what we might mean by the term. Bieri in particular is identified with this project and has defined cognitive complexity as: '...the capacity to construe social behaviour in a multi-dimensional way. A more cognitively complex person has available a more differentiated system of dimensions for perceiving others' behaviour than does a less cognitively complex individual'. (Bieri *et al.* 1966: 185, quoted Fransella and Bannister 1977: 61).

Cognitive integration

Cognitive integration is a broad concept that is used to refer to several characteristics of construing of a domain that are related to the structural relationships between constructs. Within repertory grid research these structural features are mapped using statistical procedures such as cluster analysis. Thus, this would include the hierarchical relationships between attitudes or beliefs, the probability that some views constitute a core which is relatively impermeable to change, whereas more peripheral attitudes may be more amenable to disconfirmation. Another aspect of cognitive integration is the degree of predilection of an individual to hold attitudes towards a subject that fall towards the extreme ends of bipolar constructs. Later in the chapter (p. 89), reference will also be made to a further aspect of cognitive integration, the organisation of constructs within integrated clusters.

Articulation

The concept of articulation is also used to refer to the structure or architecture of construing. Is a person able to link ideas and examine their connectedness, or is their thinking characterised by monolithic and undifferentiated clusters of views? Perhaps there may be more than one cluster of ideas resulting in contradictory or self-defeating points of view? My own research has produced some tentative evidence that the development of competence in social work is reflected by increasing articulation of constructs as thinking about practice becomes more coherent and systematic, but that this developmental process is one that becomes disrupted by new placements (Gould 1993).

Personal construct psychology is a holistic theoretical system that makes no rigid distinction between emotion and cognition but, as shown in the above concepts, suggests how psychological processes associated with change give rise to feelings and reframing of perceptions. These insights may be used as part of the theoretical repertoire that a practice teacher brings to the supervision session and introduced to the student. Thomas and Harri-Augstein (1985) refer to the use of personal construct psychology as 'conversational science'. In social work there seems to be a cultural ambivalence about the profession's status as a scientific activity, but personal construct psychology offers a conceptual framework that can be explored within the conversation of supervision. This may be approached informally or it may be introduced as a structured exercise in the form of a repertory grid.

Repertory grids as a reflexive technique

It is not the intention, and it is not possible, in the space of this chapter to give detailed instruction on how to complete repertory grids but rather to outline the purpose and some of the possibilities of the technique. Few psychological theories can be so inextricably linked with one research method as personal construct theory and repertory grid technique, although the reverse is not always the case; many researchers have used repertory grids pragmatically as a methodological tool to explore areas such as attitudinal change. The underlying method has remained relatively constant since Kelly first developed the Role Construct Repertory Test. The subject nominates a list of people who are relevant to the domain being considered so, for instance, Kelly, in his original therapeutic work, would ask the subject to nominate people from the family or other significant networks. In social work, the list might be limited to service users or it may also include colleagues, mentors or other people who seem significant. The people nominated are the 'elements' of the grid. The convention is to write each element onto a separate card, take three cards at random and identify ways in which two elements may be similar and thereby different from the third (Fransella and Bannister 1977: 14). These criteria of difference or similarity are known as 'constructs'. This process is continued until no more constructs can be identified that the subject considers to be relevant or meaningful. A grid can then be constructed with elements, or people, listed along one axis of a grid and constructs along the other axis. It is then possible to score, on a scale from say 1 to 5, how closely each person is felt to correspond to the construct.

Diverse though the use and detail of repertory grids are, the defining characteristics that differentiate them from other research tools are:

- grid completion involves the person in attempting to articulate the relationship between those constructs that have relevance to an identified topic area;
- although the researcher may be attempting to collect data that can be aggregated between subjects to produce general or normative statements about how a category of people perceive a topic, the primary use of grids is to elicit the individual's unique personal construing;
- repertory grid is a technique and not a test as it has no standardised form, the content being adapted to the research topic, therapeutic or teaching purpose. Probably the most similar schedule is Osgood's

Semantic Differential Test, the crucial difference being that this uses a standard list of dimensions supplied to all subjects alike (Adams Webber 1979: 20).

In research which is seeking to produce group data, subjects will be given the same grid to complete, with elements and constructs identified from a pilot phase of the research. For use as part of personal, reflexive learning, it is more meaningful for students to identify elements and constructs individually. In my own work students have taken as elements within the grids a cross-section of service users with whom they are working. They can be encouraged to include users with whom they experience difficulty, so that the nature of difficulty can be explored, as well as users with whom work is perceived to be going well. It can also be instructive for the student to include themselves in the form of 'self' as an element (to see whether difficulty is associated with difference, or conversely whether working well is associated with identification with people who are similar). Also, inclusion of 'the social worker I want to be' as an element that is contrasted with 'self' helps students to identify the areas of their own practice or self-presentation which they want to change. An example of a completed grid is given in Figure 4.1.

Constructs can be elicited by the 'triangulation' method described above for identifying the similarity and the differences among three people at a time. However, some find this overmechanistic or constricting and may just wish to look at all the people in the grid simultaneously to identify ways in which they think of groups of people as being similar or different; this is known in repertory grid technique as 'the full context form' (Fransella and Bannister 1977: 15). It is important that this does not continue beyond a point where the constructs identified are meaningful for the individual, as they may eventually become contrived because the individual feels under some pressure to produce a certain number of constructs. A good indicator that a grid is overelaborated or contrived is that the student then finds it difficult to score the grid, and may end up entering a lot of 'don't knows' or 'not applicables' (Yorke 1985: 385–8).

In the research field a range of statistical techniques have been used to analyse grids. These range from more simple forms of non-parametric analysis to advanced multivariate factor and cluster analyses. For a busy practice teacher or supervisor, it is not realistic to imagine that they have the time or inclination to enter all these data into a statistical software package to produce analyses which may, in any case, be obscure or baffling to the student for whom it is intended to be enlightening. However,

Construct pole rated 1

Construct pole rated 5

Construct pole rated 1	SW I wish to be like	Self	Easier client	Practice teacher	Tutor	Client 2	Difficult client	Client 1	Client 3	SW I don't wish to be like	Construct pole rated 5
Autonomous	2	3	3	3	3	4	5	5	3	5	Not autonomous
Feel empathy for	2	2	2	2	3	4	3	5	2	2	Don't feel empathy for
Functional family	2	3	2	3	2	2	2	5	4	2	Dysfunctional family
Feel comfortable with	1	3	3	2	2	2	1	4	4	4	Uncomfortable with
True to themself	1	1	3	2	2	2	4	2	3	5	Not true to themself
Polite	1	1	2	3	3	1	1	2	5	5	Impolite
Gentle	1	3	4	4	3	3	1	3	5	5	Abrasive
I like	2	2	3	3	3	3	2	3	5	5	I dislike
Personal relationship with	1	1	3	3	3	4	3	3	5	2	Impersonal relationship
Approachable	1	2	1	1	1	3	4	4	1	1	Unapproachable

*Self
*SW I wish to be like
*Easier client
*Practice teacher
*Tutor
*Client 2
*Difficult client
*Client 1
*Client 3
*SW I don't wish to be like

Figure 4.1 Example of a clustered student repertory grid.

there are two issues to emphasise. First, my own research evaluating the use of repertory grids reported that students found completion of the grid itself was helpful; it helped to articulate values and assumptions relating to work with particular people (Gould 1991). Second, there are approaches to using grids that do not depend upon computer analysis and statistical aptitude.

The simplest pencil, paper and scissors approach to looking for the patterns within a grid is as follows. In order to investigate the grid both in terms of how elements cluster (i.e. which people does a student construe as having similarities or differences?) and how constructs cluster (i.e. what attributes of people does the student perceive as connected?) the completed grid can be copied out twice. It is then cut into element strips, and the grid is reconstructed placing those strips adjacent to one another which are scored most similarly, with a gap left between strips where there seem to be significant differences. A second grid can be treated similarly by cutting it into construct strips that can be rearranged to show similarity or difference between how constructs are used. This is an approach that requires some approximation to be made about whether elements or constructs are similar or different when the scores differ relatively marginally; it is a 'low technology' exercise that can be instructive.

A slightly more ambitious but straightforward option when a personal computer and a user friendly statistical package, such as SPSS for Windows, are available is to use McQuitty's (1964) cluster analysis. The repertory grid is entered as a data matrix and the package is used to produce a correlation matrix that will show levels of similarity between elements or constructs depending on whether rows or columns are being analysed. (Those of us whose research careers go back far enough will have experience of producing correlation matrices manually, but with the contemporary availability of computer power life seems too short to recommend this as a course of action.) McQuitty (1964), and statistical textbooks explaining McQuitty's cluster analysis, explain how correlations can be read to identify clusters within the grid.

So far we have dealt with the elicitation and completion of grids, but now we will look at how they can then be used to support reflection on practice. As indicated, my own evaluation of using repertory grids reported that students did find grid completion in itself a useful exercise, but the full value came from using the grid and its analysis to support further discussion. This may be undertaken in the same session, but my experience is that it is more practical and allows deeper reflection to complete the grid in one session and then use it as the focus for reflection in a subsequent meeting. The process of discussing and learning from the grid can be given some structure by using open-ended questions as prompts. How do people in the grid cluster and why do the students think that some people are seen as being similar or different? How do students construe themselves and are there other people in the grid who are similarly construed? Are there constructs that are used similarly by the students? If grids have been completed in a previous placement, or earlier in the same placement, what seems to be happening as regards the students' perception of self and others? How does the grid correspond to the students' general judgement about their process of learning in the placement and their future learning needs or objectives?

Issues and opportunities

My evaluative study of the use of repertory grids followed a matched pair experimental design and included social work students from two qualifying professional programmes, one undergraduate the other diploma level. Repertory grids were completed by eighteen students twice during each of their two placements. Thus, students were able to reflect on their learning within each placement but also on their transfer of learning between placements. All but two of the participating students rated the experience of using grids as an adjunct to supervision as being significantly helpful and in an evaluation questionnaire gave comments such as:

> It created tangible awareness of change in myself.

> It helped me to see how my perception of clients changed as time went on.

> An occasion to sit and work out where I stand.

> It gives time to reflect on one's development – compensate for lack of supervision, gives structure to thinking.

Although we should be cautious in generalising from a small evaluation study – particularly because of a possible but unlikely Hawthorn effect – it was also found that the students who completed grids received grades for practice-based assignments which were significantly higher than the matched control group (Gould 1991: 47). Structural analysis of the grids completed in the same study also gave some interesting perspectives on the process of transfer of learning (Gould: 1993). Using a form of cluster analysis it was shown how students in the early stages of final placements experienced a fragmentation of personal models of practice that had developed in the previous placement. Reintegration of thinking about practice re-emerged over the duration of the final placement. This gives some tentative confirmation from psychometric data of some of the experiences reported by students when transferring to new practice settings, such as feeling disorientated and de-skilled. More optimistically, the data also showed that students did move on from this stage and, measured statistically from the grids, the final placement was when most change took place. The research sample did not include any students who failed their practice, which might have thrown helpful light on factors that impede students from learning from new settings.

Although there has been sporadic attention given over the years to the contribution that personal construct psychology and the repertory grid technique have made to social work education (e.g. Gould 1989; O'Connor and Dalgleish 1986; Tully 1976; Ryle and Breen 1974) and the evidence from this research that this contribution can be productive, it is only realistic to acknowledge that this approach will not become mainstream. This is because within social work, as (appropriately) a humanistic practice, deterrents arise to methods that are numerical in format, reinforced by a professional curriculum (unlike clinical psychology) which does not give many practitioners confidence with statistical analysis or familiarity with computer-based data analysis.

The intention of this chapter and my earlier writings on personal construct psychology and repertory grid technique has not been to proselytise for those approaches but rather to see them as part of a repertoire of methods that can support reflective learning and transfer of learning. During recent years there has been discernible growth in the range of 'technologies', understood in its original sense of the 'systematic study of practical arts' (*Oxford English Dictionary*), and we should see repertory grid as part of that emergent repertoire. In part led by the growth of open and distance learning, software packages for computer-assisted learning (CAL) are becoming more widely adopted in social work education. Some of these, such as the University of Bath's 'Unlocking Care Management' (see Gould and Wright 1995), are specific to domains of practice such as child protection or care management but contain interactive elements that allow students to record and reflect on their learning. Another ongoing project involving social work educators at the Universities of Bristol, Bath and West of England is 'Self-Assessment in Professional and Higher Education', which is producing and disseminating materials to be used by social work students as part of their reflection on practice. In this climate of the development and evaluation of learning methodologies what seems to be important is not that one theoretical model has hegemony in supporting experiential learning and its transfer, but that students and educators can find structured methods that are useful for them.

Bibliography

Adams-Webber, J.R. (1979) *Personal Construct Theory: Concepts and Applications*, Chichester: John Wiley & Sons.

Bannister, D. (1962) 'The nature and measurement of schizophrenic thought disorder', *Journal of Mental Science* 11(8): 825–42.

Bannister, D. and Fransella, F. (1986) *Inquiring Man: The Psychology of Personal Constructs,* London: Croom Helm.

Collins, H. (1992) *Changing Order: Replication and Induction in Scientific Practice,* Chicago: University of Chicago.

Dalton, P. (ed.) (1983) *Approaches to the Treatment of Stuttering,* London: Croom Helm.

Dalton, P. and Dunnett, G. (1992) *A Psychology for Living: Personal Construct Theory for Professionals and Clients*, Chichester: John Wiley & Sons Ltd.

Dewey, J. (1963) *Experience and Education,* Kappa Delta Pi Lecture Series. New York: Collier.

Fransella, F. and Bannister, D. (1977) *A Manual for Repertory Grid Technique,* London: Academic Press.

Gilbert, N. and Mulkay, M. (1984) *Opening Pandora's Box: A Sociological Analysis of Scientists' Discourse,* Cambridge: Cambridge University Press.

Gould, N. (1989) 'Reflective learning for social work practice', *Social Work Education* 8(2): 9–20.

—— (1991) 'An evaluation of repertory grid technique in social work education', *Social Work Education* 10(2): 38–49.

—— (1993) 'Cognitive change and learning from practice', *Social Work Education,* 12(1): 77–87.

Gould, N. and Wright, J. (1995) 'Unlocking care management: Developing computer assisted learning materials for community care', *New Technology in the Human Services* 8(2): 16–21.

Kelly, G.A. (1955) *The Psychology of Personal Constructs*, New York: Norton.

Kolb, D.A. (1984) *Experiential Learning: Experience as the Source of Learning and Development,* Englewood Cliffs, NJ: Prentice Hall.

Lewin, K. (1951) *Field Theory in the Social Sciences,* New York: Harper & Row.

McQuitty, L. (1964) 'Capabilities and improvements in linkage analysis as a clustering method', *Educational and Psychological Measurement* 24: 441–56.

O'Connor, I. and Dalgleish, L. (1986) 'Cautionary tales from beginning practitioners: the fate of personal models of social work in beginning practice', *British Journal of Social Work*, 16, 431–47.

Piaget, J.(1955) *The Child's Construction of Reality*, London: Routledge and Kegan Paul.

Ryle, A. and Breen, D. (1974) 'Change in the course of social work training: a repertory grid study', *British Journal of Medical Psychology* 47: 139–48.

Schön, D. (1987) *Educating the Reflective Practitioner: Towards A New Design For Teaching and Learning in the Professions,* San Francisco: Jossey-Bass.

Thomas, L.F. and Harri-Augstein, S. (1985) *Self-Organised Learning: Foundations Of A Conversational Science For Psychology,* London: Routledge and Kegan Paul.

Tully, J. B. (1976) 'Personal construct theory and psychological changes related to social work training', *British Journal of Social Work* 16: 481–99.

Wood, M. (1997) *In the Footsteps Of Alexander The Great*, London: BBC Books.

Yorke, D.M. (1985) 'Administration, analysis and assumptions: some aspects of validity', in N. Beal (ed.) *Repertory Grid Techniques and Personal Constructs*, London: Croom Helm.

Chapter 5

Enquiry and action learning
A model for transferring learning

Viviene E. Cree and Ralph Davidson

Introduction

Since its first introduction to UK social work training at the University of York in 1981 (see Downes and McCluskey 1985), the enquiry and action learning (EAL) approach has become increasingly popular on social work courses; it is currently being used in the Universities of York, Bristol, North London, Nottingham Trent, Derby and Edinburgh. It is also commonly used within nurse training, more often referred to here as problem-based learning (PBL). (See Creedy *et al.* 1992; McMillan and Dwyer 1990.) The EAL approach is operationalised differently in different places. Some courses (such as Bristol University) build the entire social work programme around EAL. Other courses (such as the University of Edinburgh) use the EAL framework as only a part of the professional training. Whichever model is in use, there are, nevertheless, some common features in the EAL approach. Expressed most simply, learning is based on 'study units' – scenarios and problems encountered in practice – rather than on subject-based courses (Burgess and Jackson 1990: 3). Students in EAL work together in small groups on a case study that derives from social work practice. Their task is to find out as much as they can about this particular 'case': identifying useful resources, setting learning objectives, breaking down the work into manageable tasks and coming to a decision about an appropriate course of action for the 'case' (Downes and McCluskey 1985). The knowledge that students can expect to gain from each EAL study unit thus includes conceptual knowledge (knowing that – facts, theories and propositions), procedural knowledge (knowing how – skills), strategic knowledge (knowing what to do when), personal knowledge (knowing about their own values and belief systems) and professional knowledge (knowing about social work's values and codes of practice) (Cree *et al.* 1998; Eraut 1994).

The first EAL study unit relates to the social work role in the provision of community care, since this is the area of practice in which the majority of our students have had some pre-course experience. The second EAL focuses on social work with families, children and young people and the third with social work in the criminal justice system. EAL units begin in the first week of the programme and are preceded by an introductory lecture explaining the purpose, principles and methods of the EAL approach.

The rest of the teaching in the first year of the programme takes the more traditional form of lectures, seminars and small group teaching, as does all the teaching during the second year. Lecturers who are providing this teaching are aware of the timing and the content of the EAL study units and can, whenever possible, connect their teaching to them. Inevitably, however, time-tabling difficulties mean that the appropriate sequence of themes in the teaching of these subject areas does not always coincide with the central issues in the EAL study units. For example, sociology teaching about crime may take place before the criminal justice EAL study unit begins. This requires students to be flexible in their learning, at times being able to make direct connections with current teaching and at other times having to anticipate or review their learning.

Preparation of EAL study units

Preparing the resources for each study unit involves identifying suitable case scenarios, initial reading lists and reading materials, making contact with specialist consultants and producing material for study unit facilitators.

Initially a staff member working with a number of practitioners examines a range of actual case material, suitably anonymised, in order to choose a realistic case scenario that students will work on. The group then considers the knowledge, values and skills that are likely to emerge for the students in their consideration of the case scenario. This material can be used later by the facilitator, who may not be a specialist in this area of practice. It is not, however, given to students as a template for their work, but may be discussed with them at the end of the unit as part of the process of reviewing learning.

Staff also prepare some starter reading materials, which are located in a box file that will be easily accessible to the study unit group, and a list detailing further reading and Internet resources for students to access from the library before pursuing their independent literature and on-line searches.[1]

In this chapter, we propose that the EAL approach is a ł
teaching and learning method in terms of transfer of learn
key aspects of the EAL method that are particularly \
encouraging students to transfer learning. These are as fo

- use of students' previous experience as a learning res
- use of 'live' case study material;
- use of active learning approaches;
- use of peer learning;
- use of facilitators;
- use of consultants.

We will begin the chapter with a detailed examination
the EAL approach in our own institutional context, that is t
of Edinburgh's Department of Social Work. We will the
ways in which EAL may be seen to promote transfer of le

EAL at the University of Edinburgh

The Department of Social Work at the University of Ed
adopted the EAL approach on its Master of Social V
programme in 1992. The decision to move towards EAL ż
of programme delivery reflected a desire on the part of tea
move towards a more active, adult-centred approach to lea
felt that not only would this encourage students to
responsibility for their learning during their social work
that they would learn a way of solving problems through
would be useful throughout their careers in social work pr
recognised, however, that because individuals learn in diffe
theme explored by Kolb 1976; Cree *et al.* 1998), not all stu
appreciate the interactive approach of the EAL to the same
this reason it was decided that EAL should be complemente
conventional lectures and seminars. It was also considered i
spell out to all applicants in the social work programme dur
the pattern and style of EAL so that they would have an i
awaited them when they started this course.

The pattern of EAL organisation is such that stude
opportunity to learn something about different areas of
practice before going on placement during the spring of the
the course. This allows them to begin to build the 'anticipat
necessary for transfer of learning to take place (Cree *et al.*

Process of EAL study units

In each study unit, students work in groups of eight or nine with a facilitator. The role of the facilitator is to assist the group in carrying out its work effectively. This does not involve conventional teaching, but rather promoting the learning process by helping the group to identify and hold to its task and commenting on any aspects of the task or the process that appear to be overlooked (see Burgess 1992).

The work of an EAL study unit is spread over four weeks. Individual and group activities take place, as well as weekly meetings with the facilitator. Seven stages of the process can be identified:

1   is a meeting of the study group with the facilitator at which the case scenario is presented and read. Students then share with each other what knowledge and experience each brings from previous personal, educational and professional situations that relate to the case scenario. They next consider what additional areas of knowledge they would want to have before being able to intervene competently in this situation, what value issues they would have to take into account and what skills would be required for the forms of intervention that might be appropriate. Students then identify the initial reading and Internet searching that each will do from the materials and reading list supplied.

2   is a further meeting of the study group with the facilitator at which students tell each other about their searches and reading. They then consider how this relates to the case scenario and what issues it raises that they would wish to explore further in order to reach an initial assessment of the situation. A discussion of these issues leads to the identification of further areas that each student will investigate and read about and defines some of the questions and areas for enquiry that the students will raise when they meet with the specialist consultants.

3   consists of the meetings with specialist 'consultants'. These are individual practitioners, managers, policy-makers, teachers or service users from a range of disciplines who have agreed to be consulted by the students because of their expertise in relation to some central aspect of the case scenario. Some of them may have been involved in the preparation of the case scenario. Usually two students from the study unit group visit each consultant. Consultants are expected to be available to the students for an hour or less, usually in their own workplace, to respond to questions which the students raise as

a result of their thinking about the case material and from the reading that they have done. Students prepare careful notes about the meeting to circulate to the other group members.

4   provides the students and the facilitator with the opportunity to review and discuss the further reading that has been done and the content of the meetings with the consultants. From this the group members develop a more detailed formulation of their assessment of the situation in the case scenario and how they would wish to respond to it.

5   consists of the preparation of a short oral presentation and an accompanying written report, both of which will be given to the other students in the class. These outline the process of the study unit group's enquiry, the learning that has taken place, the conclusions that have been reached about what would be an appropriate way to intervene and the further enquiry and learning that group members feel they would wish to undertake to deepen their understanding of the situation and of their ability to respond sensitively and competently.

6   is the presentation of the oral and written reports to the other students and a discussion of these. The reports focus on the knowledge and skills that would be necessary to reach a competent assessment of, and response to the situation in the case scenario and the value issues that would have to be considered in this process. They also provide pointers to further investigation.[2]

7   rounds off the work of the study unit group. Here the students meet with the facilitator to review the process and outcome of their work. This involves a critical consideration of the value of the case scenario, the resources, the visits to the consultants and the final presentation and discussion. Careful attention is given to the process of the group's work, the contribution of individual members, the role of the facilitator, the learning that has emerged for everyone about individual and group behaviour and the implications of this for the effective management of the next study unit, and, of course, for group membership more generally.

Boxes 5.1 and 5.2 are examples of an EAL study unit and guidance drawn up for facilitators.[3]

Box 5.1 Example of an EAL case study

Social work with families, children and young people: case study

You are a social worker working in a local authority children's centre. You have been asked to work individually with D over the next nine months to try to help him overcome some of his problems.

D is a White, three-year-old boy who has been attending the children's centre with his younger sister who is aged two years. D has experienced a series of separations and losses in addition to abuse and neglect. His mother, who had a long history of drug abuse, had AIDS and died in hospital almost two years ago. When the children were younger their blood contained their mother's HIV antibodies. Once they built up their own immunity they tested negative and have continued to do so.

After the mother's death the two children were taken into care because their father was neglecting them. He would leave the children unattended and sometimes return home drunk, leaving the children with nothing to eat. There are suspicions that he may have hurt D physically.

Both children were placed in foster care but the arrangement broke down and a second foster home was found, where they are now. D presented a big challenge to the foster carers because of his behaviour. As a result, arrangements were made for both children to attend the local children's centre twice a week. D is described as aggressive, particularly towards his sister, having bad tempers and being destructive with toys and other things. He is attention seeking but also mistrusts people. His feelings towards his father are very mixed.

All the signs are that the children's father will not resume responsibility for them and other plans, such as permanent foster care or adoption, may have to be made as there are no other family members interested in giving the children a home.

Box 5.2 Example of EAL notes for facilitators

Social work with families, children and young people: notes for facilitators

(Some or all of the following topics and issues may arise in this EAL.)

Knowledge

- how childcare need is generated
- the developmental needs of young children
- issues of attachment
- the impact of separation and loss on children and adults
- importance of play for children
- the task of parenting: what is good enough parenting?
- symptoms of stress in children
- effects of family breakdown on children and parents
- legal responsibilities of local authorities towards families in need
- support for families: concepts of prevention
- permanency planning
- resources available to support parents and children in the community
- multidisciplinary professional networks and duties of each profession
- causes and effects of violence against women and children in the home
- HIV/AIDS implications for affected children
- empirical evidence of children's capacity to overcome adversities
- psychological parenting
- sibling relationships

Values

- state intervention in family life
- children's entitlement to good parenting and protection
- respecting and valuing and observing children's rights
- attitudes to people with HIV/AIDS and those affected
- parenting and gender
- issues of class, 'race' and ethnicity

Skills

- listening to children
- communicating with young children
- engaging with parents and foster parents and children in need
- recognising and assessing children's attachment to parents/carers
- assessing parenting skills and couple and family relationships
- assisting the development of parenting skills
- planning and decision making with families, children and carers
- making effective use of resources
- taking account of 'race', class and gender issues in work with families

Personal

- own experience of childhood/parenthood and impact of this
- own experience of family breakdown, separations or childhood bereavement
- contact with people who have HIV/AIDS

EAL and transfer of learning

Use of students' previous experience as a learning resource

It has already been stated that EAL is introduced at the very start of the social work course. Beginning a new course can feel quite unnerving for students in the early stages. They may feel quite 'de-skilled', having left the world of work and returning to the position of being learners, a position that not all will remember as a positive or a valuable experience first time around. There is an additional issue for students and teaching staff alike. Students come with varying levels and kinds of experience, professional, personal and academic. There is thus no easy starting-point from which to begin the process of learning. The EAL starts with the recognition that the academic, practical and personal experiences that students bring with them are meaningful and of benefit not only to themselves but to others in their EAL group and to the class as a whole. It is by utilising and building on these experiences that students begin the process of their professional education. As indicated, the first EAL at the University of Edinburgh relates to community care, since that is where most students' pre-course experience lies.

The validation of previous experience is essential for transfer of learning. Encouraging students to draw on their own experiences allows them to feel that they are collaborators in the learning process. When students find that their previous experience is relevant in this new situation, their belief that they have a useful contribution to make is reinforced. Learning theories suggest that previous knowledge is the foundation on which students build their new understandings; accordingly, then, such knowledge has to be 'untapped'. Taylor (1996) identifies the potential for empowerment practice in EAL. Students, she writes, come from a 'structurally determined context that shapes their approach and experience to learning'. Empowerment practice thus emphasises the value of individuals 'identifying their own stories' and working from this starting-point (Taylor 1996: 176).

Use of 'live' case study material

One of the most exciting aspects of the EAL approach as far as students are concerned is that the case studies used each year are drawn from current social work practice. Students have consistently told us in review meetings and in course evaluations that the use of 'live' case material is of critical importance for them because they identify the case scenarios as the very situations that they will have to deal with in practice. This makes the work of the EAL feel 'real', rather than simply a learning exercise. Such authenticity is again identified as a key feature in research into adult education (Cree et al. 1998).[4]

Use of active learning approaches

Right from the beginning of the social work programme, EAL establishes a pattern of active learning in which students are expected to engage in a process of questioning, listening, reading, investigating, consulting, reflecting and decision-making, both individually and collaboratively. For many students, this will be a very different process from the more traditional patterns of learning encountered in their earlier educational experiences, and some may feel a degree of frustration that they are not being 'taught'.[5] Moreover, EAL encourages active engagement on the part of students through the challenge of working on case studies for which there are no single 'right' answers. This openness is liberating for some students, who find that they can share their own opinions and experience. It can also provoke anxiety, however, among those who would like the security of knowing that their approach is the 'right' way to proceed. As long as this anxiety is managed well in the group, and as long as the student feels well supported in the learning environment in general, this experience of instability can itself be a spur to learning, and as soon as effective learning begins to take place anxiety quickly diminishes. If anxiety is not handled well, however, it can lead to students adopting a 'surface' approach to learning: they memorise information needed for assessments, are unreflective about their work, fail to distinguish principles from examples and thus are unable to integrate or transfer their learning (Cree *et al.* 1998).

There are sound social work as well as educational arguments in support of the self-directed learning that EAL brings. Self-directed learning develops the ability of individuals to 'make their own decisions about what they think and do' (Boud 1988: 18, quoted in Taylor 1993: 6). It also implies a 'responsiveness to the environment and an ability to make creative responses to a situation', qualities that are pivotal to good practice (Taylor 1993: 6). Finally, working with and towards change is central to both EAL and social work practice.

Use of peer learning

EAL is fundamentally an experience of peer learning. Although individuals do pursue their own contacts and enquiries on behalf of the group, the greatest amount of time is spent on learning either in the study group or in twos or threes. This gives students the opportunity to learn not just about the case study itself, but about themselves as members of a group. Education is a social process: students learn more if they can discover and talk to other students, some of whom will have different experiences and backgrounds. Students can also try out new skills (such as chairing groups, speaking in group settings, giving feedback to group members and delivering group presentations) that will be very necessary in their future jobs as social workers and team members. Research suggests that working together in groups, where students can learn from the feedback of their peers, is highly beneficial in encouraging transfer of learning to take place (Brooks and Dansereau 1987; Resnick 1990).

If EAL groups are to be successful in enabling students to transfer their learning, they must be places where students feel both accepted and challenged. When group members feel secure, they are more able to cope with challenges from others and can experience criticism as being constructive. There are, of course, times when personality conflicts may arise between individual members, or when matters such as class, or gender or 'race' may emerge as issues within the group. When this does happen, the group may for a time need to concentrate on the group process before returning to the work of the case study itself. Here the opportunities for transfer of learning are both about the individual and about the management of group relations. Students may discover that previous ways of dealing with interpersonal discord (for example avoidance or hostility) are not tenable in the context of learning in a group, so that new ways of resolving conflict must be found.

Use of facilitators

As has already been stated, each EAL group has its own facilitator whose task it is to enable, listen to, clarify, draw out and guide the work of the group (Burgess 1992). During their first EAL group, members look to facilitators for guidance while they get to know each other, the method and the programme as a whole. The facilitator will therefore be more heavily involved in the group process in the early stages, introducing 'ice-breaker' exercises and helping the group to work out 'ground rules' for its conduct, as well as giving guidance on the management of the EAL study unit. As the EAL units progress, the facilitator's role will change to one of supporter and constructive challenger of the students' work, encouraging students to make connections and 'sign-posting' learning when appropriate. At the end of each study unit, facilitators also play a central role in helping group members to review their functioning as a group.[6]

In terms of transfer of learning, the facilitator acts as a 'coach', pointing out similarities and connections to students and giving them feedback on the generalisations and discriminations that they are making (Cree *et al.* 1998: 36). The facilitator encourages students' exploration of the relevance of their previous knowledge and experience to the scenario they are considering and helps them to link theory and practice. The facilitator also assists students to identify contrasting views, to debate their relevance and value, and to find new creative solutions in their work.

Taylor (1996: 183) suggests that facilitating student-led learning is much more complex than didactic teaching, and also 'more unpredictable'. We believe that it is this unpredictability that makes EAL a potentially exciting learning experience for staff and students, as each shares a part in the overall learning process.

The use of consultants

One of the key resources to students in their work in the study unit groups has proved to be that of the consultants. In a number of ways their role mirrors the facilitators' role. They are not expected to 'teach' the students on the basis of their specialist knowledge and indeed are actively discouraged from doing so. Instead, they respond to the questions that the students bring to them from their reading and discussion in their groups. However, if there are key issues that the students seem not to be addressing, the consultants will raise these with students and alert students to their importance.

The role of the consultant is crucial in assisting the students to integrate their theoretical understanding with the current realities of practice. It is the consultants 'on the ground' who can advise students about what works (and does not work) in the context of practice, and who can talk with them about their own professional and personal philosophies and about the policies and codes of practice operating in their agencies. Consultants may also offer different and at times contradictory views of possible outcomes for a given case scenario, and this too can increase the repertoire of responses that students have at their disposal in their learning. All of this encourages the development of the expertise[7] that is central to transfer of learning, both for the students who meet with consultants firsthand and for the group members who learn about the communications that have taken place in their subsequent group discussions.

Conclusion

Students who have participated in EAL at the University of Edinburgh since 1992 have consistently reported that they have appreciated the active learning approach, the vividness of the case material and the face-to-face contact with experienced practitioners and policy-makers. They have felt that EAL has enabled them to make the transition from unqualified practice into the course in a way which uses and values their pre-course learning and experience. Practice teachers in their turn have commented to us that students who have completed three EAL case study units come on placement eager to put into practice their new learning. In doing this, they approach their work in a dynamic way, transferring to their practice the skills of enquiry developed in the EAL model. They recognise the knowledge and skill that they are bringing with them and actively seek out the additional knowledge and skill that they will need to acquire to intervene competently and creatively in their new environment.

It has to be acknowledged that EAL in social work education at the University of Edinburgh is one part of a larger programme that includes many other methods of teaching, all of which may also enable students to achieve effective transfer of learning. We believe, however, that EAL has a particularly useful contribution to make in establishing the process of transfer of learning as fundamental to students' professional development during the period of their social work training. Beyond this, EAL will give them a positive way of approaching the many personal and professional transitions and changes that they will face in their careers as social workers.

Notes

1   The department is currently working on ways to improve its use of new technology in EAL study units. In 1999, an EAL website was created for the first time, facilitating on-line searching and communications between students and between students and staff in EAL. The website was also used to display the students' end-of-unit presentations (on film and in text), thus allowing self- and peer evaluation and feedback to take place.

2   Filming the EAL presentations gave students the chance to see themselves in action, and they also provided staff with tools for learning for future EAL groups.

3   Guidance for facilitators is not shared directly with students in case this has the effect of inappropriately 'steering' the process of their learning. It is nonetheless important for facilitators to have an idea of the likely subjects to emerge and the possible parameters for exploration.

4   CCETSW's 1999 review of childcare teaching also confirms the view that case material is highly valued by students as a means of integrating learning (see Report to CCETSW's England Committee on the Focused Investigation into Childcare Teaching, Appendix K).

5   The experience of some students of anger and frustration at what may seem to be 'withholding behaviour of staff' is explored by Taylor (1996: 181).

6   Again this point is elaborated in the CCETSW review of childcare teaching, where it is pointed out that in many cases self-directed learning is insufficiently supported by a structure for goal-setting and review by tutors. It is argued that self-directed learning groups need regular tutor facilitation and involvement (see Report to CCETSW's England Committee on the Focused Investigation into Childcare Teaching, Appendix K).

7   The subject of expertise is explored by Vygotsky (1978) and Fook *et al.* (1997).

Bibliography

Boud, D. (1988) *Developing Student Autonomy in Learning*, London: Kogan Page.

Brooks, L.W. and Dansereau, D.F. (1987) 'Transfer of information: an instructional perspective', in S.M. Cormier and J.D. Hagman (eds) *Transfer of Learning. Contemporary Research and Applications*, San Diego: Academic Press.

Burgess, H. (1992) *Problem-Led Learning for Social Work: the Enquiry and Action Approach*, London: Whiting and Birch.

Burgess, H. and Jackson, S. (1990) 'Enquiry and action learning: a new approach to social work education', *Social Work Education* 9: 3–19.

Cree, V.E., Macaulay, C. and Loney, H. (1998) *Transfer of Learning: A Study*, Edinburgh: Scottish Office Central Research Unit and CCETSW.

Creedy, D., Horsfall, I. and Hand, B. (1992) 'Problem-based learning in nurse education: an Australian view', *Journal of Advanced Nursing* 17: 727–33.

Downes, C. and McCluskey, U. (1985) 'Sharing expertise and responsibility for learning on a postgraduate qualifying course in social work', *Journal of Social Work Practice* November: 24–40.

Eraut, M. (1994) *Developing Professional Knowledge and Competence*, London: Falmer Press.

Fook, J., Ryan, M. and Hawkins, L. (1997) 'Towards a theory of social work expertise', *British Journal of Social Work* 27: 399–17.

Kolb, D.A. (1976) *Learning Style Inventory: Technical Manual*, Newton MA: Institute for Development Research.

Macaulay, C. and Cree, V.E. (1999) 'Transfer of learning. Concept and process', *Social Work Education* 18(2): 183–94.

McMillan, M.A. and Dwyer, J. (1990) 'Facilitating a match between teaching and learning styles', *Nurse Education Today* 10: 186–92.

Resnick, L. (1990) 'Instruction and the cultivation of thinking', in N. Entwistle (ed.) *Handbook of Educational Ideas and Practices*, London: Routledge.

Taylor, I. (1993) 'Self-directed learning and social work education: a critical analysis', *Issues in Social Work Education* 13(1): 3–24.

—— (1996) 'Enquiry and Action Learning: empowerment in social work education', in S. Jackson and M. Preston-Shoot (eds) *Educating Social Workers in a Changing Policy Context*, London: Whiting and Birch.

Vygotsky, L. (1978) *Mind in Society*, Cambridge, MA: Harvard University Press.

Chapter 6

Intentional observation

Exploring transfer in action

Karen Tanner and Pat Le Riche

Social work, in common with other professions, needs to train 'individuals who can live in a delicate but ever changing balance between what is known and the flowing, moving, altering problems and facts of the future' (Rogers 1993: 229). In this chapter, we will discuss how in a fast-changing world the use of intentional, focused observation can provide one means of facilitating the transfer of learning. We understand the transfer of learning to mean 'prior learning affecting new learning or performance' (Cree *et al.* 1998: 10). The approach to observation that we are adopting in this chapter contrasts with everyday ideas about looking and seeing, which most sighted people do without thinking. If this everyday, informal observation is located at one end of an observational continuum, then intentional observation, which is purposeful and leads to action, is at the other (Weade and Evertson 1991). During a placement, for example, a practice teacher may observe a student informally in a number of situations but may use intentional observation as a specific tool for learning and assessment.

The use of intentional observation in social work is most commonly associated with the Tavistock Model of Infant Observation developed by Bick (1964). This model is informed by psychoanalytic ideas, most notably those of Bion (1962). The aim of Bick (1964) was to compliment theoretical learning about children with experience grounded in direct contact. In the Tavistock model, an infant under the age of five is observed every week for one hour at the same time each week for a fixed period, usually one or two years. The focus of the observation is the development of the child and the emerging relationships with his/her family. Although the observer is expected to be emotionally engaged with the situation, active participation is discouraged. The observed material is recorded from memory after, rather than during, the observation and is constructed in the form of a continuous written narrative. The observation material is subsequently discussed in a small seminar group. This approach to observation recognises the importance of the emotional impact of the observational material as well as the uniqueness of the observer role.

Trowell and Miles (1991) and Trowell *et al.* (1998) recognised the value of this approach to learning within the social work context and adapted the Tavistock framework to the needs and time constraints of social work students and practitioners. In their adaptation the methodology of the Tavistock model remains largely intact. The main changes involve a shortening of the length of the observations and a reformulation of some of the objectives, for example the relationship between observation and the development of assessment skills. Trowell and Miles's (1991) adaptation of infant and child observation has been incorporated into both qualifying and post-qualifying levels of social work training in a number of colleges across the United Kingdom.

The contribution of intentional observation to the professional development and learning of practitioners has been similarly recognised by the Central Council for Education and Training in Social Work (CCETSW). Observation of a student's practice by the practice teacher was formally included in the Diploma in Social Work (DipSW) in Paper 30 (CCETSW 1989, 1991a). The introduction of the practice teacher's award in Papers 26.3 (CCETSW 19991b) and 26.4 (CCETSW 1996) also heralded the arrival of observation as part of the assessment process for trainee practice teachers. In both situations, the observer adopts a non-intrusive stance and pays close attention to the student's practice on a number of predetermined occasions. The material generated is used for the purposes of learning and assessment according to a set of defined core competencies. The effect of these developments is a set of arrangements that includes the student undertaking a series of observations of a service user, observation of a student's practice by a practice teacher and the observation of the practice teacher's supervision of the student by a practice assessor. These arrangements could be described as a hierarchy and we will discuss the implications of this structure later in this chapter.

At Goldsmith's College, in the first term of the first year, the DipSW includes an infant and child observation project (ICO) modelled on the Trowell and Miles adaptation of the Tavistock approach. Students undertake an observation of a child under the age of five for one hour a week for ten weeks. The methodology is exactly the same as that used in the Tavistock model. We encourage our students to make use of the observational learning generated by ICO in their diverse practice placements. Similarly, we emphasise the importance of this aspect of learning with practice teachers and practitioners undertaking post-qualifying training. One of the frameworks for doing this is within the context of the three formal observations that take place during a DipSW placement. At Goldsmith's we have developed guidance for the conduct of these observations which outlines the diversity of learning that such observation can generate and links this learning to the competency framework.

On the basis of this experience we will argue that intentional observation has the potential to be a powerful aid to learning, particularly in relation to the transfer of learning. This transfer is facilitated by the following characteristics of observation:

- Observation is rooted in the experience of the learner. Whether the student is the observer or the observed the material generated is based on experience. Working with immediate material that has personal meaning for the student can be an important catalyst for making connections with previous learning in other forms and contexts.

- Intentional observation provides the space for reflection, 'an opportunity to be in a situation in a qualitatively different way. Rather than being preoccupied with activity or action, the observer role creates a space for thought and reflection. The everyday priorities are reversed, enabling attention to be focused on fine detail and the feelings evoked by the process' (Tanner 1998: 57). The ongoing use of observation helps students to develop a reflective approach to the subjectivity of the resulting data. The student is encouraged to think critically about the impact of values, beliefs and prior learning on the interpretation of the material. The development of this deep and reflective approach helps to internalise learning, a significant prerequisite if the transfer of learning is to take place.

- Linked to reflection is reflexivity. A reflexive concept of observation not only takes account of these internal, subjective processes but is also located within and takes account of the impact of social processes: '[reflexivity] involves three things: reflection on ourselves (including our thinking) and others (including their intentions and motivations); monitoring the acts of ourselves and others; and the creation of ways of explaining situations in which we are involved or social phenomena in which we are interested' (Sheppard 1995: 173–4). Reflexive observation has a part to play in all three processes described by Sheppard. By adopting a critical and active stance, students can take responsibility for developing and transferring their knowledge, skills and values (Boud and Knights 1996).

- Observation is flexible enough to complement a number of learning approaches discussed in this volume. The complementary use of different approaches to the transfer of learning helps to consolidate the transfer and builds triangulation into the process.
- The observation hierarchy provides a microcosm of power relations. If this experience is made use of in the educational setting, students can transfer it to all aspects of their social work practice.

Intentional observation: the process of transfer

We will now establish these ideas about observation and its relationship with the transfer of learning through the use of a case study. We will focus on the practicalities of observation and the nature of the transfer that it makes available to the student and practice teacher.

Jenny, a Black first-year student on placement in an adult team in a Social Services Department, has been allocated a piece of assessment work. Her client is Sidney Smith, a White man, aged 78, who has been referred by his GP for assessment for nursing home care. Sidney lives with his wife, Sarah, who is also White and aged 74. Sarah is Sidney's main carer and she suffers from arthritis and diabetes. Sidney has become increasingly confused and disorientated during the last few months. He is becoming physically aggressive to Sarah and suspicious of other visitors to the house. Sarah is finding this behaviour more difficult to manage as Sidney refuses to accept help from her or their two sons, Frank and Peter. Frank lives nearby with his wife and three children but he has little sympathy for his parents' circumstances; Peter lives further away but remains in regular contact. Peter describes his parents as having had a close and loving relationship. He feels his mother is becoming more depressed and distressed by the change in Sidney. In the last year a care package has been arranged but this is no longer adequate. Jenny has been asked to reassess the situation but the GP feels that twenty-four-hour care is now necessary for Sidney, and for Sarah's future health.

Before starting the DipSW course Jenny's experience had been as a residential social worker with people with learning difficulties. Before the placement Jenny had undertaken a ten-week infant and child observation project as part of the college DipSW curriculum. Jenny had enjoyed the experience but could not see its relevance to her major interest in working with adults.

In a supervision session focusing on the theoretical issues involved in the Smith case, the practice teacher decides to use Jenny's experience of closely observing an infant to stimulate the discussion. The practice teacher is trying to help Jenny identify the relevance of knowledge generated in this previous learning environment and transfer it to her current piece of work. The practice teacher decides to develop Jenny's understanding of the Smith case by exploring ideas about attachment.

The practice teacher by encouraging Jenny to make links between her observation experience, attachment and the current practice situation is introducing her to a particular approach to thinking about knowledge and theoretical frameworks. She is pointing out that the development of frameworks for understanding or knowing is broader than purely propositional knowledge, that is written material in books. The practice teacher is drawing on the ideas of educationalists such as Eraut (1994) and Schön (1983, 1987), who indicate that, in reality, professional practice is complex and ambiguous. Such complexity and uncertainty demands more than a narrow interpretation and use of knowledge in which prescribed written theory is deductively applied to the practice situation. Rather, they argue that professionals need to adopt a more holistic view and use of knowledge: 'the concurrent use of several different kinds of knowledge in an integrated, purposeful manner' (Eraut 1994: 119–20). This approach explicitly requires the learner to make connections between the different layers of their knowledge in order to experiment with and extend their range of understanding.

The approach described above is an important first step in challenging the attitude that 'theory is in the books and has nothing to do with my practice'. Rather, 'theory', practice and personal experience co-exist in a dynamic, mutually influencing relationship. This integration of formal theory with experience is a central aspect of transfer of learning and the extension of the student's knowledge base.

Specifically, the practice teacher is asking Jenny to reflect upon her understanding of attachment in the context of her infant and child observation experience. When undertaking an observation of a baby or small child, students pay close attention to issues of attachment as they have a significant impact on the development of individuals.

Understanding why and how attachments develop is an important aspect of the learning process of student social workers. When reflecting on attachment in the context of infant and child observation, the practice teacher will be encouraging Jenny to make links between attachment experiences in the early years and throughout the life span. Here the practice teacher will be guiding Jenny in translating and applying the knowledge gained in one context to another. Critical to this process of transfer will be identifying the similarities in the situation but also pointing out the differences, for example avoiding discriminatory infantilisation of older people. In drawing Jenny's attention to the pervasiveness of attachment relationships throughout the life cycle she is beginning to explore some of the issues to be addressed in the assessment and planning of the Smith case. This will include the quality of the Smiths' relationship, Sidney and Sarah's feelings about being separated, their previous experience of separation and how each coped on any such occasions, what is important in helping separation to be managed and how they are likely to show their feelings. Integral to this discussion will be an exploration of Jenny's understanding of dementia and whether she is able to stay in touch with the person behind the condition (Kitwood 1997a). As Jenny considers these specific issues, she can draw upon her infant and child observation experience to make associations with the factors, frequently subtle, that influence the development of attachments. These will include how separation anxiety manifests itself, and what is helpful in managing transitions and breaks in attachments.

In helping Jenny build on the transfer of her knowledge about attachment into the Smiths' situation, the practice teacher needs to acknowledge her resourcing role. This will involve providing Jenny with specifically targeted reading material relevant to the situation, for example *Attachment across the Life Cycle* (Murray-Parkes *et al.* 1991), *The New Culture of Dementia Care* (Kitwood and Benson 1995) and good practice guidelines and research findings. The practice teacher can also encourage Jenny to make links between the factors emerging from the case and other aspects of the college curriculum. Relevant issues will be anti-discriminatory practice, particularly ageism, and the links between anti-oppressive practice and theory. Jenny can be invited to critique attachment theory based on her experience and introduce materials that locate attachment within a racial/cultural and gender context (Rashid 1996; Tizard 1986).

The next stage in the use of observation to facilitate the transfer of theory is its application to direct practice. Jenny has been helped to understand the relevance of a particular set of theoretical ideas to her work with the Smiths; the task now is to integrate into this understanding the most appropriate means of intervention. Arguably, an approach that draws upon counselling skills may be helpful in Jenny's work with Sarah. Here again Jenny can reflect on her experience of using such an approach in other situations. Sidney's circumstances are more complex and the practice teacher will need to resource Jenny with ideas specifically rooted in work with people with dementia. For example, Kitwood (1997b) has developed an approach to working with people with dementia that he describes as dementia care mapping. This person-centred approach uses observation and the resulting data as a way of making sense of the experience of later life and as a method of intervention.

In exploring the example of Jenny's work with Sidney and Sarah, we can see how ideas about attachment behaviour in children can be related to the situation of an older person with dementia. The use of observation skills and understanding are a significant resource in this process of transfer.

Building on transfer: the development of skills

So far we have discussed the use that can be made of observation in transferring knowledge from college programmes into placement. In this section we will consider how we can use these ideas in relation to the transfer of skills. In order to do this, Jenny's practice teacher needs to provide her with a range of learning opportunities so that she can acquire and demonstrate the skills required to obtain a DipSW as identified in Paper 30 (CCETSW 1995). These are core skills that Jenny will have to apply and adapt to the diverse circumstances and problems she will encounter in professional practice. We will now move on to consider how Jenny uses observation to facilitate the acquisition and transfer of skills.

On the basis of her initial assessment and in consultation with her practice teacher, Jenny decides that a two-week period of respite care in a nursing home is necessary as part of the assessment and planning process for Sidney and Sarah's long-term future. During his time in the nursing home Sidney becomes increasingly agitated and tries to leave the building to find Sarah. He appears to be concerned about her living on her own. Some of the staff feel that Sidney's behaviour is a sign of distress, whereas others feel that he is 'difficult' and hard to help. Sarah is also becoming distressed by the situation and is reluctantly wondering whether Sidney will settle in residential care or whether he should remain at home.

Jenny and her practice teacher decide that as part of the assessment of Sidney's situation Jenny will undertake an observation of Sidney in the nursing home. In agreement with Sidney and the staff, Jenny will spend some time quietly being with her client, observing rather than interacting. Jenny will aim to obtain a holistic picture of Sidney's experience and behaviour, which will be recorded in detail after the observation and include Jenny's personal reflections on what she has seen and felt. Specifically, Jenny needs to gain a full picture of how Sidney relates to staff as well as understanding his feelings and the meaning of his behaviour. The practice teacher wants to look at how Jenny transfers the knowledge generated by this observation into skilled intervention. This requires the integration of both reflective and reflexive skills.

In the first instance, the practice teacher asks Jenny to present and discuss her observation recording. The aim of the practice teacher is to see how Jenny can integrate the data generated by the observation with knowledge about different methods of intervention that she has acquired from college and other practice experience. As an assessor, she also needs to collect evidence of Jenny's competence, and she plans to use the observation of Sidney to focus particularly on the skills related to the competencies of communicate and engage, and promote and enable.

Jenny observes that Sidney's verbal communication is becoming more limited and confused. In focusing in detail on Sidney's communication behaviour, Jenny observes a number of patterns, including areas of strength and the factors that seemed to bring about 'difficult' aspects of his behaviour. In supervision she and her practice teacher draw upon the observation to explore, in terms of direct work with Sidney, a number of helpful ways in which communication with him could be enhanced. The practice teacher helps Jenny to make explicit her existing knowledge of ways of communicating, particularly in situations where this may be difficult. She encourages Jenny to apply this knowledge to the material generated by the observation and then to think about the implications of this for direct work with Sidney. This involves discussion of methods such as reminiscence, validation techniques, music therapy and the use of touch (Bright 1992; Feil 1992). In facilitating the transfer, the practice teacher recognises that skills that promote Sidney's rights are particularly important. These include listening skills and the development of accurate empathy, which is encouraged by the use of intentional observation. The practice teacher encourages Jenny to use the work of Kitwood and the members of the Bradford Dementia group to highlight how such observational assessment can make a significant contribution to improving the total environment for people with dementia. This holistic approach to Sidney's experience has the potential to emphasise his existing strengths as a whole person and thus to counteract the ageist, problem-focused responses that can often limit work with people with dementia (Marshall 1997; Hughes 1995).

The practice teacher may decide to schedule one of her observations of Jenny to take place after Jenny has observed Sidney in the nursing home. The practice teacher's observation can then focus on Jenny's direct work skills, specifically the ability to transfer her conceptual and personal knowledge about communication into the demands of a practice situation. Jenny's ability to find a way of communicating with Sidney will be direct evidence of competency. So will her ability to provide the other workers and his family with information that promotes his rights and needs. In particular, it will demonstrate how Jenny is able to move from showing she can contain anxiety and empathise with Sidney to using this understanding to enhance her intervention skills. If this understanding is developed and consolidated during the education process Jenny will have a repertoire of communication skills to transfer into her professional practice.

As this discussion has implied, the practice teacher plays a critical part in maximising the learning and making sense of the rich material generated by the observation, including maintaining a focus on the learning provided by Jenny's own responses. The practice teacher's ability to make use of Jenny's existing knowledge and experience to illuminate Sidney's situation provides Jenny with an important role model. In the context of this discussion, this is another example of the transfer of learning from the educational setting into professional practice.

The final point we wish to make in this section is that observation is flexible enough to form part of a range of learning resources that Jenny and her practice teacher can use during supervision. These include role-playing, process recording, learning diaries and focused reading. The usefulness of some of these approaches to the transfer of learning is discussed elsewhere in this book. Having developed the confidence to use observational learning in both assessment and care planning, Jenny will be able to think creatively about its use in a range of situations in her future practice.

A hierarchy of power

Intentional observation is clearly a very powerful source for facilitating the transfer of learning. However, this will only be achieved if the power relations inherent in the observation relationship are addressed. These power differentials are a characteristic of all learning environments, but they are accentuated by the hierarchy of assessment. It is essential that students work with this power dynamic otherwise there is a risk that all aspects of learning, including the capacity for transfer will be inhibited.

At all points in this hierarchy the student, practice teacher and practice assessor will be working with the interplay between experiencing power when observing and experiencing powerlessness when being observed. In the educational environment the student will be observed while on placement and, as we have suggested, may also have the opportunity to take on the role of observer. As an observer, the student can struggle to come to terms with the power and legitimacy of the role, experiencing feelings of invasion, intrusion, persecution and selfishness. Observation can seem oppressive. Feelings of powerlessness and vulnerability may be experienced when students are being observed. Practice teachers may share these feelings when setting up observations in placement, particularly if the observer role is unfamiliar. If the practice teacher is also being observed by a practice assessor, then these processes are likely to be mirrored in that relationship since practice assessors will bring their own experiences into the equation.

We also need to take account of the ways in which these feelings are affected by the complexities of working with and across differences, some of which may not be visible or acknowledged (Kemshall 1993; Leonard 1998). Differences will introduce another set of power relations, which are illustrated by Leonard in her discussion of the place of observation in practice teaching:

> For example, the practice teacher has power within the relationship to pass or fail the student. The student has power over the service offered to the service user. If the practice teacher is a Black woman, the student a White man and the service user a White woman, this has to be set in the context of the potential for racism and sexism from the student and the service user. If the male student is gay and the practice teacher and practice assessor are heterosexual, the impact of potential heterosexism for the student needs to be included in the service user–student–practice teacher dynamic.
>
> (Leonard 1998: 79)

Under supervision, the student and practice teacher can make use of the material generated by their experience of observation as a means of understanding the power dynamics within the supervisory relationship. Critically, the specific experience of how to work with and manage the feelings generated by differences can serve as a powerful piece of learning that can be generalised into the social worker–client relationship. The practice teacher needs to enable the student to learn through partnership but he/she also has to work with the power and authority of the assessor role. This situation mirrors the authority of the social worker in his/her role and the use of observation provides one forum in which this issue can be highlighted, reflected upon and understood. Once the student is employed this learning underpins good-quality social work practice.

Conclusion

We feel that two major themes have developed from our discussion of Jenny's work with Sidney and Sarah. The first of these relates to the way in which the holistic nature of intentional observation facilitates the transfer of learning of different orders. This includes the direct transfer of knowledge, which we have illustrated by our discussion of attachment, the integration of formal knowledge with experience and transfer across contexts, which we have described in relation to both similar and different contexts. The second major theme illustrates how intentional observation can facilitate a transfer that is both 'deep' and active. This is because observational learning encourages reflective and reflexive processes, both of which are central to the development of a critical approach to practice.

Bibliography

Bick, E. (1964) 'Notes on infant observation in psychoanalytic training', *International Journal of Psychoanalysis* 45: 558–66.

Bion, W. (1962) *Learning from Experience*, London: Heinemann.

Boud, D. and Knights, S. (1996) 'Course design for reflective practice', in N. Gould and I. Taylor (eds) *Reflective Learning for Social Work*, Aldershot: Arena.

Bright, R. (1992) 'Music therapy in the management of dementia' in G. Jones and B. Mieson (eds) *Care Giving in Dementia*, Vol. II, London: Routledge.

Central Council for Education and Training in Social Work (1989) *Requirements and Regulations for the Diploma in Social Work: Paper 30*, London: CCETSW.

—— (1991a) *DipSW – Rules and Requirements for the Diploma in Social Work*, London: CCETSW.

—— (1991b) *Improving Standards in Practice Learning, Paper 26.3*. London: CCETSW.

—— (1995) *Assuring Quality in the Diploma in Social Work – 1: Rules and Requirements for the DipSW,* London: CCETSW.

—— (1996) *Rules and Requirements for the Practice Teaching Award, Paper 26.4.* London: CCETSW.

Cree, V.E. and Macaulay, C. (1997) 'Transfer of learning: theory and practice' in *Learning for Competence,* York Conference, February 1997, London: CCETSW.

Cree, V.E., Macaulay, C. and Loney, H. (1998) *Transfer of Learning: A Study,* Edinburgh: Scottish Office Central Research Unit and CCETSW.

Eraut, M. (1994) *Developing Professional Knowledge and Competence,* London: Falmer Press.

Feil, N. (1992) 'Validation therapy with late onset dementia populations', in G. Jones and B. Mieson (eds) *Care Giving in Dementia,* Vol. II, London: Routledge.

Hughes, B. (1995) *Older People and Community Care,* Buckingham: Open University Press.

Kemshall, H. (1993) 'Assessing competence: scientific process or subjective inference? Do we really see it?' *Social Work Education* 12(1): 36–45.

Kitwood, T. (1997a) *Dementia Reconsidered. The Person Comes First,* Buckingham: Open University Press.

—— (1997b) *Evaluating Dementia Care, the DCM Method,* Bradford: Bradford Dementia Care Group.

Kitwood, T. and Benson, S. (1995) *The New Culture of Dementia Care,* Bradford: Hawker Publications.

Le Riche, P. and Tanner, K. (1998) *Observation and its Application to Social Work. Rather Like Breathing,* London: Jessica Kingsley Publishers.

Leonard, K. (1998) 'A process and an event. The use of observation by practice assessors and practice teachers', in P. Le Riche and K. Tanner (eds) *Observation and its Application to Social Work. Rather Like Breathing,* London: Jessica Kingsley Publishers.

Marshall, M. (1997) *The State of the Art in Dementia Care,* London: Centre for Policy on Ageing.

Murray Parkes, C. Stevenson-Hinde, J. and Marris, P. (1991) *Attachment Across the Life Cycle,* London: Routledge.

Rashid, S.P. (1996) 'Attachment reviewed through a cultural lens', in D. Howe (ed.) *Attachment and Loss in Child and Family Social Work,* Oxford: Blackwell Science.

Rogers, C. (1993) 'The interpersonal relationship in the facilitation of learning', in M. Thorpe, R. Edwards and A. Hanson (eds) *Culture and Processes of Adult Learning,* London: Routledge.

Schön, D. (1983) *The Reflective Practitioner,* New York: Basic Books.

—— (1987) *Educating the Reflective Practitioner,* San Francisco: Jossey-Bass.

Sheppard, M. (1995) *Care Management and the New Social Work,* London: Whiting and Birch.

Stevenson, O. (1998) *Neglected Children: Issues and Dilemmas*, Oxford: Blackwell Science.

Tanner, K. (1998) 'Toward an equality model. Observation through a power lens', in P. Le Riche and K. Tanner (eds) *Observation and its Application to Social Work. Rather Like Breathing*, London: Jessica Kingsley Publishers.

Tanner, K. and Le Riche, P. (1995) '"You see but you do not observe." The art of observation and its application to practice teaching', *Issues in Social Work Education* 15(2): 66–80.

Tanner, K. and Le Riche, P. 'Work in Progress: the contribution of observation to the development of good practice in evaluation' in I. Shaw and J. Lishman (eds) *Evaluation and Social Work Practice*, London: Sage.

Tizard, B. (1986) 'The care of young children: implications of recent research', Thomas Coram Research Unit, Working and Occasional papers no. 1, University of London Institute of Education.

Trowell, J. and Miles, G. (1991) 'The contribution of observation training to professional development in social work', *Journal of Social Work Practice* 5(1): 51–60.

Trowell, J., Paton, A., Davids, Z. and Miles, G. (1998) 'The importance of observational training: an evaluative study', *International Journal of Infant Observation and its Applications,* 21: 101–11.

Weade, G. and Evertson, C. M. (1991) 'On what can be learned from observing teaching', *Theory into Practice* XXX(1): 37–45.

Chapter 7

Using a reflective diary in student supervision

Mike Tait

This chapter focuses on the use of reflective diaries as a way of promoting transfer of learning in social work students. Drawing on my experience as a practice teacher over the last ten years, I will first consider why reflective diaries are useful before going on to explore their use in some detail. I will use excerpts from reflective diaries that will show their usefulness. The chapter is not intended to be an academic investigation of the use of reflective diaries in supervision. Instead, I hope that it will serve as an informed account of a particular approach to the use of reflective diaries and an examination of some of the issues that have arisen while working with social work students and helping them transfer learning.

My starting-point is the belief that conscious and reflective practice is the key to transfer of learning and that much of the ability to be conscious and reflective is guided by the students' openness to learning and by their willingness to review and apply previous learning. We all have our own thinking processes and ways of learning. Students coming on placement draw on past ways of thinking and being that have been useful to them in their lives – at least in some respects. Beyond this, however, is the difficult discovery that some of these ways are less useful in social work than in other areas of work and life. In that sense, transfer of learning, although an essential component of competent practice, has to be discriminating, informed by knowledge and experience, and sometimes by a different value system than that held previously. Not all knowledge, skills and values are usefully transferred to social work practice.

Before going on to consider the reasons for, and use of reflective diaries in practice, it is important to say something about what we are talking about: what is a reflective diary?

What is a reflective diary?

There is only passing reference to diary-keeping in the literature on practice teaching in social work (see Boud and Knights 1996; Harris 1996; Moffat 1996). As a therapeutic and personal development tool, it is a well-known approach, but in formal education and training it seems to be more commonly used in nurse training and in some of the paramedical disciplines than in social work (see Button and Davies 1996; Niemi 1997; Sedlak 1992; Shields 1994). It is also described by Morrison (1996) as particularly beneficial for higher degree students undertaking modular courses. The term 'reflective diary' is in fact used in many different ways in different places, and can mean different things to different people (Ghaye and Lillyman 1997: 43). It is closely aligned to the term 'learning log' or even 'learning journal', with which it is often used interchangeably. Cowan (1992) has helpfully identified five different purposes of diaries or journals, and these give an indication of the different ways that diaries may be used in practice.

1   Absolute privacy: students are encouraged to keep an 'old-style diary', privately recording incidents and mulling over them themselves later.
2   Reflection on reflection: students are invited to reflect on their experiences and their thinking, and hand in their journals for comment from 'empathetic members of staff'.
3   Reflection on learning: students keep a journal that focuses on their learning, noting issues in order to 'receive facilitative comment'.
4   Privacy, with dialogue 'on the side': students keep a private diary, but discuss issues from it with the practice teacher.
5   Students keep a learning journal based on work experience: this is more task-centred, and is set up as a question that the student must then go on to answer. It may also focus on a specific 'critical incident' (see Chapter 8).

(Cowan 1992: 139–40)

What makes this discussion even more complicated is that on many occasions, the use of diaries or journals will encompass a number of these different styles and purposes. In my own situation, reflective diaries may draw on models 2, 3 and 5, at different times and at different stages over the course of a placement, as I will describe in more detail later. Over and above this, it is my overriding wish that students will feel free to record anything that touches them in their practice; this, then, has the spirit of model 1 or model 4. The writing of the diary is, however, only one part of the learning process. It is predominantly the dialogue or exchange with the practice teacher that takes place through the dairy notes that allows learning (and transfer of learning) to take place.

Some social work programmes routinely require students to keep a 'learning log', and this is sometimes submitted as part of their overall assessment material. The guidance and prescription for such a log tends to be loosely defined and the use made of it may not be clear. This is one of the times when my own requirement of students to keep a daily diary can create problems. On the one hand, students will (justifiably) want to combine the college requirement with that of the placement, to avoid writing two versions of the same events and processes. On the other hand, a 'sanitised' log that is designed to be read by Assessment Boards is ineffectual for the purposes I hope the diary will fulfil on placement. On these occasions, it has been necessary for me to negotiate with college tutors to allow the students some leeway so that they will be allowed to concentrate on the placement requirements and tasks and, if appropriate, submit edited abstracts of the placement diary to meet the college expectations. Although I will also be assessing material from diary notes, my assessments (unlike those of the academic institution) are formative and diagnostic, helping to guide the content of supervision sessions and, together with the student, guide priorities for learning during the placement.

Why use reflective diaries?

As a 'tool' to aid long-arm supervision

When I was first appointed as a full-time social work practice teacher in a unit funded by the voluntary sector, I found myself developing placements for social work students in voluntary agencies where I had only theoretical knowledge of the day-to-day work of the agencies, service users and staff members. Of course, in setting up the placements, I paid close attention to the ways in which learning opportunities were constructed in order to make a judgement about their suitability for students and to avoid what Thompson *et al.* (1990) have referred to as the 'Duff Agency'. This results when, for example, by virtue of poor learning opportunities, lack of preparation for a student, staff who are unprepared or unwilling to support a student or a lack of clarity about the requirements for a placement the placement setting is unsuitable. At that time, the idea of 'long-arm' practice teaching was one that was still fairly new and was by no means readily accepted, especially when the practice teacher was based in a quite different agency. Today, the student unit where I work is an approved agency for practice learning, in partnership with over forty independent voluntary agencies and long-arm practice teaching is established and accepted. As well as a considerable amount of time spent in establishing and maintaining contact with agencies and building and maintaining relationships with agency staff, one of the main 'tools' I use is the student's daily diary, which I have always required students to keep and to share with me on a weekly basis. The diary notes, at their most basic level, serve to inform me prior to the supervision session of the context of work undertaken by the student. In that way, limited supervision time need not be taken up with descriptions of work – or at least not as much time as might otherwise be necessary.

As a 'diagnostic tool' for practice teachers

Although it has been suggested that reflective diaries are particularly useful for 'long-arm' placements, they are also invaluable for working with students whatever their placement setting. Reflective diaries provide an opportunity for practice teachers to find a way into the thoughts and feelings of students that would otherwise be difficult to access even if they were working alongside one another. Ideas, thoughts and feelings cannot always be inferred from behaviour alone and the commentary that a reflective diary provides allows that additional input from the student. Knowing that students not only learn in different ways but think differently and view the world differently (Pask 1976; Entwistle 1987, 1990), the reflective diary has the potential to give the practice teacher some insight, fairly quickly, into those differences. I have different ways of viewing the information that emerges, and I am watchful for patterns that may be less helpful to social work ways of thinking about and framing situations and contexts. For example, diary entries which are highly judgmental or which overly generalise from personal experience or which indicate a high level of inevitability or fatalism will set off warning bells and, at the least, alert me enough to explore those entries. I will, in reading the diary notes, attempt to identify the predominant existing qualities of the writer.

The requirements for the DipSW are designed to identify the competences to be demonstrated by students. The task of practice teaching involves working with the underpinning qualities and attributes that allow competence to develop. My own list of what to look for in students and in students' diary notes is drawn from Alinsky's (1972) 'elements of an organiser' (paraphrased for social work purposes):

- Curiosity: here I would look for students to be wondering 'why?', particularly in relation to the conditions of the people's lives in which they are training to meddle.
- Irreverence: inextricably linked with curiosity, irreverence will recognise no limits to the question. Paradoxically, there must be extreme reverence for life, humanity, rights, freedom and people, combined with irreverence for dogma, unthinking tradition and (dare I say) theory in the quest for meaning and understanding.
- Imagination: this allows the student not only to consider the other person's perspective (which social work more traditionally calls empathy) but to consider outcomes not already experienced and is a prerequisite for any change-related work.
- Sense of humour: this allows contradictions and dilemmas to be coped with, assimilated, and worked through, maintaining perspective, without either entering into despair or developing negative ideologies.
- Blurred vision of a better world: with a sense of one's own place within it, this allows the student to avoid exclusive focus on the mundane tasks of social work and the marginal effects that one social worker can have and to see one's efforts as part of a variety of change-related approaches that can, over time, make a difference. Perhaps an ability to trust and have faith are part of this 'element'.
- Organised personality: this is a different quality from being able to keep accurate records, turn up to the placement agency on time and make sure that deadlines are met. It has more to do with being able to function in disorganised situations, to find rationality in irrational acts and to work with chaos while not becoming chaotic.
- Well-integrated bipolarity: this allows the student to 'see' and appreciate both (or multiple) 'sides' of a situation at the same time and work with both, accepting neither wholly nor rejecting either entirely, working towards solutions (and sometimes compromises).
- Ego: this, as opposed to egotism, allows the student to develop belief and confidence in her/himself to be effective in the face of sometimes overwhelming odds.
- A free and open mind and a sense of relativity: this allows the student to meet the unexpected and work with uncertainty without becoming disillusioned, cynical or disintegrating.
- Joy in creation: this allows the student to maintain a marginal

position in relation to the work and the people that he or she works with, concentrating on the change that is the target for work, avoiding being sucked into unhealthy striving for personal power and taking pleasure in the development of power in others.

Of course, the work in practice teaching is more about facilitating the development of personal and professional attributes, rather than simply noting their relative presence or absence. Using the diary notes enables students to become more conscious of which characteristics are more or less present and to open discussion about possible ways of developing new approaches or styles. Although I believe that some people have a greater predisposition to these attributes and qualities than others, my own experience is that they can be developed. Research into the concept of Critical Thinking (always capitalised), which is receiving much attention in North America, suggests that whereas students who are predisposed towards Critical Thinking will develop the ability faster, those who do not score highly on this predisposition can, nevertheless, develop the capacity when engaged with learning programmes designed with that focus.[1] (Whether the present trend towards shorter practice placements will continue to allow time for sufficient development is another matter.)

As an aid to students' personal and professional development

In addition, reflective diaries allow students to actively participate in their own learning processes. Students are in control of their sharing of thoughts and feelings in their diaries in a way that we aspire to in adult learning but which is sometimes not much more than an aspiration for those who are in what is, inevitably, the less powerful position of learner. Diaries also encourage students to make necessary connections between personal/professional and academic/practice learning. Morrison (1996) expresses well the usefulness of a learning journal, arguing that it enables students' 'own personality and personal needs to feature in a course of higher education that is marked by a concern with the academic and professional areas of development ... it provides them with an opportunity ... to integrate personal, intra-personal, private, public, intellectual and professional aspects of themselves' (Morrison 1996: 327–8).

As a 'tool' for developing reflective practice

The main use of diary notes is as a tool for developing reflective practice. Schön writes:

> The student cannot be *taught* what he [sic] needs to know, but he can be *coached*: He has to *see* on his own behalf and in his own way the relations between means and methods employed and results achieved. Nobody can see for him, and he can't just see by being 'told', although the right kind of telling may guide his seeing and thus help him see what he needs to see.
>
> (Schön 1987: 17)

Although Schön is not concerned principally with social work education, this view of teaching and learning is as applicable to social work as any other field of education. It is particularly apt for students learning about social work in practice situations with the analogy of the practice teacher as coach.

Schön argues that there are stages of the learning process in any professional's practice. He describes these as 'knowing-in-action', 'reflection-in-action' and 'reflection-on-reflection-in-action'. One student on a criminal justice placement demonstrates in her diary notes 'knowing-in-action' as she reflects on a role-play I had suggested during a previous supervision session. She was able to look back on her actions (and feelings) and reflect on them:

> During supervision Mike took the service user's role which I found to be false. I find I am not too good with role-play. Mike played the service user's role at the review stage for the [Probation] Order. Every suggestion I came up with, he said 'I don't fancy that' or 'I never liked that'. This left me unable to solve the problem of allocating the service user an appropriate activity. I also had difficulty thinking 'where do I go from here?' ... In hindsight, I could have made better use of the information and my impressions of the service user and I feel this would have helped me in formulating some plan with the service user to enable us to look at his areas of interest and future plans.

There is no indication in this extract of reflection-*in*-action, that is reflecting while the task is still going on and when reflections can still affect the performance. Schön's final stage, reflection-on-reflection-in-action, is nearer to what we are asked to help students develop as reflective practitioners. The 'reflection-on-reflection-in' is a conscious and thoughtful process where students become aware of their performance and consciously refine it, applying understanding and knowledge and critical self-evaluation. When reflective diaries are used well, this process can be readily discerned. An abstract from one student's diary notes illustrates this:

This morning was taken up with a direct observation by Mike of myself with service user X and his father, Y. I deliberately tried to include the emotional aspect within the meeting after the last feedback I had. I was aware of not feeling very comfortable which was partly due to being observed. On the occasions when I asked X how he was feeling, I was caught off guard when he responded with an answer relating to his physical health. This caused me to panic a bit as I was unsure of how to get a response relating to emotional rather than physical feelings. I think because I wasn't sure how to progress, I found myself actually having a conversation with Y (X's father), about him, while he was present. I caught myself and suggested to Y that it would be better if X spoke for himself. I was embarrassed at my own collusion in excluding X and I did get a sense that X was relieved that I was at least acknowledging what was going on. He spoke more strongly and assertively after that. Looking back, I think I was trying too hard to include the emotional aspects and as a result, I was not listening as well as I might. On reflection, I think that one way of checking out his emotional state would be to 'guess' how he might be feeling and check it out by asking. I think I could also have paid more attention to his body language instead of relying on him to put into words what was a difficult area for him. As I left, I arranged to meet X on Thursday without his father present.

In ideal terms (and not uncommonly), the student begins by doing and then reflecting on practice, gradually moving to incorporate reflection into practice, and the diary notes and subsequent discussion allow reflection-on-reflection in practice.

As evidence of transfer of learning

Diary notes are also useful in two further distinct but connected ways.

They can contain the evidence of consciously transferred experience, learning and practice, or, just as importantly, that evidence might be missing from the diary notes. For example, a student with previous experience in a statutory sector children and families' placement wrote as follows about an incident while on a second placement in a voluntary sector setting working with adults who were chemically dependent:

> Although P's parenting skills are not great, there is no immediate risk to the children. If another crisis like this one occurs, though, I think we would need to discuss referral to the Area [Social Work] Team. In the meantime, I think I will work with her on ways to manage her crises while making sure that the children do not have to support her through them, especially as she has a great fear of them being taken into care. As it is, she is in danger of slipping up on parental responsibility under the Children (Scotland) Act if she does not plan for a possible relapse.

In this extract, the student was able to indicate prior understanding of 'good enough' parenting skills, knowledge of the relevant legislation and an understanding of the role of statutory social workers in child protection. In supervision, we were able to explore (from the student's own suggestions) crisis management as an approach, motivational theory and, ultimately from our discussion, task-centred work as her preferred method.

In contrast, another student (final year) who had worked for some years before entering training with teenagers who had been sexually abused was unable to make appropriate connections when working with a young woman with learning disabilities, even though this woman had an eating disorder, self-harmed and was known to have been abused. The student, in a surface-learning way, proposed a training programme focused on healthy eating and assistance with shopping, together with referral to a 'befriending' service to counter her feelings of isolation. My attempts, in supervision, to encourage her to draw on her existing knowledge and experience of working with abused young people met with resistance. It became clear that she saw the intellectually disabled service user as so different from the young people she had worked with that the human processes she appeared to know about in another context could not apply.

As a 'tool' for assessment

Finally, I have found that the diary notes are helpful in the assessment process generally. With such a detailed record of not only the student's activities but of how the student's experiences have been processed, it is possible to track developmental shifts in the student and, perhaps more importantly, for students to review their own learning and development. With such a record, writing a report (whether at interim or final stage) becomes far less a matter of two subjective impressions hopefully coinciding and more of a collaborative process drawing on the student's own material, which is available to both of us. When a student is going to fail a placement, she/he will also be less likely to argue that the evidence for a pass was available and that the practice teacher was simply unable to see it. Diary notes, although not sufficient in themselves, can thus be part of the triangulation of evidence with other sources, including discussions in supervision, direct observation, process recording and case records, feedback from other agency staff and from service users.

How are reflective diaries used?

For students whose placements I supervise, the reflective diary is standard practice and institutionalised into the Placement Working Agreement. This states:

> The main written requirements of the placement are the daily diary notes. These should be a record of (the student)'s thoughts, activities, impressions, feelings, assessments, dilemmas, difficulties, and questions; they should be submitted two days prior to the supervision session and they will be used as a basis for supervision.

Students' perceptions of reflective diaries

I have found that students are, in the main, receptive to the need for keeping a reflective diary and, at the beginning of a placement at least, trust the process to this extent. It is fairly common for me to be asked: 'what do you expect me to write?' Although this is a sensible and reasonable question, it is not one which can be answered in the way that most students might expect. I usually say that I have no expectations, that each student will use the diary in their own way and that once I am able to discover how the student writes and thinks I may make suggestions how he or she might change its use over time. I do, however, set some parameters initially. A diary that is purely descriptive will be of limited use, so I ask for comments and impressions and (if possible) feelings to be recorded. At the start of placement, I might ask a student: 'What did you see?', 'What was going on for you?' or 'How do you feel about being in this new situation?' Later in placement, as students feel more comfortable with the process of dialogue and exchange that takes place through the diary notes, I may ask them: 'What changes in your practice are you noticing?'; 'What do you find yourself avoiding or leaning towards?'; 'What are you having consistent difficulty with?'; or 'How do you feel about having to take more responsibility?'[2] This open approach and the lack of externally imposed structure[3] is the major difference between this kind of diary and the more formal 'learning logs' that I have seen used by some programmes and case records and process recordings (which I will also use with students).

Students' feelings about supervision as expressed in diaries

All students beginning placement are asked to undergo changes in ideas and behaviour and, like any change, this may set up feelings of anxiety and a sense of betraying significant people in the student's life as familiar ideas are rejected in favour of unfamiliar ones. In relation to the feelings that are obvious in supervision, Currie and Guttridge (1977) describe 'the step before reflection', which is the process of beginning to be open to review received ideas. That process is often articulated in the diary notes as discomfort in the supervision session itself. Although I can, of course, usually discern discomfort when I am directly engaging with a student, diary notes are useful both at the beginning and later in the supervision process. The diary notes often allow the student to make comment on feelings as the discussion points from a session are retrospectively processed. Given the power difference inherent in the practice teaching relationship, it is rare that a student will feel able to respond immediately with considered and reflective feedback. Sometimes, by the time we hear verbal feedback, there is an issue that has grown out of proportion and it is, consequently, much more difficult to deal with. Students often give 'clues' about their experience of supervision with me in their diary notes. Sometimes the clues are very direct and at other times they are more obtuse and obscure. I have learned to be alert in either case and, as a matter of principle, follow up by inviting open discussion on the process (however threatening it might feel to me at the time). The range of diary comments on uncomfortable feelings in supervision is diverse, but key words can be 'exhausted', 'confused', 'angry', 'felt stupid', 'overloaded', 'wrong' and other apparently negative descriptors. Sometimes the ensuing discussion points towards the need for changes in my approach or perhaps the pace of supervision. Equally, however, there may have been a shift between the time of writing and submitting the diary notes and the time we meet again, so that the student has had time to process the experience. Very occasionally, there can be issues that are not resolved but at least there has been the opportunity to explore and, if necessary, call in the academic tutor.

Goldstein and Harris (1996) describe a method of teaching that is useful for anti-oppressive practice, theory and legislation. Some elements that they list are, however, a prerequisite for any constructive practice teaching and learning, particularly in facilitating transfer of learning:

- a joint decision to engage with the topic;
- enabling the student to share their knowledge on the topic;
- ascertaining from them the content and process of any previous learning;
- asking the student to relate their previous experience on the topic;
- a sharing of views and feelings on the topic;
- helping the student to evaluate their understanding and competence in this area;
- helping the student to identify their specific learning needs;
- structuring the topic to include principles and value systems, theoretical underpinnings, legal and structural context, implications for practice;
- a joint identification of opportunities for practice;
- assessment through appropriate mechanisms;
- student self-assessment and identification of further learning.

(Goldstein and Harris 1996: 200)

Students' thinking processes as expressed in diaries

As well as the feelings generated during supervision, attention needs to be paid to the students' frameworks for the thinking process itself. I tend to use a variety of different ways of analysing the 'clues' that come from diary notes and subsequent discussion in supervision sessions, one of which comes from Edward de Bono (1996) where he identifies six 'Thinking Hats' that he labels with colours:

- The white hat is neutral and objective. Students wearing this hat will be likely to present hard data, facts and figures and descriptions of what was said and done.

- The red hat is emotional and intuitive. Students wearing this one will find it easier to present hunches and describe their feelings but may find it more difficult to justify and explain.
- The black hat is 'logical negative' and students may be cautious, describing legal and procedural limits and be concerned with why things may go wrong.
- The yellow hat is 'logical positive' and students will be optimistic and probably strong in planning and forward thinking, describing advantages and benefits of intervention approaches.
- The green hat is creative. Students will be likely to present plans, proposals, ideas, suggestions and alternatives.
- The blue hat is the 'meta hat' where students are able to control and organise their wearing of some or all of the other 'hats' and shift in and out of different ways of thinking about a situation in a conscious way.

Just as with current and conventional ideas about 'learning styles' (e.g. Honey and Mumford 1986), there is no intrinsic value placed on each way of thinking, but it is valuable for students (and practice teachers) to be able to identify their preferred styles and to be able to work towards broadening and developing into others. This is one of the developmental uses of the diary notes. Once a student's 'pattern' has begun to emerge and we have been able to discuss it in supervision, I like to reach agreement with her or him about the changes that it would be useful to see. For example, many students (predominantly, but not exclusively, male students in my experience) arrive on placement with relatively little experience of being asked to describe their feelings. Commonly, this will be associated with a restricted emotional vocabulary and may be related to male socialisation and upbringing (Segal 1990; Phillips 1993). In situations like this, it has been helpful to ask the student to try to consciously include the 'red hat' when writing diary notes. The student is asked to give himself permission to simply note his feelings in situations without having to rationally explain them (at that stage). One interesting addition to the notion of a gender-related emotionally restricted code is that I have found that male students (when they do give permission to themselves) usually find it easier relate to their anger and resentment before some of the other emotions can surface.

For example, a final year student in a setting concerned with drug and alcohol misuse was working with a man who had been told by medical staff that he would be dead within three months if he did not stop his intake of alcohol altogether. The student had been working patiently with the man, maintaining a calm and thoughtful stance, which I thought was slightly detached and clinical (perhaps wearing his 'white hat'). This was not inconsistent with the college reputation of the student as solid and academically very able, described informally to me as a 'high-flyer'. About a third of the way through the placement, he wrote in his diary:

> J was admitted again today to X hospital. Within an hour of me cleaning him up and taking him there, he had discharged himself just as he did last week, against all medical advice. I was really angry and I went right round and told him so in no uncertain terms.

The significant information here was not that feelings of anger could arise in such a situation or that resentment about a service user might arise towards someone who appeared, to the student, to 'sabotage' his best helping efforts or that feelings of helplessness might manifest as anger, but that this student, who had claimed to have all of his feelings under control and to be caring but contained, should not only feel anger towards the service user but express it directly to the service user. In supervision, I asked the student, first, to cover the same ground as he had written about. If anything, it seemed to me that his anger was even more evident than it had been on the page. I asked if he had any insight into why this incident should trigger that reaction when he had (in previous sessions) been quite resistant to my attempts to explore feelings related to work situations. I found myself faced with a very different student from the one I had experienced up to this point. This student was emotional and vulnerable as opposed to the (apparently) strong (protected) and rational one I was more used to. He was able to identify earlier experiences in his first family that were connected to the service user work he was engaged with. Clearly, there were serious unresolved issues for the student in his own life as well as questions about his service user work in this instance. Fortunately, his college tutor was very helpful and supportive, identifying a counselling resource in the academic institution. This was one of those 'cusp' situations where the student was able to use some remaining placement time to develop his emotional range and vocabulary and to engage with issues of empathy that might otherwise have been missed in the guise of containment. Interestingly, he was also able to begin to appreciate that service users' actions and decisions are not always based on logic and rationality. For J, the service user described above, the logical and rational action would have been to accept medical intervention and to cease drinking. I was encouraged when the student began to speculate that perhaps J was frightened and found it safer to deny the real danger he was in by not 'hearing' the warnings given to him by health professionals and his family.

Personal issues in diary notes

In my experience, it is not unusual for personal issues to arise, given a catalyst, during placement experience. In terms of transfer of previous learning, we could think about this student as having 'learned' that all actions are based on rationale and logic and, therefore, that dysfunctional behaviours must be consciously designed to frustrate and impede. This can be seen as 'negative' transfer in the sense that a long-held belief was applied to a situation where its applicability was inappropriate and unhelpful. It is important to note that when the learning is related to beliefs and values, there is an emotional attachment to the learning which comes from the person's memory of situations where that learning has been applied previously. In the example above, we can speculate that the student had, in a family context, 'blamed' someone for their inability to deal with an alcohol addiction, thereby relieving himself of feelings of responsibility, blame and guilt. Inevitably, learning that there are different explanations for dysfunctional behaviour can give rise to feelings of guilt and incongruence and the notion of cognitive dissonance comes into play. It is often more comfortable to frame new situations into familiar moulds than to review our past responses and, perhaps, judge them (and ourselves) retrospectively as uncaring or insensitive.

Reflective diaries and teaching

Diary notes are also used as springboards into the deep end of teaching. Because social work placements are time restricted, it is helpful to find any short cut in identifying the most pressing gaps in knowledge, skills and values. Again, the diary notes only give clues that need to be explored through direct discussion, but they usually give a helpful starting point. Sometimes, a student will be keen to 'name-drop' in their application of theory. Commonly I will find a naive or underdeveloped understanding of an approach or intervention method (for example 'I decided to use a task-centred approach' or 'I approached him in a person-centred way' or 'I employed crisis intervention as my principle approach'). With these openings, there are a number of options for practice teaching. First, it is necessary to check out whether the student's understanding of the concept is accurate and useful in the first place. When it is not, it is possible to offer direct teaching or referred reading. Where it is accurately understood, it allows the discussion of 'why that approach?', and the world is opened up to assessment and planning discussion as well as possible teaching on alternative approaches. Where issues of skill are identified, I would tend, after discussion, to follow up with both process recordings and focused direct observation of practice.

Diary notes, values and anti-oppressive practice

The diary notes can be especially useful in exploring issues of values and anti-oppressive practice. For example, a woman student, in a criminal justice placement setting, had been working with a single mother who had two teenage daughters. The student had helped to organise another agency to decorate the shabby house that the family had recently been allocated. She recorded in her diary notes:

> B said she was really grateful. She told me that she had begun to feel that nothing would be done after the (male) social worker did nothing about the problem. She had said to her daughters, 'it takes a woman to get things done.' I knew this was discriminatory against men so I challenged her and said that there were probably all kinds of reasons why the social worker hadn't got it done yet.

I knew from previous diary notes and case recordings that this woman service user had had a string of unhappy (and often violent) relationships with men and spent considerable time and effort in presenting herself to men as attractive and available for relationships and that part of the student's assessment of the situation was that the woman suffered from low self-esteem and felt worthless unless she was in a relationship with a man. It seemed to me that there had been other possible responses from the student when B had described her conversation with her daughters. I tried to check, first, whether the student had felt uncomfortable with B's expression of gratitude towards her. It soon became clear that it was the requirement to demonstrate anti-discriminatory practice in social work itself that was problematic: the student was attempting to 'evidence' anti-discriminatory practice as she 'ought', rather than responding spontaneously or with considered and critical thought to the service user. In discussion, I developed a picture of this student, who actually related personally to B's expressed view of 'men as useless' (alongside her other personae of 'wife' of a man and 'mother' of two sons), allowing some work on the concept and more genuine expression of anti-discriminatory practice to begin, as well as thinking about more appropriate responses to this welcome shift in the service user, using the student's own assessment.

Conclusion

The main thesis of this chapter is that what determines transfer of learning is the ability to think in transferable ways across different dimensions as well as to apply developed skills and knowledge appropriately in new situations as they are deemed to be required. The creative, empathetic, aware and reflective student who can draw on some relevant theory and her/his own experience will be able to enter most new situations and offer something – even if that something is an open recognition that new thinking, consultation and further development is required before a competent response can emerge. Keeping a reflective diary during placement, and getting feedback on the diary from a practice teacher, is a practical and helpful way to develop this process.

Notes

1   Note that McPeck (1990) argues that attempts to generalise something called 'general Critical Thinking skills' are misguided, the term is largely meaningless, and that specific subject content determines the required ingredients of thinking critically in each case.
2   It is difficult to offer a blueprint for practice since every student is different and comes with different learning needs and different experiences to draw on.
3   This approach is also demonstrated in Niemi's (1977) account of the use of learning logs with first year medical students.

Bibliography

Alinsky, S. (1972) *Rules for Radicals,* New York: Vintage Books.
Boud, D. and Knights, S. (1996) 'Course design for reflective practice', in N. Gould and I. Taylor (eds) *Reflective Learning for Social Work,* Aldershot: Arena.
Button, D. and Davies, S. (1996) 'Experiences of encouraging student-centred learning within a wellness-oriented curriculum', *Nurse Education Today* 16(6): 407–12.
Cowan, J. (1992) 'Learning journals: what are they for?', *British Journal of Educational Technology,* 23(2): 139–40.
Currie, R. and Guttridge, P. (1977) 'Student Supervision: the step before reflection', *Social Work Today* 8: 22.

De Bono, E.(1990) *Six Thinking Hats,* London: Penguin Books.

Entwistle, N. (1987) 'A model of the teaching-learning process', in J.T.E. Richardson, M.W. Eysenck, and D. Warren Piper (eds) *Student Learning,* Milton Keynes: The Society for Research into Higher Education, Open University Press.

—— (1990) 'Teaching and the quality of learning in higher education', in N. Entwistle (ed.) *Handbook of Educational Ideas and Practices,* London: Routledge.

Ghaye, T. and Lillyman, S. (1997) *Learning Journals and Critical Incidents: Reflective Practice for Health care Professionals,* Dinton, UK: Mark Allen Publishing.

Goldstein, B.P. and Harris, V. (1996) 'Innovations in practice teaching', in M. Preston-Shoot and S. Jackson (eds) *Educating Social Workers in a Changing Policy Context,* London: Whiting and Birch.

Harris, A. (1996) 'Learning from experience and reflection in social work education', in N. Gould and I. Taylor (eds) *Reflective Learning for Social Work,* Aldershot: Arena.

Honey, P. and Mumford, A. (1986) *Using your Learning Styles,* 2nd edn, Maidenhead: Peter Honey.

McPeck, J.E. (1990) *Teaching Critical Thinking: Dialogue and Dialectic,* New York: Routledge, Chapman & Hall.

Moffat, K. (1996) 'Teaching social work as a reflective process', in N. Gould and I. Taylor (eds) *Reflective Learning for Social Work,* Aldershot: Arena.

Morrison, K. (1996) 'Developing reflective practice in higher degree students through a learning journal', *Studies in Higher Education* 21(3): 317–32.

Niemi, P.M. (1997), 'Medical students' professional identity: self-reflection during the pre-clinical years', *Medical Education* 31: 408–15.

Pask, G. (1976) 'Styles and strategies of learning', *British Journal of Educational Psychology* 46(2): 4–11.

Phillips, A. (1993) *The Trouble with Boys,* London: Pandora.

Schön, D.A. (1987) *Educating the Reflective Practitioner,* New York: Basic Books.

Sedlak, C.A. (1992) 'Use of clinical logs by beginning nursing students and faculty to identify leaning needs', *Journal of Nursing Education* 31(1): 24–8.

Segal, L. (1990) *Slow Motion. Changing Masculinities, Changing Men,* London: Virago.

Shields, E.A. (1994) 'A daily dose of reflection: developing reflective skills through journal writing', *Professional Nurse* (August): 755–8.

Thompson, N., Osada, M. and Anderson, B. (1990) *Practice Teaching in Social Work,* Birmingham: Pepar.

Chapter 8

Critical incident analysis
Facilitating reflection and transfer of learning

Hilary Davies and Helen Kinloch

Introduction

Critical incident analysis (CIA) has been developed as a tool for social work educators and learners to assist in the process of learning from current practice by reflecting on past experience and anticipating future action. A useful definition of a critical incident is 'a personal experience – snapshot, vignette, brief episode – which epitomises a situation or encounter of interest to the student ... from professional settings' (Minghella and Benson 1995: 212). Putting such incidents under the microscope creates opportunities to analyse experience in order to develop practice by reflection-on-action (Schön 1987). In this way 'a practitioner looks back at what has been done and, through reflecting on it, learns lessons from what did, or did not, work' (Rich and Parker 1995: 1051).

A major challenge in learning is that of appropriate transfer from one situation to another. Until this has been achieved, any learning that has taken place is of limited value. A key element in the continuing cycle of learning is the process of reflection (Kolb 1984). Practice teachers may use CIA to encourage students to focus on specific incidents from practice, reflect on these, find links with experience and knowledge from other contexts, develop conceptualisations and put new learning into practice. Thus the social work student and professional worker, as reflective practitioners, are assisted in the process of learning, which moves from limited knowledge and skill to informed and skilful action.

The development of CIA

The concept of CIA was first documented by Flanagan in 1954 (Rich and Parker 1995). He used it as a research tool for identifying the effective and the ineffective performance of fighter pilots after analysing data from the pilots' own detailed accounts of successful and unsuccessful flying missions. Subsequently, critical incident techniques have been used in many different contexts. In personnel selection in management, for example, interviewers may present specific incidents to candidates and ask them to respond as if they were in a work context, with their answers being measured against bench-marks of good, average or poor performance (Cook 1998). In nursing and nurse education, CIA has been used extensively for developing reflective practice and integrating theory and practice (Minghella and Benson 1995; Rich and Parker 1995).

Within social work CIA has been used as a technique for studying human errors in the management of child abuse through the analysis of data from child protection incidents (suitably anonymised) to identify common errors and take appropriate action to improve practice (Mills and Vine 1990). CIA has also been used as a method of supervision in student placements in social work education and training. In the 1980s, Butler and Elliot (1985) outlined a framework for using CIA in practice learning with groups of service users as an aid to 'understanding the events and processes taking place and in exploring alternative ways of responding and their possible impact on the group' (Butler and Elliott 1985: 70). This was offered as an alternative to the more familiar tool of process recording with its primary focus on one-to-one rather than multiple interactions. (Process recordings are discussed in Chapter 9).

CIA was also used in the 1980s for training residential and day care staff in Scotland. Students studying for the Certificate in Social Service and other care staff on in-service training were invited to examine in detail some of the ordinary events of daily life in group care settings and the opportunities these presented for helping people grow and change (Kinloch and Fulcher 1983). This work drew on Redl's (1966) concept of 'life space' intervention in residential childcare: 'making use of momentary life experiences in order to draw out ... something which might be of use for long range ... goals' (Redl 1966: 47). In training sessions, each student was given one and a half hours to focus on an incident or interaction from work that they wished to review. After presenting this to their learning group of five people, the event was replayed with actors taking the role of service users and each student taking his/her own role as the worker. The scene was video-taped then analysed by the small group and the course tutor. The anxiety level among students was high. The safety and support of the learning group was crucial. The outcome was that students consistently reported feeling more confident, having greatly increased understanding and/or being aware of new skills that they were keen to put into practice. The tutors were struck by the excitement, energy and learning emerging from this use of CIA.

We have used CIA over a period of years in a range of practice contexts to illuminate the potential for learning from a moment of practice and the complexity of its dynamic interactions. This experience has confirmed the value of CIA as a tool for professional growth. The rest of this chapter explores its recent use in the DipSW courses in Scotland.

CIA frameworks in use

From the experience of using CIA in the training of residential and day care staff described (Kinloch and Fulcher 1983), we have developed and adapted CIA frameworks for the training of social work students. Two frameworks in current use are presented and discussed. The first framework is envisaged primarily as a tool for taking inexperienced and/or unreflective students gently but firmly into reflective analysis of their practice. It invites students to work as whole people – thinking, feeling, acting – acknowledging and valuing positive and negative feelings as they affect, and arise from, their work. It is expected that Framework 1 (Box 8.1) will be experienced as less daunting for 'beginners'.

The second framework (Box 8.2) is intended to meet the learning needs of students who have already begun to reflect on and analyse practice. It is a tool for in-depth reflection and analysis of specific events or interactions. From one such incident, students are encouraged to unpack significant factors contributing to what happened and to explore what they have learned from the experience. In doing so, they are asked to make links between prior experience and the transfer of new learning for future practice.

We undertook a small-scale study to evaluate the effectiveness of CIA. Ten Barnardo's Scotland social work practice teachers were asked to describe their experience of using these two CIA frameworks. From these data and feedback from a number of students valuable pointers and questions emerged.

CIA was seen to be particularly useful at the beginning of a placement in creating a learning climate and enabling the practice teacher 'to get inside the student's thinking and feeling about practice'. It is important to have such frameworks available from the start of placements and to have them explicitly stated in the Working Agreement. This idicates how the practice teacher sees the contribution of supervision to the development of reflection and transfer of learning. For the CIA frameworks to be effective, we found that it was important for practice

Box 8.1 Critical incident analysis: framework 1

Framework 1: examining critical incidents

Below are listed examples of events that all of us experience. Think of things that have happened in your placement within the last week of work which fit some of these descriptions. Choose one event that seems to you to be significant. When we meet for supervision, we will talk about the event that you have chosen. Beforehand, note what happened, what you and others did, how you felt and what you thought. Be as specific as you can. It may help to write a few notes to enable us to focus on learning from your experience.

1   When you felt you had done something well...
2   When you made the wrong decision...
3   When something went better than expected...
4   When you lacked confidence...
5   When you made a mistake...
6   When you really enjoyed working with someone/a group...
7   When you had a feeling of pressure...
8   When you found it difficult to accept or value a service user(s)...
9   When you realised you did not know enough...
10 When you felt unsupported...
11 When you were worried about a service user(s)...
12 When you took a risk and it paid off/didn't pay off...

teachers to engage with the material, adapt and make it their own, and offer it enthusiastically to students. It is essential that negotiation takes place between practice teachers and students on issues such as the selecting and timing of the use of frameworks, and whether the student's written analysis of the incident is made available to the practice teacher before supervision or whether it may be sufficient to present the material verbally on the day.

As with all teaching/learning tools the skill of practice teachers is crucial. It is their role to draw out and develop students' learning through using the frameworks. This includes ensuring that students crystallise the knowledge that they have drawn on (e.g. Framework 2, questions 3, 6, 8). It is also the practice teacher's task to bring in additional theory to support and extend the student's understanding, for example theory that is fundamental to the placement agency practice but has not yet been

Box 8.2 Critical incident analysis: framework 2

Framework 2: critical incident analysis

Any event or interaction in work is potentially significant for students as learners. Critical incident analysis is a tool for examining in detail what happened and drawing out learning, so enabling the student to become a more skilled worker.

You are encouraged to use this framework as relevant for you.

Identify an incident for reflection and make brief notes on the following:

1 Describe the event: what happened, where and when; who was involved.
2 Put this event in its context, e.g. what had happened previously; what you had achieved/tried to achieve and your relationships with those involved.
3 What was your role in the event, e.g. as participant, observer, co-worker?
4 What was the purpose and focus of your intervention at this point?
5 What did you think and feel about what you were doing at the time?
6 Did it remind you of any previous experience or learning?
7 As you look back, what do you think and feel about the outcome?
8 What have you learned, e.g. about yourself, relationships with others, the social work task, organisational policies and procedures?
9 Are there things that you might do differently in future? What help might you need to achieve this?
10 What issues out of this reflection will you take to supervision?

addressed on the course. Likewise, it is the responsibility of the practice teachers to ensure that the student is making links between past experience and learning and with future action, for practice teachers carry a central responsibility for the continuity and transfer of the student's learning over different contexts (e.g. by encouraging the student to draw from previous experience of ending work with individuals and apply this to the final phase of group work).

The practice teachers who took part in the study were aware that doing justice to one CIA could take over the whole supervision session. They recognised this as acceptable so long as they held the balance of depth and breadth across the range of supervision sessions. One practice teacher, recognising the student's need for help in moving from descriptive, superficial accounts into a much deeper level of analysis, had found CIA very helpful in achieving this objective. The student's initial response had been to answer every question in Framework 1 with a one word response. The practice teacher had taken this on by putting flip charts up round the room to work with the student on 'unpacking' what was behind each one-word response. She said that they ended up with such a vast amount of material about what was going on for the student, that it had a great impact on the student's understanding of complexity and on the practice teacher's sense of moving forward in her teaching role.

Another practice teacher commented that the frameworks were a way of 'introducing students to the squirm factor' in placements – getting them to the uncomfortable zone where significant learning might happen, what Reynolds (1942) referred to as the stages of acute consciousness of self- and 'sink or swim' adaptation. Here students move from earlier certainty, through the disequilibrium of 'not knowing', to more complex understanding and the ability to respond appropriately. In this context the importance of trust and a safe enough learning environment were emphasised, so that discomfort was enabling rather than disabling.

Among the responses from practice teachers on the use of Framework 2 (Box 8.2) were comments such as 'it's what we do in supervision anyway but more thorough' and 'this gives me the framework I've been using in supervision' (i.e. it is written down in contrast to it being carried in the practice teacher's head). Making this explicit for the student as well as the practice teacher was seen to have the potential to increase power sharing within the supervisory relationship, giving the student more choice of what to work on when in supervision.

How did the students experience the frameworks? Feedback was generally positive. One commented: 'it quite quickly manages to raise various issues around the incident plus links with use of self, theories and knowledge, understanding of service users, and own strengths and weaknesses as well as those of the organisation.'

Another student wrote about the value of CIA in her final placement report. In supervision she had raised her difficulties in relation to appropriate challenging of discrimination. Her practice teacher suggested she use CIA and following this:

When the next incident occurred I therefore felt more prepared. A member of staff was recounting a story to a group of workers about a 'gypsy' of foreign extraction in a manner that was inappropriate and derisory. I gently pointed out that the comments she was making involved frequently used stereotypes and that this was one of the ways in which this particular group of people are socially excluded. I felt that I had made this challenge in a sensitive way and was pleased to be told by my link worker later that she had overheard the same member of staff recounting the story again with the discriminatory remarks removed.

(student self-evaluation, DipSW 1998)

It is relevant to note that feedback from the practice assessor to the practice teacher, following direct observation of work with the student, included the suggestion that use of CIA might help to develop the student's learning from the earlier difficult and uncomfortable experience.

Making CIA work for reflection and transfer of learning

It is important to recognise the demands that CIA makes. This is particularly true for students who wish to demonstrate their competence through busy activity with little time for reflection. It is also a fact that other tools for learning (e.g. process recording) may be similarly demanding. Hence, it is vital that students have a supportive, enriching learning experience as a result of doing their work and sharing it with their practice teacher. Commitment to the use of the frameworks for developing reflection and transfer will diminish if the students experience only a superficial engagement with the outcome of their work from the practice teacher. The philosophy of adult learning which underpins this use of CIA is that of a learner-centred experiential model of education (Friere 1972; Knowles 1978; Rogers 1983). As indicated previously, CIA makes the agenda for supervision explicit and more within the control of the students who can initiate and lead the discussion. Thus, the threat of supervision may be reduced.

Each student brings to supervision his/her own unique balance of motivation and ambivalence about learning on the placement. Factors that influence this include those which come from social and cultural experiences, conditioning and social norms. The social context of their lives so far, including ethnic origins as well as experiences of being valued or marginalised, are all part of what the students bring to their placement learning. We are aware that the practice teachers and students with whom we shared this study of CIA were all White. This reflects the under-representation of people from minority ethnic groups in social work education in Scotland at this time (see Singh 1999). Likewise disabled people were under-represented in each group (see CCETSW 1999). All the students were female, and there were slightly more female than male practice teachers involved. There are many questions to be addressed about how those with significant experiences of disempowerment will respond to CIA as a learning tool. Might it be perceived as a threat by its invitation to self-disclosure? This could be particularly relevant in practice teacher–student relationships in which the students are aware of a significant power imbalance and feel that their unique experiences are not being understood or valued. Practice teachers, whose personal and social experience results in them needing to hold on to their power in the learning context, may also find CIA a threat.

CIA can raise issues for students who have difficulty in doing justice to their practice in written communications. While the management of writing tasks are worked on elsewhere, it may be helpful for CIA to be audio-recorded. If the student is successful in doing this, it might enable the practice teacher to encourage the use of audio-recording on other occasions when the student is required to produce written material.

It is anticipated that practice teachers will choose to use CIA within a repertoire of teaching/learning tools. Earlier, reference was made to CIA as an alternative to process recording. It may be particularly useful when the student's practice focuses on a multiple interaction rather than one-to-one interventions (e.g. in group work, group care settings, community development). Because of the requirement to focus on one brief passage in ongoing work, it may offer a way of registering and retaining the complexity, without the student becoming overwhelmed by a mass of detail. Practice teachers may also choose to use it selectively alongside process recording of one-to-one interactions.

Practice teachers have suggested that CIA may be useful for students having difficulty in writing their reflective diary by providing one way of reflecting on and recording their learning. It would be necessary for the practice teacher and the student to agree the boundaries of confidentiality regarding CIA if these need to be different from those in place in relation to the rest of the diary.

Further development of CIA

In our discussions with practice teachers and students, some of them were uncomfortable with the term 'critical incident'. This is partly because of unhelpful connotations with crisis and emergency. It would be unfortunate if this resulted in ignoring the opportunities for analysis of ordinary events and practice that went well. Other more accessible terminology might include 'significant interaction analysis' or 'significant incident analysis'. The question remains whether these terms more accurately convey the intention behind CIA.

Colleagues have suggested other uses of CIA. Practice teachers who were line managers were enthusiastic about its use in staff supervision, particularly when staff were confined to work with individual service users. It could be used by co-workers in their private analysis of their work in preparation for discussing and planning future work together. A student used Framework 1 on her own initiative as a checklist for reviewing and debriefing herself at the end of each day of working at a demanding play-scheme.

We have already indicated that the video-recorded simulation of critical incidents in group learning is a fruitful tool for reflection, skill development and transfer. CIA has been used in nursing education primarily as a tool in group learning and teaching (Minghella and Benson 1995; Rich and Parker 1995; Parker et al. 1995). We have also experienced its use in groups of staff and students. New understanding was achieved through feedback from peers as well as trainers and from the links made between the experiences of different people. It can be useful to focus on an incident experienced by all members of a group, or an event experienced by one member (e.g. a violent outburst by a young person in a residential setting). In addition CIA may be used as a focus for groups of staff experiencing difficulties in terms of roles and relationships to open up their issues and create motivation for change.

The possibility of using CIA for assessment has been discussed by Minghella and Benson (1995). They suggested that students keep portfolios of their critical incident writing over a period of months to record their development as mental health practitioners. Social work practice teachers have confirmed the value of CIA for gathering evidence for assessment of students. Other uses may include inviting students to write a CIA using Framework 2, focusing on an incident from their practice that has been observed by their practice teacher. This could help to deepen the analysis of that practice. The practice teacher's ability to draw out the learning and to gather evidence for assessment could also be enhanced.

The use of CIA in social work practice, education and staff training has not been widely studied, and questions remain about the validity of

CIA as a tool that students can take with them as qualified practitioners. If agencies are dominated by a task culture which is about 'right' and 'wrong' ways of doing things at the expense of time for reflection and learning from practice that has not gone well, workers may be able to use CIA as one means of pursuing their individual professional development. It is important not to underestimate the size of this challenge and the need for professional support wherever it can be found.

In our view, CIA is an appropriate tool for promoting learning throughout professional life and, as we have seen, it can be used in a range of contexts with individuals or groups. At this time of major transition for social work in Scotland and throughout the United Kingdom, government statements affirm that 'people using social work services have a right to expect high quality services delivered by a competent workforce committed to continuous improvement' (Social Work Services Inspectorate 1998: 2). One element of this is the demand for staff to take 'personal responsibility ... for their proper and continuing education and the development and maintenance of their own practice standards' (Social Work Services Inspectorate 1998: 6). It is important to recognise that this requires an organisational context that values the need for reflection and transfer of learning to inform action, and thus promotes best value services for individuals, groups and communities.

Acknowledgement

The authors wish to thank the practice teachers and students who collaborated in this work.

Bibliography

Butler, B. and Elliott, D. (1985) *Teaching and Learning for Practice*, Aldershot: Gower.

Central Council for the Education and Training in Social Work (1999) *The Enabling DipSW,* London: CCETSW.

Cook, M. (1998) *Personnel Selection: Adding Value Through People*, Chichester: John Wiley & Sons Ltd.

Freire, P. (1972) *Pedagogy of the Oppressed*, Harmondsworth: Penguin Books.

Kinloch, H. and Fulcher, L. (1983) *Report of the Group Care Training Project 1979–1982*, Essex: Barnardo's.

Knowles, M.S. (1978) *The Adult Learner: A Neglected Species,* Houston, TX: Gulf Publishing Company.

Kolb, D.A. (1984) *Experiential Learning*, Englewood Cliffs, NJ: Prentice Hall.

Mills, C. and Vine, P. (1990) 'Critical incident reporting – an approach to reviewing the investigation and management of child abuse', *British Journal of Social Work* 20: 215–20.

Minghella, E. and Benson, A. (1995) 'Developing reflective practice in mental health nursing through critical incident analysis', *Journal of Advanced Nursing* 21: 205–13.

Parker, D.L., Webb, J. and D'Souza, B. (1995) 'The value of critical incident analysis as an educational tool and its relationship to experiential learning', *Nurse Education Today* 15: 111–16.

Redl, F. (1966) *When We Deal with Children*, New York: The Tree Press.

Reynolds, B. (1942) *Learning and Teaching in the Practice of Social Work*, New York: Rinehart & Company.

Rich, A. and Parker, D. (1995) 'Reflection and critical incident analysis: ethical and moral implications of their use within nursing and midwifery education', *Journal of Advanced Nursing* 22, 1050–7.

Rogers, C. (1983) *Freedom to Learn for the 80s*, Columbus, OH: Charles E. Merrill.

Schön, D. (1987) *Educating the Reflective Practitioner*, San Francisco: Jossey-Bass.

Singh, S. (1999) *Educating Sita*, Glasgow: Scottish Anti-Racist Federation.

Social Work Services Inspectorate (1998) *Modernising Social Work Services. A Consultation Paper on Workforce Regulation and Education*, Edinburgh: The Scottish Office.

Chapter 9

In praise of the process recording

Gary Clapton

> The written description of the dynamic interaction that has taken place in an interview.
>
> (Dwyer and Urbanowski 1965: 283)

Process recording is a widely used but little discussed supervisory tool. It offers a unique focus on students' 'soft' personal qualities such as sensitivity and intuition, their ability to use emotional antennae to sense the need for a change of pace or direction and their preparedness to act on hunches during an interview. These and other such qualities have been called 'emotional intelligence' (Goleman 1996) and are central to the transfer of learning (Cree *et al.* 1998). Interestingly, such qualities are often associated with women (e.g. 'women's intuition') and it is these qualities that have been most sidelined during the present shift towards a more technicist (and macho?), outcomes-based, competency-driven model of social work education. This chapter is concerned first with providing a practical outline of the principles, usage and values of the process recording and second with highlighting its usefulness as a tool to facilitate the transfer of learning.

At least three DipSW programmes and four busy student units in Scotland include some input on process recordings for students. During the writing of this chapter I undertook a quick 'straw poll' among a group of Scottish practice teachers and sixteen out of the seventeen with whom I spoke said that they asked their students to complete at least one process recording per placement. Despite this (chiefly) anecdotal evidence that process recordings are regularly in use, there is little sign of any substantial reappraisal of their effectiveness in the many recent discussions of practice teaching in social work.

A literature search revealed that almost all of the contributions on process recording originate from North America. Because many works are out of print or the journals unobtainable, there is difficulty in accessing references – there seems to be little substantial writing on process recordings that is less than twenty years old. Among the few recent references on process recording, it is difficult to find a dedicated discussion that is longer than a page. Although Thomson (1990) and Ford and Jones (1987) touch on the purpose of a process recording and offer a brief content outline in which they suggest that it is an 'excellent teaching tool' (Thompson 1990: 52), they note that it is generally out of fashion (Ford and Jones 1987). Before offering a hands-on practice model of process recording that may, hopefully, begin a reappraisal of its use, I will give a brief thumbnail sketch of its history.

The development of the process recording: a brief history

It is difficult to establish the beginnings of the use of process recordings. As is the case for much of social case work and supervision in social work, the introduction of the practice of recording the *process* of an interaction (in addition to its content) as a means of gaining additional insight, seems to have its origins in psychotherapy (Kadushin 1976; Gardiner 1989). It is difficult to pinpoint the transition between it being used in therapy and it being taken up by social work supervisors. An early example appears in Hamilton (1946), although it seems that the main period of published work relating to process recordings was during the 1960s.

Ackerman's (1966) text on psychotherapeutic work with families does not discuss process recording as a student learning tool; however, it is one of the few places where the method is presented: in this case in a series of transcriptions of therapy sessions. These transcriptions are written up in two-column form. The titles of the columns are 'verbatim record' (left-hand column), which consists of dialogue and behaviour of the parties in the session, and 'interpretative comment' (right-hand column), which consists of the therapist's thoughts and reflections that occur during the session and are noted down to correspond with the 'outside' events in the session (Ackerman 1966: 5).

Through this, an insight into the subjective role of the professional during the unfolding of the session can be gained; the reader may locate the points during the interview when, for example, breakthroughs in communication occur and digressions take place. In other words, Ackerman's model provides a 'map' that can help evaluate the efficacy of the professional intervention by providing an account of key exchanges and actions during the session (the 'verbatim record') alongside that of comments by the therapist concerning his/her impressions of the unfolding dynamic of the interview ('interpretative comment'). The value of Ackerman's work is in the presentation of a method for analysing the process of professional practice.

Around the same time, a non-column form of process recording was outlined by Dwyer and Urbanowski (1965). This remains a useful statement of the purpose and value of the process recording in social work training. The process recording is described as:

> [T]he written description of the dynamic interaction that has taken place in an interview ... it is a basic tool for stimulating communication and self-awareness on the part of the student. Process recording enables the field instructor to assess quickly the student's ability to respond to a client's feelings.
>
> (Dwyer and Urbanowski 1965: 283)

Such a concern to access and improve the student's ability to 'think on their feet' is now echoed in such phrases as 'reflecting-*in*-action'. Both Schön (1987) and Carter *et al.* (1994) make this a skill distinct from such post-event activity as 'reflection-*on*-action' (my emphases). Dwyer and Urbanowski indicate that process recordings were, at the time of writing, popular in social work field education; they were therefore concerned with promoting a structure for process recordings. They suggest that the process recording ought to comprise the following elements:

- purpose of the interaction;
- general observations: the student's initial impressions;
- content: the central section, including factual information, the responses of both client and student, and a description of 'the feeling content of the interview, on the part of both the client and the student';
- impressions: a final section that provides the student's reflections on the completed practice.

> (Dwyer and Urbanowski 1965: 285)

The marriage of the column-type presentation as exemplified in Ackerman (1966) and the structured content of Dwyer and Urbanowski (1965) appears to have taken place around the end of the 1960s. Baldock (1974) indicates that process recordings were used 'extensively' in social work training at this time and offers a structural variation so that instead of columns a narrative format is used, interweaving comment on process with that of a verbatim account of the group meeting. He also broadens the use of process recording to encompass learning in a group work situation.

The content of process recording

In terms of content, it is suggested that most process recordings in social work supervision will include at least two dimensions to the interaction. The first is the verbatim report of what happened; the second is concerned with what the student felt at given moments during the session. There are also examples of a third dimension: the thinking of the student. Here students are invited to report their thoughts separately from their feelings, and these are itemised alongside both the verbatim and affective accounts of the unfolding interactions.

It can be seen, therefore, that there are a number of permutations in both form (columns, interleaved narrative) and content (verbatim, thoughts, feelings) of a process recording. There seems, however, to be general agreement regarding the overall aims. The student is to 'try to identify as many possible issues in the accounts, for example, the dynamics – the feelings, roles, cultural patterns etc. that are taking place in the interview'. The supervisor's aim, is to 'try to get at a student's processes of thinking, feeling and acting' (Ford and Jones 1987: 89).

The exact manner in which the process recording may be completed and used in supervision will vary according to the individual student and practice teacher. However, there is no doubt that a process recording takes considerable time to write up and requires substantial discussion in supervision. Box 9.1 represents part of a process recording used by a student and myself in a recent supervision session. The entire process recording consisted of five pages.

The case for process recordings

As can be seen (Box 9.1), process recording offers real potential for facilitating the transfer of learning as opportunities for insight into the student's actions and decision-making emerge. The connections between the student's thoughts and feelings and a particular course of action taken are made explicit: a 'journey' can be traced from initial anxiety to greater confidence. Contributory events such as the student's actions arising from awareness of the importance of body language can then be made apparent.

Box 9.1 Excerpt from a process recording

Process recording

M, mum

A, her young son

G, A's dad and mum's partner

Purpose of interview

I had arranged a home visit to speak to the parents of a two-year-old who had been allocated a morning placement at Parkway Children's Centre a few weeks earlier. M, a 30-year-old White Scottish woman, had come down to Parkway with her son on his first day, but neither had returned in two weeks and therefore A's place at the centre was in jeopardy. One week after A's first and only day, G (a 29-year-old White Scottish man) came into the centre looking for M, who had not come in. I showed G around the centre to introduce him to the environment and I received a telephone call from M later that morning. She apologised for A's absence and indicated he would come to the centre the next day.

Since the call I have had no direct contact with any member of the family and A has not come back to the centre. I sent a letter to M and G indicating that I would visit them at home if it was convenient. This was to identify any difficulties the family were having with the placement and to work with them to come up with any solutions.

Observations

I arrived punctually for the visit and had some difficulty getting a response from the intercom on the main door. I tried three times on the buzzer but got no response. As the family live in a ground floor flat I decided to walk back on the pavement parallel to the window of the flat to gauge whether there was anybody home. M was sitting by the window with A on her knee. She saw me, waved and stood up. I walked and M let me in to the hall. She said that she had been keeping an eye out for me as the buzzer was not working. She invited me in and asked me to come through to the living room.

I asked how she and A were and she said they were both well. I felt a little anxious as I had been considering how to obtain the information

I needed without pressurising the family or appearing judgmental about A's absence. M seemed on initial contact to have been expecting me and was open and friendly but perhaps a little nervous and defensive as she immediately started to explain her son's absence before I had the opportunity to discuss the reasons for my visit. The environment and the physical appearance of both A and M were as they had been on my first home visit. There was no sign of G. On entering the living room M sat down on the armchair with A on her lap and with her body slightly turned away from mine. I sat on the settee adjacent to the armchair.

Content*

Interaction
On going through to the living room and sitting down, M quickly related to me that A had not been down to the centre because she was looking after a friend's children while she was at work. Her friend did not get back to the house until 9.30 a.m. and M was unable to bring her son down to Parkway till 9.45 a.m.

Thoughts
Noticed M sat with A on her knee with her body turned away. It was not an open posture. Maybe she felt under pressure. I thought she was nervous and spoke quickly.

Feelings
Felt that I had to be sensitive as I did not want to put her under pressure or appear judgmental about A's absence. Anxious to put her at ease and establish a rapport.

Interaction
Without pausing she began to show me A's finger and said the doctor had treated it and that he wouldn't need a skin graft despite the fact the doctor thought it was a burn. She said that she didn't know how he had got it.

---

*In practice, students would record the interaction and their thoughts and feelings in three columns across the page, but space here does not permit this layout.

Thoughts
Tried to consider my body language. I sat with my legs uncrossed and arms unfolded and had no pad or pen this time. I did not want to interrupt and thought about how I could demonstrate that I was actively listening, i.e. by nodding and keeping an open posture.

Feelings
How could I put her at her ease and make her feel less defensive? I felt she must have been very anxious about A's finger to draw my attention to it right away.

Interaction
I looked at his finger when she showed me it and said that it looked much better and that he had healed quickly.

Thoughts
I wanted to acknowledge what she had said about his finger but not dwell on the subject as this may add to her anxiety.

Feelings
Anxious to put across that I was here to help if I could in identifying any difficulties with the placement and work with her to come up with solutions. Would this work?

Interaction
I explained the purpose of the visit - it was to see how A and the rest of the family were as we hadn't seen them in a bit. That if they were having any difficulties with the place we could try to find a solution.

Thoughts
I considered my facial expressions and smiled while I spoke to try and help her relax.

Interaction
I asked M if she felt she couldn't bring A down to Parkway at all because she'd be late.

Thoughts
I wanted to explore this issue with her in order to have some insight into what she was thinking.

Feelings
Worried. Had I overemphasised the starting time?

Interaction
M replied that she felt awkward being late and that the friend she baby-sat for had been annoyed with her for not bringing him down to the centre after she had fought to get the place.

Thoughts
Hard to gauge by body language if she was being open as she had turned to face A playing on the floor. No mention of G's thoughts on the subject.

Feelings
Unsure.

Interaction
I replied that there would be no problem about her coming down a little later in the morning as he would only miss breakfast and that other children sometimes started a little later.

Thoughts
I sat forward and tried to engage her in eye contact. She turned to face me.

Feelings
More confident.

Interaction
M replied that she still wanted A to continue at the centre as she thought it would be good for him. She also felt it wasn't fair not to take him when somebody else could have had his place.

Thoughts
Still no mention of G's thoughts on the benefit of a place.

Feelings
I felt she was being sincere about A's need for the place.

But why bother with the minutiae of these interviews? We live in a time of measurable outcomes where self-awareness may be deemed indulgent. Many students begin their courses with the notion that social work training is concerned with learning to deliver material resources to people (e.g. benefits, residential and day services, etc.). Students learn early on that the relationship they can build with a service user is a potential helping resource in itself:

> Most frequently, the principal resource the agency makes available in the process of helping people is the skill and competence of the worker herself ... In social work, where the worker is the main instrumentality, the person of the worker determines what is done and how it is done.
>
> (Kadushin 1976: 152)

This emphasis on self-awareness in social work practice has recently been restated by Lishman:

> Do we convey a non-judgmental attitude to aspects of clients' lives which are potentially shocking, for example violence, abuse or deprivation? What sense of empowerment do we convey to our users? How do we remain aware of our impact on others?
>
> (Lishman 1998: 94)

She makes the case (over twenty years after Kadushin) for reflection upon behaviour in order to 'learn, confirm good practice, analyse mistakes and develop alternative actions and responses', suggesting that in order to develop skills that are of use during practice, social workers need to ask themselves questions such as: What am I feeling? How am I presenting? Do I need to change my approach or focus? Why do I feel uncomfortable? (Lishman 1998).

Such questions are at the heart of the case for process recordings. The process recording assists students in learning how to 'interrogate' their practice. Students are taught an analytical skill that enables them to explore a key interface, the interface that exists between themselves as individuals with past and present experiences and their understanding of a professional intervention. Locating and exploring the 'gap' between the students' private self and their (imagined) professional persona is an important task of supervision, enabling students to develop an awareness of how they behave and how to use themselves in a skilled manner. The process recording allows connections to be made between past and present experience, assists in 'unpacking' the learning in a given interaction, and puts the means by which to do this into the hands of the student (Cree *et al*. 1998). Thus, the aspects of student powerlessness in the supervisory context are somewhat mitigated. As such, the process recording contrasts with other supervisory tools that normally involve the practice teacher divining meaning from student reporting or behaviour. Certainly, with the process recording, the students' account of their learning may be placed alongside that of the practice teacher, thus allowing a negotiation to take place regarding an agreed learning outcome.

As practised, the essence of the process recording is to provide a tool for a focus upon 'the how' of a student's practice. But what are the criticisms of process recordings? Aside from the lengthy amount of time it takes to write it up, a more substantive criticism is that of 'selective recall', that is the student records either consciously or unconsciously what he or she wishes to transmit to the supervisor.

It could be argued, though, that whereas there is a challenge of interpretation for the supervisor, selectivity may not be a 'hindrance' because, in the discussion of a recording that provides a 'selective perception' of the event, any 'omissions and distortions become the content for supervisory teaching and the source of supervisee learning about self' (Kadushin 1976: 415). Such interpretation and other tasks associated with the 'reading' of a process recording, for example successful extrapolation from student behaviour in supervision to behaviour in a practice setting, are 'very difficult' (Kadushin 1976). However, I would suggest that the problem of extrapolation is a common but not insurmountable drawback of other supervisory tools, for example case presentations. Students' accounts of their cognitive and emotional processes are valuable in terms of 'what makes them tick' and provide an insight into how the students may define their social work role. As conceived and designed, the process recording is first and foremost the students' version of the event and therefore not a truly objective account, but rather a means of accessing what the students believe took place, not only in terms of the event but also in relation to their thoughts and feelings. More 'objective' ways of gaining access to the students' performance include direct observation.

Other criticisms made of process recordings are presented by Ford and Jones:

- the possible creation of hyper self-consciousness in a student who may already be self-conscious;
- there is danger that the supervisor will not do justice to the effort invested in it by the student;

- process recording is out of fashion because it is associated with 'the psycho-dynamic approach to working with clients'.

(Ford and Jones 1987: 89)

The first two criticisms are not specific to process recording and may apply to any method used in supervision. In terms of the latter criticism, Ford and Jones themselves point out that students' self-awareness is necessary, because all interventions in social work practice require self-awareness on the part of social workers and a sensitivity to the feelings, attitudes and behaviour of other people.

The educative role of the process recording

Proper use of process recordings (including direction as to content, frequency and timing, and its use as part of a repertoire of teaching and learning tools) can encourage the skills of self-awareness and critical reflection that ensure that 'the how' of relationships with clients and services users is given as much importance as 'the what'. Use of process recordings in supervision can develop the capacity to 'read' an exchange between people. With its focus on the student's thoughts and feelings and the dynamics of interactions whereby the potential for the relationship to be used as a helping tool is explored, the process recording invites the student to attend to and develop senses such as intuition – the hairs on the back of the neck moment – and an awareness of the 'here and now' of interaction. Such awareness is fundamental to the transfer of learning. The meaning and importance of shifts in tempo in a discussion or the significance of movement are revealed in the use of process recordings. Through attention to such detail, a repertoire of 'micro-skills' can be formed, thus allowing the student to cast and use themselves as a resource. Furthermore, because learning often takes place in the course of reviewing an interaction through the medium of the process recording's focused framework, the student also develops the ability to learn how to learn (Gardiner 1989).

Unfortunately, in the current training climate, which is driven by performance indictors, greater self-awareness can seem like a luxury. However, criticism of the currently dominant functional analysis model of training is mounting. Horder (1998:120) indicates that since the introduction of competence-based qualifications, social work educators have been 'bogged down in paperwork, ticking boxes, jumping through hoops, struggling to hold onto a sense of the person'. Lishman is even more forthright:

The 'competency' model is inappropriate for education, training and professional development in social work because it results in fragmentation of the complexity of the social work and lacks the holistic approach to the necessary integration of knowledge, values and skills and the processes whereby these are integrated and applied.

(Lishman 1998: 92)

The process recording provides a teaching and learning method with which to introduce a student to just such a holistic approach. It is this approach that makes social work valuable and unique. Just as practising effective social work requires practitioners who have a holistic sense of the person, so too does social work education require the use of teaching methods that facilitate the transfer and integration of learning. All students will know the feeling of having been 'taught' something then instantly forgetting it. When real learning takes place it is never forgotten. Knowledge or awareness is transferred from somewhere 'out there' and passes into possession: it becomes 'in there'. The process recording provides the student with a tool that will help accomplish this crucial shift.

Bibliography

Ackerman, N. (1966) *Treating The Troubled Family*, New York: Basic Books.

Baldock, P. (1974) *Community Work and Social Work*, London: Routledge and Kegan Paul.

Brown, A. and Bourne, I. (1996) *The Social Work Supervisor*, Buckingham: Open University Press.

Carter, P., Jeffs, T. and Smith, M.K. (1995) *Social Working*, Basingstoke: Macmillan.

Cree, V.E., Macaulay, C. and Loney, H. (1998) *Transfer Of Learning: A Study*, Edinburgh: Scottish Office Central Research Unit and CCETSW.

Dwyer, M. and Urbanowski, M. (1965) 'Student process recording: a plea for structure' in *Social Casework* (May): 283–6.

Eagan, G. (1975) *The Skilled Helper*, Monterey, California: Brooks/Cole.

Ford, K. and Jones, A. (1987) *Student Supervision*, Basingstoke: Macmillan.

Gardiner, D. (1989) *The Anatomy of Supervision*, Milton Keynes: Open University.

Goleman, D. (1996) *Emotional Intelligence*, London: Bloomsbury.

Hamilton, G. (1946) *Principles of Social Case Recording*, New York: Columbia University Press.

Horder, W. (1998) 'Competence(s) without tears?' *Social Work Education* 17(1): 117–20.

Kadushin, A. (1976) *Supervision in Social Work*, New York: Columbia University Press.

Lishman, J. (1998) 'Personal and professional development', in R. Adams, L. Dominelli and M. Payne (eds) *Social Work: Themes, Issues and Critical Debates*, Basingstoke: Macmillan.

Pritchard, J. (ed.) (1995) *Good Practice in Supervision*, London: Jessica Kingsley Press.

Salomon, G. and Perkins, D.N. (1989) 'The rocky road to transfer: rethinking mechanisms of a neglected phenomenon', *Educational Psychologist* 24(2): 113–42.

Schön, D.A. (1987) *Educating the Reflective Practitioner*, San Francisco: Jossey-Bass.

Shardlow, S. and Doel, M. (1996) *Practice Learning and Teaching*, Basingstoke: Macmillan.

Thompson, N., Osada, M. and Anderson, B. (1990) *Practice Teaching in Social Work*, Birmingham: Pepar.

Yelloly, M. and Henkel, M. (eds) (1995) *Learning and Teaching in Social Work*, London: Jessica Kingsley Press.

Young, P.H. (1967) *The Student and Supervision in Social Work Education*, London: Routledge and Kegan Paul.

Chapter 10

Mature students and transfer of learning

Pam Green Lister

Introduction

The past educational, employment and life experiences of students have been shown to have a substantial impact on their ability to learn and to transfer learning (Boud and Miller 1996). For the last eleven years, I have been teaching mature students who have caring commitments and who are studying a DipSW programme in the west of Scotland; this course is specifically designed to meet their needs. I have become aware that an understanding of how students use these past experiences in new learning is vital for social work lecturers, practice teachers and students themselves. In this chapter, I will discuss the ways in which mature students approach the transfer of learning and strategies that can facilitate this process. Initially, I will examine the educational context looking at programme design and teaching approaches. I will then discuss the placement context looking at how students transfer learning from previous work and life experience to their practice and what aids this transfer. I will discuss my experiences as a lecturer and tutor with this student group and will refer to the students' own views on the transfer of learning as ascertained through a small-scale study of mature students with caring commitments undertaking the programme. In this study, I interviewed ten students who were either in the final year of the programme or had recently completed the programme; I asked them to reflect on how they transferred learning and how their life experiences as mature students with caring commitments affected this.

The context of the educational institution

The DipSW requires students 'to identify, analyse and take action to counter discrimination, racism, disadvantage, inequality and injustice, using strategies appropriate to role and context' (CCETSW 1995: 18).

As social work educators we must also devise strategies to assist disadvantaged groups to enter and succeed in further and higher education. The range of students undertaking the DipSW should match the diversity of the users of the social work service. Although I welcome the adoption of equal opportunity policies in educational institutions, in order for these policy statements to be effective, attention has to be given to providing programmes that meet the needs of disadvantaged students. There are a number of barriers preventing disadvantaged groups from entering and succeeding in further and higher education (Logan *et al.* 1996; James and Thomas 1996; Dominelli 1988). There are also particular difficulties faced by mature women students returning to education and these are compounded by caring commitments (Edwards 1993). However, access to social work training can be increased, and learning can be facilitated by the flexible design of DipSW programmes and by teaching methods that meet the needs of adult learners.

Programme design

The design of a teaching and learning programme clearly affects the ability of students to develop their learning. For example, the DipSW programme for mature entrants with caring commitments specifically aims to provide the opportunity for mature people with caring commitments to undertake social work training. It operates around a shorter timetabled day organised around school hours and school term dates. The period of training is therefore extended over three years. The majority of students on the three-year programme are White women aged between thirty and forty-five years of age. All students have a caring commitment. Usually, this involves looking after young children, with many students being lone parents, but a significant proportion of students also care for disabled partners or elderly relatives.

The importance of the programme design in facilitating student learning was emphasised by all of the students interviewed in the small study. Several students recalled first getting information about the programme and being encouraged to apply for social work training by the explicit reference to maturity and caring commitments in the programme leaflet. One student described her surprise that caring commitments were a prerequisite for a course and were positively welcomed, rather than seen as personal issues that individual students had to deal with. Another said she found it refreshing that children and education were not seen as incompatible. These views echo those reported by Pascall and Cox (1993). In their study of women returning to higher education, they found that their respondents did not view education 'as a rejection of domesticity' but rather 'placed education within the context of lives in which responsibility for others, particularly children, was assumed as a priority' (Pascall and Cox 1993: 143). Students in my study stated that the shorter timetabled day and extended three-year programme allowed them to give attention to their children at key times of the day and year. Several compared this with previous educational experiences where the additional stress of juggling caring commitments severely restricted their learning. As one student commented:

> When you are running from pillar to post, picking up, dropping off, arranging childcare, feeling guilty and all that, there is just no time to think ... in the [previous] course I was on I think all I did was pick up interesting facts – interesting but totally unconnected to each other. I never consciously thought about how I could transfer what I had learned. I was too busy keeping it all together.

Most simply but most importantly then, students returning to education later in life with caring commitments require the time and space to learn and to reflect on learning in order for transfer of learning to take place (Gould and Taylor 1996). Flexibility in course design is one way that this can be achieved. As Edwards (1993) notes, discussion about women and caring commitments has been expressed from the perspective of the higher education institution, where family responsibilities are seen as impeding women's education and are seen as 'bag and baggage' to be dealt with (1993: 9). We need, then, to reframe how we view women's caring commitments and organise our educational provision accordingly.

Teaching approaches

Teaching approaches that facilitate adult learning are clearly a key element for assisting mature students to transfer their learning in the classroom environment. The diversity of students' learning styles and the different approaches to teaching and learning have received considerable attention from researchers in education (Entwistle 1987; Honey and Mumford 1992). There are, however, some common themes that emerge from research in this field which are of particular significance when teaching mature entrants.

An open and supportive environment that encourages student interaction is a crucial element in facilitating adult learning, and the importance of facilitated class discussion for adult learners is an obvious but important consideration for educators (Brown and Atkins 1993). Many mature entrants have spent years outside the educational system, with perhaps their last contact with the system being secondary school. There may be, therefore, a basic lack of familiarity with the classroom environment of higher education and of lecturer expectations (Pascall and Cox 1993). Many universities now offer introductory courses during the summer vacation to prepare mature students. A small number of students on the mature entrants' diploma programme have attended such a course and found it a useful preparation for university life. However, if social work education wishes to increase access to disadvantaged groups, diploma programmes need to address this issue directly and extended induction and entry units may be required. The mature entrants' programme, for example, has extended the entry unit into an introductory module entitled 'Key Concepts and Values in Social Work'. This module not only examines core social work concepts and values but also includes study skills sessions and experiential work with students on group processes. Evidence from module and course evaluations of the mature entrants' diploma and from the small study suggests that class discussions and seminars are the most valued method of learning, as one student said:

> I would like to say to lecturers to allow us more time to discuss ... it's then that you make the links, or someone in the class says something which helps you clarify your thoughts. That's where our past experience can work for us... We have a myriad of experiences between us and one of us can sometimes relate the teaching to that and it opens it up for us all.

The ability to relate theory to practice is a key factor in the transfer of learning and one which some mature entrants, returning later to education, struggle with. Sometimes the wealth of their personal experiences can inhibit engagement with theory as they have taken an 'everyday social approach' to problem solving that has worked for them to this point (Secker 1993). Very often, at the early stages of their training, when asked to consider 'why' they hold a certain point of view, students refer not to a theoretical explanation but to 'common sense'. In order for students to transfer learning from their previous experience to their learning about social work theory and practice, they have to be given the tools to analyse that experience and to generalise from it. Students need specific guidance to solve particular problems, and they also require an ability 'to identify underlying principles and not just the surface features' (Cree *et al.* 1998: 36). Transferable elements need to be brought 'into consciousness' and their 'general applicability pointed out' (Nisbet and Shucksmith 1986: 21).

Several students in the small study stated that they found it easier to make connections between ideas, and between theory and practice, when the lecturer taught from an identifiable theoretical position. A theoretical framework was described by one student as 'the glue that made everything hang together', and by another as 'the blue sky in the jigsaw – difficult to do but when it is done all the rest fits into place'. Students welcomed lecturers who provided an overarching framework in which to understand new ideas: an anti-oppressive framework and feminism were mentioned by several students. They all described at length the initial struggles they had with theory and the relationship of theory to practice but that once 'the light bulb came on' their learning rapidly developed.

Even after the light bulb comes on, students may find the relating of theory to previous practice a difficult process. When working with mature students with substantial practice and life experience, it is important to appreciate the major impact of their new learning on their sense of self. Retrospectively applying this learning to previous experience can be exciting and self-confirming, as one student explained:

> I used to think everybody should know this. This is pure common sense. I never gave myself credit that I had learned it somewhere: from practice, through reading, through experience, through somebody. Now I'm so much more conscious of when I am learning something and where else I can use it.

However, the transfer process is not always an easy one for students with extensive work experience when they evaluate their previous practice in the light of new knowledge. When introduced to new concepts or challenged on beliefs or assumptions, students can feel de-skilled and find it hard to look at past experience positively. Sometimes this can lead students to be resistant to theory and to be unable to generalise from previous experience. At other times it can create self-doubt. One student in the small study had twenty years' experience in residential childcare work and as a social work assistant in a fieldwork team. She described how during classes while she was being introduced to a new theory or approach she applied it to her previous work experience in order to understand the theory. She had found the teaching in the university enabled her to critically examine her previous practice and described this as an emotional experience:

Very emotional. I just wish I had understood these issues earlier ... thinking I could have done a better job ... a feeling not of guilt but ... I wish I had understood that then, a definite, definite feeling so it's quite emotional.

Social work educators need to be aware of the emotional impact of new learning and all the changes that it brings (Curnock 1985). Before transfer of learning can take place, students may need to be facilitated in constructively and critically analysing their previous experience in the light of newly acquired learning. They may have to painstakingly deconstruct their past experiences before moving on. As one student neatly put it: 'It's hard – before you move on there are certain things you have to undo you know'.

Returning to education as a mature woman student can have an enormous impact on the student's personal and family life. In her study of mature women students undertaking social science courses, Edwards (1993) describes the different strategies used by students to manage the personal and intellectual growth that their education was creating alongside sustaining relationships with partners, friends and families. Change in the political awareness of the women students was a particular cause of strain. Students in Edward's study gave examples of challenging racism and sexism in friends and family, explaining that they felt that they 'didn't fit' any more (1993: 143–4).

My experience of teaching mature social work students bears out Edward's findings. The exploration of personal values and political beliefs is fundamental to social work training and involves students in questioning their histories, their relationships and their identities. For many students, this is the first time that they have been afforded the opportunity for such exploration and this has a profound effect on their sense of self. The theoretical frameworks such as feminism or anti-oppressive practice that help students make connections and transfer learning also pose challenges for them. The interconnectedness of personal and professional growth and development was emphasised by a number of students in the small study who were able to show how learning at the university and on placement had been transferred to their personal life. As one student explained: 'the learning you've done and the growing you've done through learning and the changes it makes to your own life ... you transfer your learning to other people'.

All students discussed how their learning about their own value-base had significantly affected their family lives. Several students described how they had begun to challenge gender roles and expectations in their own families. Two students described how their new awareness of racism in all its forms whether intentional or unintentional had had a profound impact on them and had caused them to question their own attitudes and those of friends and family, resulting in some friction and resentment from others.

The context of the placement

I have argued that in order for students to transfer learning from their previous experience to their learning about social work theory and practice in the classroom, they first have to be given the tools to analyse that experience and to generalise from it. I have also emphasised that we should not underestimate the impact of this new learning on students' personal lives and their sense of self. After making connections between new knowledge and previous experience, successful transfer of learning requires the application of the learning to new situations (Salomon and Perkins 1989). However successfully students have analysed previous experiences in the light of newly learned theoretical frameworks in the classroom environment, their competence in transferring knowledge, skills and values is primarily assessed through their practice while on placement.

The mature students I have worked with vary considerably in how well they can transfer their learning from previous experience to placement. Inevitably, this student group of carers, the majority of whom are women, will be working with service users with experiences very similar to their own, including poverty, childcare issues and caring commitments. All these students have some knowledge and skills in the fields of parenting, child development, and some areas such as separation and divorce, the death of a partner, having a child with a disability or adopting a child. They may have received a service from the Social Work Department or other voluntary agencies. This can give them important insights into the needs and feelings of service users and the opportunity to identify commonalities and differences in their respective experiences (Hanmer and Statham 1988).

In the small study, all students were clear that they viewed their experiences as women, mothers and carers as assets in practice and thought they could positively transfer their learning. Students brought to the interviews a wealth of examples of how learning from their life experiences had been transferred to social work practice. One student felt that she was 'less likely to be dogmatic' because of her wider experiences of people and family, because 'you know there's not a right way'. Another student felt her previous parenting experiences helped her work with parents because she had:

> [A] real awareness of the contradictory nature of parenting, of the tender spots, that it's difficult to be good at being a parent and that we all have our ways of going about it. The common ground though is that it's not likely to be easy ... You make the connections but you see the differences.

Students stressed the need to be careful about how personal experiences were used to throw light on their practice. They were aware that assumptions could be made about the similarity of experiences. Several expressed the view that as student social workers they needed to be flexible about approaches to issues and open to different explanations and perceptions of people's problems. One student talked about how she used her experiences as a mother and a widow:

> You get a broader view rather than directly transfer your experiences as a widow or as a mother ... your personal experience does help a lot in understanding people but you don't use yourself as a yardstick to measure people's lives.

One student, who had an adopted child who eventually required respite care, had been a service user of the Social Work Department for a number of years. She felt that the struggle she had had coping with the social work system radically influenced her approach to service users:

> It took me a lot of time of serious thinking and confusion to work through my experience ... but I have to make sure in working in social work that I don't transfer the pain; that I listen to where clients are and not make assumptions.

In the above examples we can see some students reflecting on the knowledge they have gained from their past experience. They are considering what aspects of this knowledge might be useful in working with people in similar situations, but they are able to own what is unique to them about the experience and the value they invest it with.

However, some students struggle with the adoption of the professional role when encouraged to make use of their previous experience. Although they may be aware of the commonalities between themselves and service users, they may be neglectful of differences and inappropriately transfer from previous experience. This manifests itself most obviously in actions such as inappropriate self-disclosure, exchanging of gifts, inviting service users into their private lives and becoming overinvolved in the service user's private life. In my experience, all student social workers are challenged at some point in their training in one of these areas. However, the degree of similarity between the lives of mature students and service users can increase the likelihood of inappropriate transfer. In the latter part of this chapter I will describe and analyse three extended examples of situations in which students have attempted to transfer learning from previous experience to placement with varying degrees of success. These examples broadly illustrate the approaches to learning proposed by Secker (1993): 'the everyday approach', 'the fragmented approach' and the 'fluent approach'.

The everyday approach

Secker characterises the 'everyday social approach' as one in which

> the student did not draw at all on the kind of knowledge which is usually described as theoretical. Instead they drew solely on knowledge derived from their personal, everyday social lives.
>
> (Secker 1993: 24–5)

This approach can lead to students treating 'clients as if they were friends, family or casual acquaintances' (Cree et al. 1998: 11). Students using this approach have not consciously analysed previous experience using a theoretical framework, and they are not able to identify the knowledge or skills that they are using. The following example, taken from a placement meeting I attended with a first placement student and a practice teacher, illustrates how this approach might manifest itself in a student's practice.

At the placement meeting the student and the practice teacher described how, in a group session with mothers of children with learning disabilities, that was being directly observed by the practice teacher, the student failed to pick up on a serious childcare issue. One mother in the group had described the difficulties she had with her thirteen-year-old son with learning difficulties who kept threatening to leave. She had sent her son out into the back yard on the spot in his underclothes and made him stay there for a period of time. As the student later explained, she entered this encounter with the previous experience of coping with the difficult behaviour of her teenage daughter. On one occasion she had allowed her daughter to walk out of the house with a suitcase of clothes without protest and her daughter had been out for several hours and the student had felt guilty about this.

The student's reactions to the mother's contribution in the group had been one of friendly sympathy and of humorously sharing her own experience. When this encounter had been raised by the practice teacher in the debriefing session, the student realised that she had not listened closely to the parent, she had made assumptions about what the parent was going through and had as the student herself said 'confused empathy with identification'.

In the placement meeting, when asked to further analyse her practice, the student explained that she had lost sight of what her role in the group should be. She attributed this to a number of factors. Most obviously, she had felt nervous about being observed and this had affected her ability to listen as she had self-consciously been trying to 'perform'. However, the student stated that she had also previously been given positive feedback by her practice teacher about her abilities to communicate and engage with people and in her 'use of self'. The practice teacher had encouraged her to make use of her previous skills developed during her voluntary work and use her knowledge and experience as a mother when working with mothers of children with learning disabilities. The student explained that she had, therefore, decided, 'just to act naturally' during the direct observation session.

It can be seen then that, although the student inappropriately transferred skills that she had previously developed, this had not been an unthinking process. The student had given some thought to how she would approach the group, particularly when under the stress of being observed. She had listened to her practice teacher's feedback but had interpreted it in a very concrete way. During the placement meeting the student was encouraged to identify her communication skills and consider what knowledge she had gained about parenting from her own experience. She was then encouraged to reflect on what aspects of both areas were readily transferable to the new situation and what features would change depending on the specific situation. Finally, she was asked to consider what might help her in undertaking the transfer task. Interestingly, she suggested more knowledge about theories of parenting to enable her to analyse her own experience so that she would be more aware of general issues for all parents and possible differences between parents. The student required assistance in identifying her learning needs and in bringing into consciousness the learning process. The role of the practice teacher and tutor here was to structure the student's reflection by assisting her in the dialectical process of generalising from her experience and then discriminating in her use of generalisation (Houston 1991).

The fragmented approach

My second example illustrates how a 'fragmented approach' might manifest itself in a student's practice. In this approach, students experience conflict between their everyday and theoretical knowledge and this causes dilemmas in practice. Again, this example arises from my experiences at a placement meeting with a first year student and her practice teacher. During the meeting the student described how she had compiled a social work background report on a thirteen-year-old boy for the Children's Panel.[1] He had shoplifted on a number of occasions and his mother, a lone parent, had told the student that the boy was getting beyond her control. In the conclusion to the report the student had argued that the boy's behaviour could be attributed to the lack of a father figure and she recommended that he be placed on supervision to a male social worker. When asked to explain how she had come to this conclusion the student gave a number of reasons, including the past experience of a family member, a recent television documentary and some reference to adolescent development, attachment and modelling. The conceptual confusion of the student was evident in her explanation. Her difficulties arose from some conflict between theoretical and everyday knowledge and also the uncritical and haphazard application of theory to practice. Her approach to the transfer of learning agrees very much with Secker's fragmented approach, where students are self-conscious about their theoretical justification (Secker 1993: 46–7).

Harris (1996) argues for the importance of the tutor in assisting students to learn from past experience. Tutorial work with this student centred on assisting her to outline a theory, pulling out its key features, considering the value issues it raised and then looking at how it might assist her understanding of a person's situation. We used examples from her past experience as well as from her practice. We also used vignettes to compare and contrast theoretical approaches. Unfortunately, these strategies did not assist the student who became more anxious and tended to look for 'the correct answer' and consistently tried to 'get it right'. This is reminiscent of a 'surface approach' to learning. Entwistle (1987) suggests that learners who use a 'surface approach' concentrate on completion of what they consider to be an externally imposed task in an unreflective way. These learners are not able to distinguish principles from examples and do not integrate the different aspects of their learning.

The fluent approach

My final example is a good illustration of Secker's 'fluent approach' in which students 'made use of ... ready made theory in constructing their own theories' (1993: 78). One student in the small study described how feminist theory and attachment theory had assisted her in working with a young male drug user during her first placement in a prison. The student explained how feminism had assisted her in making sense of her own background. She also described how feminism had provided her with 'an overarching framework' to understand not only the oppression of women but also different sites of oppression; in this case, the disadvantaged position of this young man living in poverty with poor educational achievements and few employment opportunities. The student continued to explain how attachment theory had first helped her in understanding her adopted son's behaviour. This awareness of attachment theory then further helped her when undertaking work with the young man, who had undergone a number of separations that compounded his disadvantaged position. The student described a complex dialectical process of the transfer of learning from past experience to placement through the use of theory. She had introduced concepts of oppression and had explained the nature of attachment to the young man to assist him in understanding some of the reasons behind his drug use. She had drawn personal strength and practice wisdom from the critical application of the theories. When asked what teaching or supervision processes had assisted her, she identified the ability of lecturers to provide frameworks for understanding and to make the connections and the ability of practice teachers to analyse a practice situation from a number of perspectives. This final example of how transfer of learning takes place illustrates both the complexities of the task and the rewards it can bring. It exemplifies Yelloly and Henkel's definition of a reflective practitioner in whom 'professional competence is the product of a complex, shared and negotiated process which also involves the responsibility for continuous professional growth and development' (1995: 27).

In this part of the chapter, I have identified a number of strategies that social work educators might find useful in assisting the transfer of learning on placement. When students in the small study were asked to identify strategies that would facilitate transfer of learning on placement, an open and trusting relationship with a practice teacher where students were not made to feel defensive was most frequently mentioned. Students welcomed practice teachers who were themselves reflective of their practice, in that this modelled for them the process of reflection. All students described how they had learned from their mistakes and indicated that if they were in a supervisory relationship where they were free to make mistakes, received good honest feedback and were encouraged to try again, their ability to transfer learning increased. Finally, students felt that it was important that they were given the space to rehearse their inadequacies, encouraged to take risks and then given the time and space to discuss how to move forward. These findings broadly mirror those of Gardiner (1984) and Gould (1993), whose research highlighted the importance of reflection and structured support in practice teaching.

Conclusion

Mature students are a valuable resource in social work education, and we must ensure that the design of our programmes and our teaching approaches attract them to social work education and support them throughout their education and training. They bring to social work education a rich pool of past experience that is not only available as knowledge for transfer to new situations but also determines how the transfer takes place. As Edwards (1993: 10) succinctly puts it, 'mature students ... do not just bring their experience with them, they are their experience'. Transfer of learning is a complex process with theoretical, practice and personal dimensions. We need to develop a range of strategies based on our knowledge of how adults learn to facilitate this process. This final quotation from one of the students in the small study indicates how all-encompassing transfer of learning can be:

> You have no idea of the personal changes I have gone though as a result of this training ... you go back and interrogate all that you have done in the past, you analyse all that is going on around you. This term 'transfer' doesn't do it justice – you don't just transfer learning you transform yourself.

Notes

1. The Children's Hearing system was established by the Social Work (Scotland) Act 1968 as an alternative to a juvenile justice system. Children's panels are convened to decide on appropriate measures of care for children.

Bibliography

Brown, G. and Atkins, M. (1993) *Effective Teaching in Higher Education*, London: Routledge.

Boud, D. and Miller, N. (1996) *Working with Experience. Animated Learning*, London: Routledge.

Central Council for Education and Training in Social Work (1995) *Assuring Quality in the Diploma in Social Work – 1: Rules and Requirements for the DipSW,* London: CCETSW.

Cree, V.E., Macaulay, C. and Loney, H. (1998) *Transfer of Learning: A Study,* Edinburgh: Scottish Office Central Research Unit and CCETSW.

Curnock, K. (1985) 'Educational principles and education for social work', in R. Harris (ed.) *Educating Social Workers*, London: Association of Teachers in Social Work Education.

Dominelli, L. (1998) *Anti-Racist Social Work*, London: Routledge.

Edwards, R. (1993) *Mature Women Students. Separating or Connecting Family and Education,* London: Taylor & Francis.

Entwistle, N. (1987) 'A model of the teaching-learning process', in J.T.E Richardson, M.W. Eysenck and D.W. Piper (eds) *Student Learning,* Milton Keynes: The Society for Research into Higher Education, Open University Press.

Gardiner, D.W.G. (1984) 'Learning for transfer', *Issues in Social Work Education* 4(2): 95–105.

Gould, N. (1993) 'Cognitive change and learning from practice: a longitudinal study of social work students', *Social Work Education* 12(1): 77–87.

Gould, N. and Taylor, N. (1996) *Reflective Learning for Social Work*, Aldershot: Arena.

Hanmer, J. and Statham, D, (1988) *Women and Social Work: Toward a Woman-Centred Practice,* London: Macmillan.

Harris, A. (1996) 'Learning from experience and reflection in social work education', in N. Gould and I. Taylor (eds) *Reflective Learning for Social Work,* Aldershot: Arena.

Honey, P. and Mumford, A. (1992) *The Manual of Learning Styles,* Maidenhead: Peter Honey.

Houston, J.P. (1991) *Fundamentals of Learning and Memory,* San Diego: Harcourt Brace Jovanich.

James, P. and Thomas, M. (1996) 'Deconstructing a disabling environment in social work education', *Social Work Education* 15: 34–45.

Logan, J., Kershaw, S. Karban, K., Mills, S., Trotter, J. and Sinclair, M. (1996) *Confronting Prejudice. Lesbian and Gay Issues in Social Work Education,* Aldershot: Arena.

Nisbet, J and Shucksmith, J (1986) *Learning to Learn,* London: Routledge, Kegan Paul.

Pascall, G. and Cox, R. (1993) *Women Returning to Higher Education,* Milton Keynes: The Society for Research into Higher Education, Open University Press.

Salomon, G. and Perkins, D.N. (1989) 'Rocky roads to transfer: rethinking mechanisms of a neglected phenomenon', *Educational Psychologist* 242: 113–142.

Secker, J. (1993) *From Theory to Practice in Social Work,* Aldershot: Avebury.

Yelloly, M. and Henkel, M. (1995) (eds) *Learning and Teaching in Social Work. Towards Reflective Practice,* London: Jessica Kingsley Press.

Chapter 11

Understanding and managing conflict in the learning process

Christians coming out

Yvonne Channer

Introduction

The purpose of this chapter is to examine how learning can be affected when one's personal values are undermined, threatened or berated. A consideration of the process of transfer of learning is central to the discussion. The general issue to be explored is how students with a coherent set of beliefs and values derived from their membership of a 'faith community' cope with a social work course when the values they hold dear are publicly rejected by staff and peers.

CCETSW recognises the significance of personal values and the community context in which these values are formed and supported:

> Values are distinguished from personal preferences in that they have been accepted and articulated to some degree by a group, of which the individual is a member. We certainly speak of 'personal values' but in this sense are referring to those of various group values which the individual has selected as most significant for his or her personal conduct and to which a large measure of commitment is felt.
>
> (Working Party on the Teaching of the Values of Social Work 1976: 15)

The groups referred to here may be political, religious or other reference groups that hold particular significance for the individual. Social work students who hold traditional religious views often find that their beliefs are in conflict with secular social work curricula. I have met White, Black, Christian and Islamic students who have some difficulty in harmonising professional and personal values. This is illustrated by the following excerpts from a personal testimony that was recently shared by a student with her peers and staff at Hallam University. She wrote this in response to a comment made by a member of staff in a teaching session:

A comment has been made that 'some Christians believe that suffering and the cross are what human beings are entitled to rather than happiness'. This opinion has been given as a testimony, and if we really believe in anti-oppressive practice, anti-discrimination, equal opportunities for all, justice and mercy, then I appeal to this teaching that I am allowed the same opportunity to give my opinion and testimony about the work of God and Jesus Christ in my own life – and of his purpose to bring happiness into everyone's life, contrary to the above statement.

The student then describes her journey from occultism to Christianity and concludes:

I cannot remain silent when the person I owe the most to in the world, has given me hope and a future – brought me happiness beyond my wildest dreams, is vilified. If it wasn't for him I wouldn't have today or tomorrow. Therefore I offer an alternative viewpoint and personal testimony that it is Satan who desires only suffering, sorrow and unhappiness for human beings. Because it certainly isn't the Christ I've met and know personally.

As a third year student just about to complete her social work degree, it is noteworthy that she felt the course had failed to provide her with sufficient opportunities to disclose, discuss or examine her personal beliefs. The testimony may seem extreme and unrepresentative of the views of many students. However, many individuals have strong religious beliefs that are integral to their life experiences. Students may rely on their religious communities and belief system to support them, especially in stressful times, such as completing a degree – an academic and personal challenge.

For the purpose of this chapter, I have chosen to focus on Black Christian students as a specific example of a group whose membership of a faith community and personal value-base is challenged by the pressure to absorb certain professional values. I would suggest that these students experience traumatic learning because their learning is inhibited because of the ongoing conflict between personal and professional values.

The evidence for this chapter is based on a small-scale study consisting of interviews with fifteen Black Christian social workers. These included a probation officer, a manager in social services, a residential worker and one person who had failed to complete her course. Both in the formal, taped interviews and in the unstructured conversations, interviewees reflected on their learning experiences, giving specific consideration to issues of conflict between personal and professional values.

'Race', religion and social work

A number of writers in recent years have examined the experiences of Black students on social work programmes. Some have catalogued the difficult and negative learning experiences of Black students, focusing on course content, rates of retention and failure (e.g. de Souza 1993; de Gale 1991).[1] Graham (1999) in particular considers the nature of the social work knowledge base, exploring the value and role of an African-centred paradigm for social work. She points out that 'social work consciously and unconsciously has become an instrument of the Eurocentric worldview' (1999: 255):

> Epistemologies – sources of knowledge – are intrinsically bound by historical period, culture and ideology; the questions we ask about the world and human behaviour reflect our life experiences, our culture and our historical development. The existing knowledge base for social work has emerged from epistemologies that are an expression of European historical and cultural development.
>
> (Graham 1999: 256)

This has implications not only for social work education but also for social work practice. The nature of oppression must remain at the forefront of an analysis of social work with Black service users and practitioners: 'A people whose paradigms of thought and practice are borrowed from its oppressors clearly have limited human possibilities' (Asante, 1987, in Graham 1999: 254) and 'How can the oppressed use the same theories as the oppressor?' (Karenga, 1997, in Graham 1999: 255).

Graham (1999) is thus concerned that the foundation of established social work practice models do not reflect the diversity of worldviews and cultural values found in Britain today. More than this, she argues for an alternative paradigm that is grounded in the cultural and historical reality of Black experience. She states that: 'The African-centred worldview challenges social work to expand its philosophical and intellectual base to embrace humanity, to release the domination of the Eurocentric worldview over the psyche of the creativity and unlimited potential that is embedded within authenticity' (Graham 1999: 252–3).

Even anti-oppressive or anti-discriminatory practice as it is currently taught receives censure from Graham. She explains that the approaches are essentially a reactive stance against racism and oppression:

> Anti-discriminatory practice does not provide social work models that seek to support, nurture or understand the emotional, spiritual and development needs of Black families to advance the collective interest of African people. Instead, this social work model promotes damage limitation by infusing a Black perspective/experience articulated as an adaptation or modification of existing theoretical frameworks that serve to mask more fundamental theoretical deficits inherent within the ethnocentric nature of social work. Consequently, this model falls short of creating a social work that mirrors the worldview and cultural values of those who are heavily in receipt of social work intervention.
>
> (Graham 1999: 252–3)

Many adults appear to experience difficulties in learning and applying what they have learnt, difficulties which are not associated with intellectual problems (Atherton 1986). It could be that the Eurocentric content and approach to teaching creates dilemmas for Black students. Atherton's (1986) analysis of the learning process provides a helpful framework from which to examine the educational experiences of social work students.

Traumatic learning

Atherton (1986) states that for adults, particularly those undertaking educational programmes that challenge their attitudes and aim to supplant existing knowledge and skills, the element of loss entailed by the learning can be sufficiently pronounced to give rise to a distinctive learning process, referred to as 'traumatic learning'. He suggests that such learning tends to be resisted and that in engaging upon it the learner is likely to undergo a three-stage process of destabilisation, disorientation and re-orientation. He points out that the stages are not discrete; rather, they run into each other and can only be effectively disentangled with hindsight:

> Stage one is distinguished by the difficult initial move away from the old, stage two by the completion of that manoeuvre and the state of limbo which goes with it; stage three by the gradual acquisition of the new but all three are in some measure present in each one.
>
> (Atherton 1986: 30)

Atherton argues that the process of traumatic learning is normal rather than pathological: all learners are affected at some time. He also notes the role of the tutor as the key to providing conditions that offer the least hindrance to such learning.

Destabilisation

Destabilisation is described as an induced crisis that upsets a cherished set of beliefs. Atherton (1986) indicates that there are some forms of 'education' in which the destabilisation process assumes considerable importance, for example the experience of initiates who join religious or political cults. These individuals are encouraged to suspend their critical faculties and keep them suspended in order to take on board a closed frame of reference that explains everything. For those in more conventional learning settings, however, such changes may be short lived because subjects find it possible to reconcile apparent inconsistencies between old beliefs and new ones. Interestingly, for the purposes of this chapter, Atherton notes that only destabilisation at the level of the self-concept will result in long-term change.

Disorientation

Stage two – disorientation – is seen as the trough in Atherton's (1986) model. Here the learner experiences a sense of confusion. Atherton notes that not only is the learner who is trying to do things differently likely to be relatively unskilled and occasionally 'at a loss', but the trough may go beyond the practical dimension to affect morale. A degree of psychological confusion and possibly depression is expected. Atherton argues that the depth of the depression, and hence the degree of loss and disorientation, is related to 'the level of implication of the area of change for the rest of the person's life. (In other words, the salience of the values involved)' (1986: 31). At this stage of the learning process, students may leave a course stating that they 'can't cope'; the difficulty implied is not necessarily intellectual.

The second-stage phase has a number of other significant features. A level of suggestibility accompanies disorientation:

> The drive to make sense of the apparently meaningless situation is a powerful one and thus people will grasp at straws to orient themselves … This phase of learning is also a time of 'costing' when the price of the change comes home to the individual, and the uncertain benefits

of the future and the new way of working are balanced against the security and familiarity of the past. Even when the change is obviously for the better – from an outsider's point of view – it may not seem so to the learner. The facilitator of change, whether tutor or therapist, has to strike a balance – holding out both an assurance of the benefits to come, and yet respecting the price being paid for them.

(Atherton 1986: 35)

Re-orientation

After juggling with a number of possible titles, including 'Return', 'Recovery' and 'Renewal', Atherton (1986) chooses 'Re-orientation' as the most fitting for stage three. He regards 're-orientation' as that stage which focuses on the learner's experience and highlights 'the change in understanding of his [sic] situation which it appears necessarily accompanies traumatic learning' (Atherton 1986: 35).

Re-orientation is the end product of successfully managed traumatic learning. However, Atherton points out that the long-term nature of this stage is not guaranteed and is affected by the length of time the learner is influenced by the facilitating environment:

If it [the facilitating environment] is withdrawn too soon, the learner may be unable to cope and may revert to his [sic] previous conduct – and once he has done that, and 'proved' that the new way 'does not work', any subsequent attempt at change will be even more difficult, if not downright impossible. If it persists too long, there is no opportunity for the new conduct to grow and mature and be fully internalised through normal interaction with others – but the variables here are not only those of the strength of the learner's new conduct but also the receptiveness or hostility of the environment to it.

(Atherton 1986: 36–7)

I will now draw on Atherton's perspective to help in my analysis of the experiences of Black Christian students on social work programmes with specific reference to transfer of learning and the impact of assessment.

Transfer of learning

Atherton's (1986) model provides a useful instrument through which we can examine various aspects of transfer of learning as outlined in Cree *et al.* (1998). This study concludes that the ability or capacity to successfully achieve transfer of learning is possible if students engage in a 'deep' rather than a 'strategic' or 'surface' approach to learning. Open reflexive learning requires the absence of threat and anxiety: 'Adults must be appreciated for the diverse experiences which they bring; their experiences must be acknowledged and validated. If not, they are likely to feel 'de-skilled' and unable to transfer learning appropriately' (Cree *et al.* 1998: 25).

Atherton (1986) notes that many learners experience feelings of loss and depression. They may therefore experience difficulty in relating new ideas to previous knowledge (seen as a defining feature of a deep approach to learning). This may be because they are reluctant to trade the old for the new or even permit facets of the new to impinge on valued, safe previously held ideas (Atherton 1986). Feelings and emotions are an integral part of both the learning and the critical thinking process. Cree *et al.* (1998) note that 'an intellectual student who was cut off from their feelings would find it hard to reflect … people need to be able to use both their heads and their hearts' (1998: 31). Similarly, Brookfield (1987) asserts that as we try to think critically and help others to do so, we cannot help but become aware of the importance of emotions to this activity.

It seems clear that learners and educators should not ignore the role of feelings and emotions while engaging in the learning process.

The impact of assessment

Assessment is known to have a major impact on learning, whatever the setting (see Chapter 2). Black social work practitioners interviewed for this chapter about their experiences of being assessed reported that they had not been willing to fully immerse themselves in course material and integrate it with their belief systems when they had been social work students. They stated that they had felt unsettled or, to use Atherton's word 'disoriented', by some of the teaching material. Some reported that they had actually left teaching sessions where there was clearly no space for them to voice their opinions. They felt that the tutors who had facilitated these sessions did not have an awareness of the range of views that deserved recognition. In consequence, tutors may have thought that their students had learnt and internalised new concepts being taught, but the students had reverted to their own original beliefs when they encountered practical application of new ideas. In terms of Atherton's (1986) model, it was not possible for stage three, re-orientation, to occur.

The framework of CCETSW's DipSW demonstrates an underlying assumption that by assessing the behaviour and use of the language of social work students, it is possible to draw conclusions about their attitudes and values. However, as Atherton notes, there may be some discrepancy between what students say they believe, what is expressed in their behaviour and what they genuinely believe, but conceal. A student's personal set of values may therefore in practice be at some distance from a professional or theoretical set of values. This has important implications for direct observation of students' practice. As Evans (1990) points out, observed performance does not of itself produce what is totally unequivocal evidence – students may do the 'right thing' for the 'wrong reason' and vice versa.

This connects with the issue of what has been called 'political correctness' (Dunant 1994), a popular but at times controversial crusade to 'clean up' the language of prejudicial practice. Attention to the meaning and use of language has played a necessary, and on the whole, positive part in the development of an anti-oppressive approach within social work. However, it may also have had the effect of encouraging some students to pay 'lip-service' to anti-oppressive ideas, while others have been silenced, not daring to express an opinion in case they were set upon by 'politically correct' tutors or fellow students. Atherton (1991) suggests that some students learn to play the role of 'unprejudiced social worker' while at the same time retaining the prejudices they had before coming on the course; they learn what is required to satisfy their assessors without necessarily absorbing 'the essence of social work values'.

This has important implications for learning. On the one hand, real learning (Atherton's 'traumatic learning') is unlikely to take place, because the originally held views have not been sufficiently challenged and unhinged. On the other hand, there may be too great a distance between new belief systems and old ones, leading to difficulty in making the learning stick or in accepting that the learning is necessary.

Implications for practice

It is a privilege for me to be given the opportunity to examine, in public, issues of such personal and professional interest. From the perspective of a Black Christian social work educator, I have often been challenged by the experiences of social work students who find that their personal beliefs and values are threatened or undermined during social work training. Unless social work education and training identifies and values the role that religion can play for the African Caribbean student, service user, community and educator doors will be closed to a network of unique resources.

The experience of being a Black student in a largely White educational institution is potentially, and often in reality, one of being a powerless, vulnerable observer. Mature, Black students selected for social work programmes are by no means a homogeneous group. Some grapple with the evidences of racism in White educational institutions, whereas others are more concerned with realising their ambitions than critically examining a variety of personal and professional issues.

The general concerns of Black students can be highlighted in the approach many social work programmes take to the subject of religion. In my experience of over almost two decades in social work education and practice, I have found that there is invariably a negative view of the role that religion plays, with views such as the following being expressed:

- African Caribbean families are often deemed to be too strict and too religious and there is a feeling that children should be removed from such a restrictive environment (Channer and Parton 1993).
- Religion is seen as an oppressor of homosexuals (Burgess *et al.* 1997).
- Women are generally regarded as victims or subservient in religions such as Islam (Ahmad 1990; Thakur 1998).

A popular teaching activity demonstrates this further. Students are invited to construct two lists, one concerning groups who are often oppressed and one concerning those who are often oppressors. The outcome of this exercise is often that 'religion' or people with fundamentalist, religious ideas are usually listed in the latter. The tenor of the group discussion usually highlights the role religion is deemed to play in undermining choice and freedom of action. Rarely are students, without some guidance, willing to examine the positive role that religion may play for individuals, groups and communities.

An interesting and common phenomenon I have observed is that students who hold clear religious beliefs and are participating members of various religious organisations often feel unable to defend their position and 'testify' to the place of religion and spirituality in their personal values against a barrage of secular liberal Western ideas. Many such students keep their views to themselves, for they fear that they may be 'marked down' by assessors for being 'too religious'. Black students whose Christian views lead them to value heterosexual relationships and the 'traditional family' may also be challenged by the expectations that as members of an oppressed group they should be sympathetic to issues around homosexuality.

Channer (1995) and Gillborn (1990) have outlined the ways in which British Black students find themselves having to use strategies of personal and political resistance in order to succeed in an academic arena. Gillborn (1990) regards resistance, accommodation and negotiation as key strategies used by Black students. However, strategies that enable Black students to function in institutions of learning may be identified as unhelpful or counterproductive by tutors and assessors. In such circumstances, family members, wider social networks and belief systems will all play a vital role in protecting the self-esteem and repairing the damaged egos of Black learners.[2]

In conclusion, the following points deserve consideration to enable the debate to move forward:

1 The process of the learning experience needs to be given as much consideration as the content.
2 Social work tutors need to appreciate the significant role personal values play in the lives of student social workers.
3 Social work programmes need to make transparent and ongoing the examination of personal values, at least giving space for students to articulate and acknowledge the difficulties they experience.
4 Those concerned need to identify strategies that may help to square the circle of conflict between personal and professional values.

Acknowledgement

I would like to gratefully acknowledge the support of Alan Sanders and Dr Viviene Cree, who read the paper and provided useful suggestions.

Notes

1 At a recent national conference on the experience of students who fail in higher education, the presentations and discussions took no account of issues of 'race'. I was particularly disappointed that Professor Yorke's (1999) study 'Leaving Early' commissioned by HEFC, regarded as the most up-to-date national picture found no place for these issues. In plenary sessions when I noted the significance of these issues in social work education it felt as if many conference participants were content to view the failure of Black students as a matter of concern only for social work education.
2 I have experienced this kind of support myself, particularly on The Black Practice Teacher's course that I attended in 1996. The Black Practice Teacher's course was one of the few events in social work education and indeed other education experiences where Black teachers

and students had the opportunity to attempt a counter-hegemonic act. Much criticism and concern could be levelled at the concept of an all Black course; however, the advantages were evident to facilitators and course participants. My observations of teaching social work courses with varying but small percentages of Black students have shown that the request for safety in the classroom is often a euphemism or rhetorical camouflage for permission to avoid challenging issues of oppression. Racism is often at the top of the list deemed to be the most 'challenging or threatening' topics. On these occasions the vested interest of the majority significantly curtails the learning opportunity of minority groups. On the Black Teachers' course the chance to thrash out significant practice and theory issues without conflict arising from these areas left space for the examination of equally challenging areas. The permission to unclutter the creative, critical channels for learning allowed adults on the course to examine and interrogate. The permission for Black facilitators to the teaching space to support critical thinking without the suspicion of favouring 'their own race' was an additional dimension to the teaching and learning on the course' (Channer 1996).

Bibliography

Ahmad, B. (1990) *Black Perspectives in Social Work*, Birmingham: Venture Press.

Asante, M. (1987) *The Afrocentric Idea*, Philadelphia: Temple University Press.

Atherton, J.S. (1986) *The Natural History of Traumatic Learning*, Manchester: Centre for Adult and Higher Education University of Manchester.

—— (1991) 'The management of traumatic learning', unpublished PhD thesis, Manchester: University of Manchester.

Brookfield. S.D. (1987) *Developing Critical Thinkers: Challenging Adults to Explore Alternative Ways of Thinking and Acting*, Milton Keynes: Open University Press.

Burgess, R., Healey, J., Holman, J., Hyde, P., McBride, S., Hilburn, H., Killican, K., Nnaji, J., Prest, P., Spence, J., Stainsby, P., Trotter, J. and Turner, K. (1997) 'Guilty by association: challenging assumptions and exploring values around lesbian and gay issues on a Diploma in Social Work course', *Social Work Education* 16(3): 97–108.

Channer, Y. (1995) *I am a Promise: The School Achievement of British African Caribbeans,* London: Trentham Books.

—— (1996) 'Adult learning and practice teaching; issues for Black teachers and learners', *Social Work Education* 15(2): 57–68.

Channer, Y. and Franklin, A. (1995) ' "Race", curriculum and HE: Black lecturers' reflections', *Journal of Further and Higher Education* 19(3): 32–46.

Channer, Y. and Parton, N. (1993) *Taking Child Abuse Seriously*, London: Routledge.

Cree, V. (1996) *Social Work: A Christian or Secular Discourse?*, Edinburgh: University of Edinburgh New Waverley Paper.

Cree, V.E., Macaulay, C. and Loney, H. (1998) *Transfer of Learning: A Study*, Edinburgh: Scottish Office Central Research Unit and CCETSW.

de Gale, H. (1991) 'Black students' views of existing CQSW courses and CSS schemes', in CCETSW (ed.) *Setting the Context for Change. Anti-Racist Social Work Education*, London: CCESTW.

de Souza, P.A. (1993) 'Review of the experiences of Black students in social work training', in CCETSW (ed.) *One Small Step Towards Racial Justice*, London: CCETSW.

Dunant, S. (ed.) (1994) *The War of Words. The Political Correctness Debate*, London: Virago.

Evans, D. (1990) *Assessing Students' Competence to Practise in College and Practice Agency*, London: CCETSW.

Gillborn, D. (1990) *'Race' Ethnicity and Education. Teaching and Learning in Multi-ethnic Schools*, London: Unwin Hyman.

Graham, M.J. (1999) 'The African-centred worldview. Developing a paradigm for social work', *British Journal of Social Work* 29(2): 251–67.

Halmos, P. (1969) *The Faith of the Counsellor*, London: Constable and Company.

Karenga, M. (1997) *Kwanzaa: A Celebration of Family, Community and Culture*, Los Angeles: University of Sankore Press.

McCarthy, E.T. (1999) 'Spirituality and political correctness', *Health and Social Work* 24(1): 80.

Maltby, J., Lewis, C.A. and Day, L. (1999) 'Religious orientation and psychological well being: The role of the frequency of personal prayer', *British Journal of Health and Psychology* 4: 363–78.

Patel, N. and Kausbika, A. (1998) *Faith, Communities and Social Work. Shifting Identities and Changing Realities*, London: CCETSW.

Philpot, T. (ed.) (1986) *Social Work: A Christian Perspective,* London: Lion Publishing.

Seden, J. (1998) 'The spiritual needs of children', *Practice* 10(4): 57–67.

Thakur, S. (1998) 'The case for religion in social work education: an independent view of social work and ethnicity' in N. Patel, D. Naik and B. Humphries (eds) *Visions of Reality. Religion and Ethnicity in Social Work*, London: CCETSW.

Working Party on the Teaching of the Values of Social Work (1976) *Values in Social Work. A Discussion Paper,* London: CCETSW, Paper 13.

Yorke, M. (1999) *Leaving Early,* London: Falmer Press.

Chapter 12

From the blackboard to the web

Liz Timms

Introduction

Information technology serves a variety of functions within social work and social work education. Computers may be used simply for their word processing facility, particularly in writing up case notes. At a more sophisticated level they may be used as a storage and access facility through the creation of databases for holding information on service users or procedures. Used to their full potential they provide opportunities for networking with other workers and agencies, for accessing up-to-date research and information and as an aid to learning and teaching. Social work has generally been slower than other professions to grasp the full import of information technology [Human Service Information Technology Applications (HUSITA) Conference 1999; Pierce 1995], and as Hick (1999) points out, surprisingly little has been written about social work education and the Internet.

In terms of education, information technology may serve a variety of functions. It may merely provide a means of accessing and delivering information from, for example, bibliographic databases. It may enable distance learning through computer-mediated communication (CMC), or it may deliver learning through highly sophisticated interactive instructional programmes, such as computer-assisted learning (CAL). This chapter describes an initiation into Internet-based teaching, relating this to transfer of learning both in terms of my own experience as a module developer and tutor and in terms of the demands on participants. The module *Community Portraits* is designed for health and welfare professionals and delivered within SCHEMA (Social Cohesion through Higher Education in Marginal Areas), a project funded by the European Commission Educational Multimedia Taskforce. The Project, co-ordinated by the University of Stirling, Scotland, has partners in Finland, Germany and Sweden. SCHEMA has four basic aims: the development and verification of a delivery system for open and distance learning using network computers or set-top boxes; the evaluation of Web-based learning environments designed to support a collaborative, problem-solving approach to learning; the development and delivery of training modules for health and welfare workers in remote areas, with particular emphasis on learning experience shared across professional boundaries; and research concerning the extent to which computer-based networks can contribute to social cohesion (SCHEMA 1999).

Community Portraits

The three main aspects of the *Community Portraits* module are:

1   the community as a context for welfare practice;
2   collaboration as a method for working and learning;
3   the Internet as an enabler of collaboration/collaborative learning (see Timms 1999a).[1]

The community as a context for welfare practice

The community focus derives from recognition that the bulk of practical and personal support and help for people takes the form of mutual help between relatives, friends and neighbours, in other words, community networks (Barclay Report 1982). It follows that professional services will be more effective if they take as their starting point understanding the community's dynamics and the implications of these for community members, rather than focusing exclusively on individual clients and their problems. Unfortunately, the predominant mode of current welfare practice exemplifies the latter approach. The outcome is, predictably, parallel welfare systems – informal caring and formal services – which may at best incur waste by duplication and at worst pathologise the recipients of services and de-skill those who care for others as part of their daily social life. We do not live in isolation from the community and social workers would benefit from capitalising 'on all available resources in that community to improve upon and take over some of our tasks' (Green 1989: 20).

Awareness that communities affect individual welfare both for good and for ill, as well as recognition of their power to undermine unwelcome professional intervention, suggests that it is both inefficient and unwise for welfare practitioners to ignore the dynamics of the community in which they practice. The argument for dovetailing formal social work services with their community contexts is logical and powerful (Martinez-Brawley 1990). In Scotland it is built into core social work legislation [The Social Work (Scotland) Act, 1968]. Guidelines, still extant, are permeated with directions to attend to the community context of the service (Scottish Office 1968, 1969).

The prime thrust of *Community Portraits* (Box 12.1) is to inculcate in participants habitual and active curiosity about the communities in which they practice, with a view to developing an appreciative understanding of the people, their relationships, their norms and their perspectives on social life and the world about them. The long-term vision is of welfare practitioners better able to dovetail their services with existing helping exchanges in the community and to offer support to that community provision in ways which are recognisable by, and acceptable to, the community.

Collaboration as a method for working and learning

Despite the fact that collaboration has been an invariable and crucial feature of welfare, it has frequently been found wanting. Although structures and procedures have been established, such as child protection committees and guidelines, these, predictably, are likely to deal only with problems in collaboration that are structural or procedural. Essentially, collaboration is relational: people working purposefully with people, across boundaries of various kinds and regardless of personal congruity. Whether face to face or computer mediated, it is not easy to maintain such relationships. It is, therefore, regrettable that, whereas a great deal of social work literature and education concentrates on workers establishing and sustaining effective working relationships with clients, the processes of productive worker-to-worker relationships are given little emphasis.

It might be suggested that relationship skills established in one context will automatically be transferred into the whole range of a worker's interpersonal relationships. Research on child protection suggests the fallacy of this (Department of Health 1995). Although the worker–client relationship is recognised as a base for collaboration, the components of that relationship are systematically different from worker–worker relationships, at least in terms of purposes, processes, knowledge bases and power, and are not automatically transferred. There is a need for social work education to address the situationally specific relational requirements of collaboration in social work practice and the kind of learning required to support good collaborative practice both with clients

Box 12.1 *Community Portraits* programme

Week 1 Introductions

Opportunity to browse and meet the module tutor, other module participants and members of the small group with whom you will be working during the module. You can also read about the *Community Portraits* module, look at some of the course material and familiarise yourself with the TELSIpro learning environment - the framework which will support your collaborative learning process.

Week 2: The concept of community

Exchange of views and experiences in Portrait Task Groups (PTGs), developing a view from the small group, debriefing with reference to literature (Web search).

Week 3 Thinking about collaboration: a start

PTGs consider the collaborative potential of the group in terms of similarities and differences, skill and interest mixes, the added value of cultural and/or professional differences.

Week 4 Introducing the communities

Within their PTG, participants exchange 'snapshots' of their communities that have been prepared in advance, leading to comparative questions and preliminary comparisons of the focus communities.

Week 5 Planning for the task

PTGs plan collaborative approach to preparing their community portraits, decide and allocate tasks, agree procedures and 'meetings'. Report plans to other groups. Groups comment on one another's action plans.

Weeks 6–9 Doing the work

PTGs get on with the task of exploring the communities, as agreed within the group and supported by on-line 'staffed' tutorials and back-up, on-line consultation as requested.

Week 10   Taking stock

PTGs review material gathered to date, take stock of progress; identify information still needed and decide the shape of the final presentation. Prepare action plan for completion of task. Report on progress and action plan for completion of task to other groups. Exchange of comments/ideas between groups. Group reflection on collaborative process to date and plan for any changes needed.

Weeks 11–12   Preparation for the presentation

Time to check material collected and assemble it as planned for presentation on the WWW.

Week 13   Presentation of Community Portraits on WWW

Week 14

1   Submission of assessments of Community Portrait presentations.
2   Conclusion: On-line plenary debate on similarities and differences between communities, the learning gained through the collaborative process of the module, the learning gained through the use of the technology, the advantages and disadvantages of the technology.

Week 16

Participants submit reflective study of collaborative process.

and with co-workers. At the core of *Community Portraits* is a problem-solving exercise to be completed by people working together, via the Internet, across professional, cultural and personal boundaries.

The Internet as an enabler of collaboration/collaborative learning

The final strand of the rationale for *Community Portraits* is based on recognition of the potential that communication via the Internet may have for collaborative practice and learning in the field of health and welfare.

The recent convergent drives for lifelong learning and social inclusion coincide with the development of the World Wide Web, the rapid increase in personal ownership of computers and technological developments that have the potential for universal access, in terms of both equipment and user-friendliness. The realistic goal of SCHEMA is a system that simply requires the user to plug in, switch on and go: two-finger typing and the ability to follow simple instructions will be the skill level required. This has created exciting opportunities for educational development and involvement. Not only can use of the Internet overcome problems of distance in the provision and exchange of information but also computer-mediated communication can overcome many other barriers: difficulties with mobility, restrictions on timing, social exclusion, shame or fear in interpersonal encounters, difficulties with unbalanced status or power in relationships. The flexibility and anonymity of the Internet can encourage and support access for everyone to information, learning, networking and socialising on a phenomenal scale, where quantity and selection can be controlled entirely by the participant. People can learn what they want, when they want, where they want: the locus of control shifts from the teacher to the learner.

The Community Portraits task

Community Portraits requires participants to work collaboratively in small groups to produce comparative 'portraits' of the communities in which they work. Groups of three participants, each from a different country, work together to produce a comparative portrait of their three communities. Participants are expected to use their cultural, professional and individual differences of perspective to sharpen each other's awareness of their own work community. This collaborative process is also expected to enhance the participants' awareness of their own, as well as each other's, perceptual frameworks and should encourage them to recognise the advantages of collaboration for extending ways of gathering and interpreting information, deepening understandings and developing ideas and innovations.

The module is presented entirely via the Internet. Participants do not meet face to face and therefore must establish and sustain their collaborative relationships through electronic communication alone. This arrangement is rare in Web-based group learning for social welfare and runs contrary to the perceived wisdom that some face-to-face contact is essential because the technology is not able to foster the desired quality of interpersonal linkage. It does, however, encourage inclusion which any face-to-face requirement may restrict.

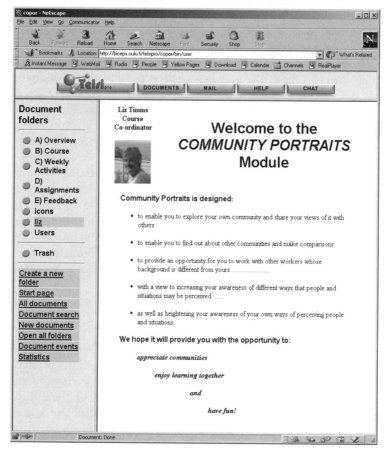

Figure 12.1 Community Portraits homepage.

For *Community Portraits*, the walled and windowed space of conventional teaching, with its tables and chairs, black/white-board, overhead projector and ancillary equipment, is replaced by a structured learning environment (TELSIpro) that is mapped out on the participants' computer screens. Once logged on to *Community Portraits*, participants see four buttons across the top of the screen allowing them to choose one of three activities (Document preparation, Sending mail or Chat) or to seek help. The selection of a button will lead to a list of options in the vertical column on the left of the screen. The main work area occupies the rest of the screen (Figure 12.1).

Participants decide and allocate permissions for reading and revising any document that they enter into the system but the tutor has access to all material apart from private mail. These differential levels of access enable small group and plenary activity to take place with tutor observation, consultation and support while providing the confidentiality of the private mail box as required by Finnish law, where the learning environment TELSIpro was originally developed. Throughout the sixteen-week module, supervision and support for participants are supplied via the Internet. Technical and pedagogic expertise is available to the tutor and to participants to enable them to optimise use of the technology and to produce and present their portraits of the communities on the Internet. Although participants are encouraged to make demands on the technology, efforts are made to ensure that any demand the technology makes on the participants is minimal. As already indicated they should, according to the principles of SCHEMA, be able to plug in, switch on and go.

The first trial of *Community Portraits* took place in the spring and summer of 1999. The participating group consisted of three men and five women distributed across five sites and three countries: Finland (four), Germany (two) and Scotland (two). Three small groups were formed before the start; each group was made up of participants from different countries, where possible, or at least from different sites. The *Community Portraits* trial run settled down to two groups as the third group ceased communication after six weeks. Despite awareness of the received wisdom that relationships start with the very first signals of communication and that the messages sent and received at that point, whether through content or process, may determine the future of the relationship, the start of *Community Portraits* was flawed. The course was launched with a mass of information and too little guidance to participants about how to begin to engage with it. Not enough time had been allowed for people to join in and familiarise themselves with the system. Neglecting the significance of informal interchanges in the development of collaborative relationships, it was short-sightedly decided to use a substantive course exercise as a vehicle for people to begin their interpersonal exchanges.

Ultimately, two groups collected the necessary information for completing the *Community Portraits*, one of which did not assemble its material into a presentation. In its trial delivery, *Community Portraits* did not fully achieve the planned learning outcomes, but feedback from the participants and the tutor (Timms 1999) together with participation data collected within TELSIpro (Bangali *et al.* 1999) indicates both that it is an initiative worth pursuing and that there are identified changes to the technology and to the module presentation that need to be made.

Community Portraits *and the transfer of learning*

A feature of *Community Portraits*, implicit in its rationale, is that effective practice will draw resourcefully on any relevant knowledge, ideas, and experience that might promote intervention goals, or welfare generally, regardless of source, that is the relevance of information and ideas to professional practice should not be determined by the context in which they appear. Module guidelines advise participants to 'keep your eyes and ears open at all times ... to think of yourself as having antennae that should be kept alert to information of any kind that might enrich your understanding of community contexts' and point out that 'it is important to recognise that vital clues to the context of community life are often presented outside strictly professional tasks but are nonetheless important pieces of professional information' (Timms 1999b). Thus the learner is encouraged to be active and to access knowledge from everyday life. A similar foundation for learning, wholly consistent with transfer of learning goals (Cree *et al.* 1998), is presented by Bentley (1998) in his proposals for an education system made relevant for life and lifelong learning:

> This learning ... requires a shift in our thinking about the fundamental organisational unit of education, from the school, an institution where learning is organised, defined and contained, to the learner, an intelligent agent with the potential to learn from any and all of her encounters with the world around her.
>
> (Bentley 1998: 1)

The notion of continual transfer of learning underpins the *Community Portraits* module. Knowledge is seen as 'all of a piece' – the participants are expected to be alert to information and ideas from any source and open to their usefulness in any new situation. Lateral, creative and 'desegregated' thinking is necessary (De Bono 1970). The module process reflects this goal by supporting student initiatives and ideas and prompting developments of innovative thinking based on a wide range of information. Teaching, it was felt, should be modelled on the pattern of practice towards which the students were working; thus the learning outcome should not only guide the content of courses but also be woven into the educational process (NISW 1983, 1989;[2] Smale 1996, 1998).

The role of the tutor in *Community Portraits* is of crucial importance. Presenting the module via the Internet required the ability to convey encouragement and enthusiasm via the written word with no supportive non-verbal signals. 'Real' classroom skills had to be transferred to the 'virtual' classroom. There was some transfer in terms of 'technological' skills, which mirrored other such shifts in my varied teaching career, for example moving from chalk and blackboard teaching in secondary school classrooms for thirty pupils to university lecture rooms for 300 students. Apart from oral traditions there is a technology associated with all teaching and learning: slates, books, blackboards, overhead projectors, computers, televisions, and so on. Transferring lecture material into a Web-based course framework is often criticised for being 'mere page turning' making only limited use of the presentation and learning opportunities provided by current communications and information technology (IFETS 1998). In order to make best use of CAL, it is essential to be clear about the purpose of any teaching/learning unit. Thereafter, it is necessary to be imaginatively alert to the relevant capacity of the available technology and to creatively marry the technological opportunity with the educational goals in such a way that technology is transparent and inconspicuous to the student and learning is thrown into high relief.

Transfer of learning was implicit in the development of *Community Portraits* rather than an explicit learning outcome. Participants were active learners, just as collaborative learning encourages them to be. There is some evidence, drawn particularly from early feedback on the experience and meanings of community, that the habits of extensive and strictly academic learning may have favoured vertical thinking and 'intellectualising' for some, so hindering their use of personal experience. The relational process of collaboration emphasised in *Community Portraits* encouraged more integration of personal experience with 'academic learning'. Some commented that more thoughtful contributions to the collaboration were encouraged by computer-mediated communication because, in contrast to face-to-face discussion, electronic mail allows time to think before responding. The students were all well motivated to learn, even when this module was a burden on an already heavy schedule, perhaps because they were free to time their learning to suit themselves.

Given differences of age, gender, experience, nationality, communities and occupations within the small groups, a richness of exchange and learning about communities and about self was expected and promoted. However, on observing early online exchanges it was striking to note the disproportionate efforts being made to identify similarities rather than differences. One might speculate that similarity was being pursued to ease the development of harmonious collaborative communication. This is probably a feature of face-to-face as well as online collaboration. Given that best collaboration capitalises on differences rather than on similarities, sustained politeness inhibits the development of collaboration and this is more obvious in the slower pace of computer-mediated communication. This politeness may also inhibit transfer of learning: if it is necessary to perceive differences as well as similarities between situations in order to effectively transfer, then such a desire to avoid potential debate or conflict will inhibit learning.

Collaborative learning, whether computer mediated or face-to-face, requires to take on board the process demands of both relationship building and of learning. The evidence of *Community Portraits* suggests that this will affect responses to differences and similarities which will need sensitive guidance by the teacher. Feelings and attitudes also need careful monitoring, though we need longer experience with computer-mediated communication to develop skills in identifying feelings and attitudes being expressed online and in conveying an appropriate emotional response. Some participants in *Community Portraits* suggested that this was a safer context for expressing themselves and for trying out ideas. They were in control. They engaged within the familiar setting of their own homes, at times of their own choice (often midnight or the small hours) with people whom they might never meet. On the other hand, any technical unreliability may disturb novices to the computer or unconfident users of unfamiliar computer programmes and it needs to be made clear that technical problems are the responsibility of equipment and technical advisers, rather than of users.

Development of collaboration during *Community Portraits* may reflect equivalent face-to-face collaboration, but in slow motion. Given the importance of improving collaborative practice in health and welfare and our need to understand better what helps and what hinders good collaboration, the experience of *Community Portraits* and other online collaborative learning and working may yield valuable insights for transfer across technologies. The early indications of the strength of computer-based technology here, including the visibility of the processes online, might well be taken up in the wider research on collaborative processes. Effective collaborative relationships exemplify transfer of learning horizontally in terms of partners learning from one another as well as an accumulation of pooled experience for transfer to future situations.

SCHEMA has been able to bring together professional, pedagogic and technical experts into educational developments that rely on the interdependence of different areas of expertise. At this stage in the diffusion of communications and information technology, the skill mix is crucial since the social work educator cannot match the technologist's awareness of cutting-edge technology that might enhance professional education; the technologist does not have the professional expertise to plan the substance of professional education and both may not be aware of the hazards of computer-mediated learning for pedagogy. As the use of communication and information technology becomes more common across the educational spectrum, the skills and understanding will doubtless be more broadly shared and the current need for a specialist skills mix is likely to be less pressing.

For the near future it will be important to ensure that there is adequate technical support for social work educators and students seeking to enhance learning by taking up the opportunities that the communication and information technologies have added to existing educational resources. Furthermore, the quality of that support will be more important than the quantity. In SCHEMA technical specialists are dedicated to tolerant encouragement of the technically illiterate educators and technophobic learners. These technical experts accept full responsibility for easing access to and acceptance of computers: the technology can and must be made accessible to people rather than placing demands on users to adjust to the demands of the technology. The quality of this support is vital for sustaining user motivation and facilitating learning. Such attitudes, as much as technical development, will be vital to the widest dissemination of computer literacy and the most accessible exploitation of computer-mediated communication for learning.

Notes

1   E. Timms and L. Timms both refer to the author of this chapter.
2   The National Institute for Social Work in London developed these ideas in seminars in 1983 and in their consultancy development programme between 1989 and 1990.

Bibliography

Bangali, L., Booth, S., Crompton, P., Klein, B., Schnuekel, B., Timms, D. and Timms, E. (1999) *The Learning Process and Online Collaboration*: Brussels, European Commission. Available online at http://www.stir.ac.uk/schema/deliverables.htm

Barclay Report (1982) *Social Workers: Their Role and Tasks,* London: Bedford Square Press.

Bentley, T. (1998) *Learning Beyond the Classroom*, London: Routledge.

Cree, V.E., Macaulay, C. and Loney, H. (1998) *Transfer of Learning: A Study*, Edinburgh: CCETSW and Scottish Office Central Research Unit.

De Bono, E. (1970) *Lateral Thinking: a Textbook of Creativity*, Harmondsworth: Penguin Books.

Department of Health (1995) *Child Protection: Messages from Research*, London: HMSO.

Green, R. (1989) 'The Badenoch and Strathspey Social Work Team', in G. Smale and W. Bennett (eds) *Pictures of Practice: Community Social Work in Scotland*, London: National Institute for Social Work.

Hick, S. (1999) 'Learning to care on the Internet: evaluating an online introductory social work course', *New Technology in the Human Services* 11(4): 1–10.

HUSITA (1999) 'Social services in the information society: closing the gap', Human Service Information Technology Applications Conference, Budapest, 29 August to 1 September 1999.

IFETS (1998) 'Web-based documents – electronic page turners?', *Discussion Board* at http://zeus.gmd.de/ifets/discuss/messages/41/35.html

Martinez-Brawley, E. (1990) *Perspectives on the Small Community*, Washington, DC: NASW Press.

Pierce, R. (1995) 'Computers in social work education and training – introductory talk', *New Technology in the Human Services* 8(2): 2–3.

SCHEMA (1999) *SCHEMA Information Leaflet*, Stirling: Centre for Research and Development in Learning Technology, University of Stirling.

Scottish Office (1968) *Circular No. SW 6/98*, Edinburgh: Social Work Services Group.

—— (1969) *Circular No. SW 11/69*, Edinburgh: Social Work Services Group.

Swale, G. (1996) *Mapping Change and Innovation*, London: The Stationery Office.

—— (1998) *Managing Change through Innovation*, London: The Stationery Office.

Timms, E. (1983) 'On the relevance of informal social networks for social work intervention', *British Journal of Social Work* 13: 405–15.

—— (1999) *Community Portraits: Interim Report*, Brussels: European Commission. Available online at http://www.stir.ac.uk/schema/deliverables.html

Timms, L. (1999a) 'Communities and welfare practice: learning through sharing', *New Technology in the Human Services*: 11(4): 11–17. Available online at: http://www.soton.ac.uk/~chst/nths/etimms.htm

—— (1999b) *Guidelines for Community Portraits Module*, at http://biceps.oulu.fi/telsipro/copor/bin/user (password-protected site).

Index